The Narcissistic/Borderline Couple

A Psychoanalytic Perspective on Marital Treatment

The Narcissistic/Borderline Couple

A Psychoanalytic Perspective on Marital Treatment

Joan Lachkar, Ph.D.

BRUNNER/MAZEL, *Publishers* · New York

Library of Congress Cataloging-in-Publication Data
Lachkar, Joan.
    The narcissistic/borderline couple : a psychoanalytic perspective
on marital treatment / Joan Lachkar.
    p.   cm.
    Includes bibliographical references and indexes.
    ISBN 0-87630-634-2
    1. Marital psychotherapy. 2. Borderline personality disorder.
3. Narcissism. 4. Psychoanalysis.   I. Title.
RC488.5.L348   1991
616.89'156—dc20   91-28228
                                                         CIP

Published by
BRUNNER/MAZEL, INC.
19 Union Square West
New York, New York 10003

Manufactured in the United States of America

10   9   8   7   6   5   4   3   2   1

Contents

v

Acknowledgments

My thanks to those who were helpful and supportive in my writing of this work, as well as those who were the sources of my pain and suffering. The latter contributed much to my efforts to understand the psychic pain and conflict that occurs in the mental lives of the conflicting couples reported in the cases to be found here.

Incongruous as it may appear at the inception of a work of this nature, I feel impelled to acknowledge the special contribution to my practice of psychoanalytic psychotherapy of Carmelita Marcacci, noted ballet dancer and master teacher of classical dance, with whom, for some 12 years, I had the good fortune to study dance. It was there that I learned the importance of artistic expression, the blending of technique and feelings, and more important, the effect that one human being can have on another. She was a role model. To develop one's own sense of style. To move with grace within the strict constraints of a tightly structured medium, be it at barre or within the constructs of the consultation chamber. Like the dance, the practice of psychoanalytic psychotherapy involves the subtle blending of scientific principles with art.

Master blenders to whom I owe much are Drs. Wilfred Bion, James Grotstein, Albert Mason, and my ex-husband, Robert Kahn, M.D. Bion brings to psychoanalysis the world of passions, dreams, and myths to probe the depths of human understanding. Grotstein probes the depths of primitive mental defenses. Mason integrates with precision Kleinian psychoanalytic theory, and Dr. Kahn taught me more about psychoanalysis than any supervisor.

Many of the perspectives you will find presented in this book are concepts of my own blended with the products of such rich and fertile minds of other clinicians, theoreticians, and colleagues: Drs. Otto Kernberg, Heinz Kohut, Donald Meltzer, and Mrs. Melanie Klein have provided not only profound contributions to psychoanalysis, but have offered challenging and unique insights. I am also compelled to acknowledge Marie Briehl, Ph.D; Gottfried Bloch, M.D.; Samuel Eisenstein, M.D.; Melvin Lansky, M.D.; John Lundgren, M.D.; Donald Marcus, M.D.; Marvin Osman, M.D.; Michael Paul, M.D.; William H. Rickles, M.D.; the late Alexander Rogawsky, M.D., M.A.; Frederick Vaquer, M.D.; Katherine Welds, Ph.D.; and Murray Weiler, M.D.

I am indebted to Kay Lyou for her editorial efforts, Blanche Reyes for her word processing, as well as to the late Ann Alhadeff, chief editor of Brunner/Mazel, and to Natalie Gilman and Suzi Tucker, for their editorial guidance. There are many others who have provided unfailing encouragement.

More directly I wish to acknowledge my fiancé Robert Snader, my family, my patients, and the many couples who have endured the rigors of intensive marital psychotherapy—without them, this book would never been published.

Introduction

BACKGROUND

Although a great deal has been written about narcissistic and borderline disorders—and though such authors as Kohut (1971, 1977), Brandchaft and Stolorow (1984), and Stolorow and Lachmann (1980) have increased our understanding of the narcissistic vulnerabilities in individuals and in couples (clarifying such clinical concepts as empathy, mirroring, and self-object functions)—the conflicts that occur when the two pathologies are found in a marital relationship or in a primitive bond seem to have been ignored in the professional literature. Few therapists have recognized the potential wealth of material an object-relations point of view of the borderline syndrome offers in understanding marital discord.

In treating couples, I have found the use of self psychology constructs to be not enough. In this book, clinical constructs abstracted from self psychology, object-relations, and group psychology theories are blended with couples therapy, and case illustrations are given to indicate that a positive therapeutic experience can occur when these theoretical contributions are applied. Although the ideas abstracted from self psychology (including the open field of intersubjectivity) offer an in-depth listening stance for both pathological organizations, I find self psychology more applicable to the narcissistic personality disorder, and object-relations theories more applicable to the borderline personality. Both of these pathologies are in need of self objects and self-objects functions; however, the narcissist responds more to mirroring needs and the borderline responds better to containment. Because of the complexity of these pathologies, both approaches are useful when both personality types are involved within a marital conflict (Lachkar, 1984, 1985b, 1991). I hope not only to contribute something new to the treatment of these couples, but also to demonstrate how self-psychology and object-relations approaches to treatment complement one another.

Perhaps the reason many clinicians are encountering more and more of this familiar kind of couple in their practices is because of increasing percentages of single-parent families, higher divorce rates, decreasing parental availability to children, more parents working, the extinction of extended families, and, in general, social isolation.

I have tentatively diagnosed as the narcissistic/borderline couple individuals who, when they are together, form a shared couple myth that gives rise to many collective fantasies. "If only the other would change!" The idiosyncratic nature of their relationship arouses many distorted views related to archaic longings, yearnings, and unfulfilled wishes. We wonder why such couples stay together, united in a bond, even when their relationship is painfully destructive and nongratifying. Even when narcissist/borderline couples divorce, or depart from one another, they still stay joined or connected in similar ways. The very thing that bonds them also may be, paradoxically, the element that perpetuates the conflict between them. Together they play out a scenario of earlier conflictual experiences similar to those that occur in groups as described by Bion (1961), Freud (1921/1955), and Kernberg (1975).

Although I use the terms "narcissistic" and "borderline" as though they were distinct, well-understood entities, neither disorder is the same across individuals, or even within an individual over time. Discussion would be impossible, however, without making certain abstract distinctions between the narcissist and borderline syndromes in order to provide a structural framework in which to view the conflictual relationships.

The view presented in this book is that an individual with a borderline character is inclined to attract, or to draw as an object choice, a narcissistic person. I believe it is not necessarily their pathologies that attract them to each other, but rather it is their pathologies that keep them together in a primitive bond, in that they meet each other's infantile needs (N. Pevsner-Thorpe, personal communication, 1985). Together the partners play out a drama of earlier conflictual experiences, characterized by their circular, painful, and never-ending patterns of behavior, which I have described as "the dance." These partners form a type of parasitic bond that leads not to growth and development, but instead to destructive, repetitive behaviors. Two narcissists or two borderlines do not "make it," do not "do the dance," because of their dynamics and defenses, but a narcissist and borderline together, although they are oppositional types, seem to maintain a bond. Each appears to be the perfect counterpart for the other.

Although this book is not about diagnosis, I believe that a number of relationships can be diagnosed accurately as narcissistic/borderline relationships because of the symptoms each partner manifests. The uncertainties of diagnosis are acknowledged: The question arises, Is an individual truly narcissistic or borderline, or may that individual merely be exhibiting a proclivity toward, or vulnerability to, either of these pathologies when involved with the other specific individual in the dyad? The dramatic interrelationship of borderline and narcissist can baffle even the most experienced clinician.

In this book, how two theoretical constructs, self psychology and object relations, can be integrated into conjoint treatment of a specific kind of marital conflict is demonstrated, with the focus primarily on maternal bonding, attachment, containment, empathy, and mirroring needs. Patients engaged in these primitive, preoedipal relationships who are in this form of conjoint treatment are helped to face their internal deficits and to take more responsibility for their own behaviors.

Today, a now significant number of psychoanalysts and psychoanalytically trained researchers who understand both fields are increasingly directing their attention to marital conflict (Dicks, 1967; Lachkar, 1984, 1985b, 1986; Lansky, 1981, 1987; Rutan, 1985; Scarf, 1987; Scharff & Scharff, 1987;

Schwartzman, 1984; Sharpe, 1981, in press; Slipp, 1984; Solomon, 1985, 1986; Strean, 1980, 1985; and Willi, 1982).

Although many theorists have made valuable contributions bridging classical theory to marital conflict, few of these authors distinguish between narcissistic and borderline vulnerabilities within a particular dyadic relationship. Lansky (1981), for instance, referred to "narcissistic vulnerability in marriages"; however, he did not distinguish diagnostically between narcissistic and borderline disorders. Lansky did specify certain dynamic processes that might evoke considerable stirring up of existing psychopathologies.

THIS BOOK

In Chapter I, the focus is on the narcissistic personality disorder, the construct of self psychology, the ever-changing ideas of Heinz Kohut, and the views of other authors who have investigated narcissism.

In Chapter II, the borderline syndrome is discussed from an object-relations point of view. The works of a number of authors are reviewed, with particular emphasis given to the theories of Grotstein, Klein, and Bion. In this chapter, I describe the concept of the borderline's "black hole," and explain my view of the borderline's need for bonding, attachment, and reenactment of old, archaic, painful experiences.

A detailed account of a narcissistic/borderline dyadic unit is presented in Chapter III, and the manner in which particular configurations merge to join in a primitive bond is described. The metaphor of the dance is used to describe the complexities of behavioral patterns of the narcissist/borderline couple. The bond between the partners and the drama of these relationships are discussed. Diagnostic differences between borderline and narcissist as they exist in the dynamics of couple interaction are also clarified.

Attention is given in Chapter IV to psychodynamics and their qualitative differences in the two disorders, including the interlocking systems of needs, pain, rage, and self-sacrifice. In Chapter V, I address dynamic positions and transference formations including the various countertransferential issues evoked in the therapist. In this chapter the focus is not on teaching the partners to perform self-object functions for one another but rather on the therapist as the self-object. Theoretical implications and techniques used in the therapeutic settings are discussed in detail in Chapter VI.

In Chapter VII, ideas from group psychology are used as an approach toward expanding our view of the primitive aspects of these preoedipal relationships. The primitive nature of the couple as a form of a group is elucidated. Concepts from group psychology are applied to marital discord, and the role of society is addressed.

Bion's (1961) "work group" and "basic assumption group" are discussed as they apply to the couple. I use Bion's group dynamics theories along with my own earlier work (Lachkar, 1984, 1985b) on "real relationship" versus "fantasized relationships" to explain the regressive nature of these couples. The Tavistock model is considered as it offers a deeper dimension in which to think about persons as part of a group.

Chapter VIII is the forum for the model of the treatment proposed as an application of the theories presented. A six-point systematic treatment procedure is suggested within the paradigm of three specific developmental phases. In Chapter IX, I offer clinical cases and illustrative material to demonstrate some of the points made in this book.

The psychodynamically oriented therapist learns from self psychology to allow both partners to have their own subjective experiences, so that ultimately they may become more grounded and rooted in their own individual convictions and perceptions. While an object-relations perspective helps pave the way to help couples with their intense, interlocking systems, enabling them to take more responsibility for their behaviors. Through object-relations theory, we can gain a clearer understanding of the reasons these couples remain in painful relationships.

IN BRIEF

The purpose of this book is to offer an improved understanding of marital pathology from a psychoanalytic perspective, that is, an emphasis on the intrapsychic as well as the interpersonal experience using ideas from the constructs of self psychology, object-relations theory, and group formation to illuminate the paradigm of the narcissistic/borderline couple.

The progressive movement in psychoanalysis through ego psychologists, object-relations theorists, and self psychologists has been away from the Freudian instinctual drive theory toward an emphasis on interpersonal experience as explored in object relations and self psychology. Melanie Klein expanded Freud's structural model and paved the way to object relations. Her ideas were revolutionary in redirecting psychoanalytic attention from internal objects and projections to the external world. In short, from drive seeking (Freud); to object seeking (Klein) to self seeking (Kohut).

This book is designed to make one think and to stimulate new discoveries through attention to one's own preconceptions. Science and creativity go hand in hand. To learn from our experience, our mistakes, and our misconceptions allows us to work with the narcissist/borderline couple using the appropriate theoretical constructs and our own intuitions and using both science and creativity.

CHAPTER I

The Narcissist

CLINICAL DESCRIPTION

Narcissists are individuals who need perfect mirroring, perfect stroking, perfect responses. Narcissists need to be in control. When injured or insulted, they typically withdraw or isolate themselves. They do not realize that their withdrawal evokes certain unconscious anxieties in borderlines (sadistic attacks, envy, and persecutory anxiety). The narcissist has the tendency and power to stir up enormous conflict within the borderline because the borderline is continually threatened by the potential fear of fragmentation and decompensation, and suffers annihilation anxiety as a person who already has a thwarted sense of development.

Narcissists are driven by the need to be desired and appreciated, tend to isolate themselves either physically or emotionally, fear a loss of specialness, and are easily injured or outraged when not properly understood. They are dominated by guilt and self-hatred, and have idealized and omnipotent fantasies. Preoccupied with a loss of self-regard, narcissists have an overinvestment in self, yet will do anything to preserve a sense of specialness, and attempt to prove themselves by isolation from others and concentration on perfection, power, and omnipotence. The narcissistic tendency to withdraw is accompanied by a driving need to be desired and appreciated, and the narcissist becomes easily injured, insulted, and outraged when not properly mirrored or understood by self objects.

1

Through the process of introjection, narcissists internalize an idealized image of themselves and then project this image onto others. Repeated empathic failures recreate injury to the self, resulting in self-persecution and self-hatred.

For the narcissist, there are two central issues: (1) the child's search for the missing entitlement, and (2) the sense of being the "chosen one," whose concentration on perfection, power, and omnipotence leads to a perfect harmony with God. Narcissists seek out others to confirm or justify exaggerated entitlement fantasies and distortions that the world is deeply indebted to them. A typical attitude is, "Why should I have to get a job? You know I'm special! I'm going to be an actress!"

Clinically, the narcissistic personality disorder is viewed as a developmental arrest in which the main caretakers have withheld phase-appropriate mirroring responses.

Freud (1914/1957) initially conceived of narcissism as the state of self-directed libido; the word is derived from Narcissus, the Greek youth of legend who fell in love with himself. Freud viewed narcissism as a libidinal force similar to a hormone that can be transported to different parts of the body and fixated there. These ideas are the first forerunners of the notion of self that is between the ego's relationship to its ego ideal and the ego's libidinal forces cathected to its objects. Freud meant by primary narcissism an absolute state in which all libidinal energy is stored up and which lasts until the ego begins to cathect onto other objects, when the ego is transformed from narcissistic libido into later object libido.

Freud wrote that the state of love consists in a flowing over of ego libido to the object. In states of passion, sexual desires coincide with the ego ideal. Love is like a psychotic state, a reunion between highly charged emotional and bodily experiences. This state emanates from the fulfillment of infantile conditions of love, and whatever gratifies this condition becomes idealized.

The narcissistic person who is "in love" is highly cathected to someone who has qualities that he or she wishes to have, or had and no longer possesses (beauty, power, organization, sense of self, ability to be alone). The narcissist then tries to own these qualities or to possess them through envy. Feelings of love, under these conditions, are not sustained and soon are diminished or devalued. The effort of one partner to possess the other will destroy or spoil the object, and envy will increase rather than subside.

In finding a love relationship, one will often choose someone who has qualities that are lacking in oneself. It is a common myth that in order to be complete all one has to do is to choose a love object, hoping that the beloved person will make the other whole (Freud, 1914/1957).

Elaborating on his important discoveries about splitting, Freud ("On Narcissism," 1914/1957) discussed the development of the ego ideal as a split-off and projected aspect of the ego that becomes a separate agency with observing functions. Considered by Grotstein (1981) as forerunners to Heinz Kohut's work on narcissism, these contributions between an ego ideal identified with an object and the ego and its objects in the external world have clearly laid the groundwork for the object-relations school of psychoanalysis from which D. W. Winnicott, Ronald Fairbairn, and their followers descend (Grotstein, 1981). I believe this means that there is a part of the ego that searches for an external object, a mirroring object to reflect the undeveloped part of the self.

Otto Kernberg suggested that the narcissist is one who responds defensively, is regressive in nature, and attempts to get back at the parental image for failing the child at a primitive sadistic level. The Kohutian model of narcissism depicts the more highly developed narcissist, whose primary and normal narcissistic phases were virtually unattended to at phase-appropriate times.

Of all the descriptions of narcissism, I find A. Mason's (personal communication, 1988) the most workable. He described narcissism as a pathological disorder in which the object does not recognize the need for the breast, a state in which the object "has it all" and cannot take in, get, or get excited (e.g., allow the therapist's interpretations to provide the feeding or the excitement for the patient). An illustration of this is the situation where a patient is heavily invested in trying to get the therapist sexually excited, rather than allowing the therapist's interpretations to provide the feeding or the excitement for the patient.

In narcissistic/borderline relationships, this last model is helpful because we can readily see not only how the narcissist tends to leave the therapist out, but the kinds of reactions this leaves within the borderline, who already feels discounted, left out, and displaced.

SELF-PSYCHOLOGY VS. OBJECT-RELATIONS THEORIES

I think the main difference between self psychology (mirroring) and object relations (containment) is that the former tends to ignore the internal world, which can lead to a form of collusion with the pathology—for example, the tendency to blame the other for all the shortcomings in the relationship. Certainly environmental factors are important, but if the primary focus is on the external, we are in danger of undermining the internal conflict. I have found object relations more helpful than self psychology in helping couples face internal deficits, which enables them to take more responsibility for their behaviors. Self psychology can be misinterpreted as collusion or fusion when the therapist goes along with the pathology.

Both self-psychology and object-relations theories are necessary. It is not a matter of choosing one over the other, but of there being a vital place in conjoint therapy for each.

Since self psychology places too much emphasis on the self-object tie to the therapist, when fragmentation or injury occurs, it is viewed as the disruption to the therapist, or as an "empathic failure." The implication may collude with the delusional fantasy that the danger is externalized, and the danger from within—primarily the patients' own distortions, projections, persecutory anxiety, splitting, and projective identification—may be ignored. Robert Langs (1989) refers to the wisdom of the unconscious indicating that the "subjective experience can be delusional and fool both patient and therapist."

Self psychology does not help patients face their deficits directly because of the risk that confronting deficits might induce disruption to the treatment or to the relationship. It is recommended that the techniques of mirroring, empathy, and introspection be blended with an object-relations approach to help these narcissistic individuals deal more directly with their internal deficits and with areas of conflict that contribute to the maladaptive nature of their relationships. When couples can face their internal deficits, they feel more secure and contained.

For borderlines suffering from abandonment anxiety and preoccupied with the lack of maternal bonding and attachment experiences, self psychology is not enough. Kohut's model alone does not provide a broad enough scope to aid in understanding internal deficits. Kohut saw only certain forms of narcissistic disorders as being suitable for treatment; nevertheless Kohut's ideas are useful, and can be applied to both partners in a narcissistic/borderline couple.

Object-relations theory provides us with an environmental mother, a background mother, transitional objects, a being mommy/doing mommy, a weaning mommy, and a containing/sustaining mommy to help establish different kinds of bonding relationships. The importance of mother as the container becomes more vital in a conjoint setting because the central issues revolve around separation anxiety. Self psychology does not emphasize the same importance of mother as the container, but rather presents the mirroring, empathic mother. Although both narcissist and borderline patients need self objects, there is a qualitative difference in the way they form bonds. Self psychology, in offering us mirroring and self-object functioning, allows a revival of a bond to occur in the transference. There must, however, be a self to mirror, and a sufficient sense of self to allow a revival of a bond to occur in the transference, and the borderline is not able to revive a bond because bonding never took place.

BEYOND SELF PSYCHOLOGY

At its essence, self psychology is a theory of bonding. Many authors have described the application of self psychology to the understanding and treatment of narcissistic personality disorders (Brandchaft & Stolorow, 1984; Stolorow & Lach-mann, 1980; Kohut, 1971, 1977). Several have recognized the value of self psychology, especially with respect to the ability to form self-object ties, including a narcissistic transference, the need for specialness, idealization, empathy, and its mirroring functions. According to these authors, the formation of the self-object ties with those who mirror and who affirm the narcissist's nascent self helps maintain a sense of cohesion to a developmentally arrested self. Some see borderlines as requiring different kinds of treatment. Many self psychologists view the more primitive aspects of borderline disorders as being similar to the same kinds of treatment as narcissism, but see the borderline as one who is in a more archaic state of narcissism (Adler, 1985; Lachkar, 1985b). Other theorists, including Solomon (1985, 1986) and Lansky (1981), have applied the works of Kohut in self psychology in describing narcissistic vulnerabilities in couples.

Although Lansky was influenced by Kohut and drew from many other theoretical perspectives, his focus is more on the complexities and difficulties arising from the clinical treatment itself. Although Lansky did not equate the differences between narcissistic and borderline personality disorders, his emphasis was more on the interpersonal evocation. Lansky assumed there is a high degree of narcissistic vulnerability in these marriages emanating from both these disorders. Lansky stressed the differences between normal marriages and marriages with narcissistic vulnerabilities, and expanded upon specific dynamic processes and symptomatologies that are evoked from their preexisting psychopathologies (blame, shame, demandingness, and entitlement), "which pervade vulnerable marriages so that nothing seems capable of fulfilling omnipotent expectations" (Lansky, 1981, p. 167).

To compare the applications of self-psychology and object-relations theories in a more practical way, let us consider the case of the borderline who becomes fragmented and enraged and begins to attack the therapist, claiming, "You are just like my wife, you have too many expectations of me." The self psychologist might address the archaic tie to the mother, confirming that there were too many of these expectations in the past, that as a child he could not please his mother, and that now he is expected to fill the therapist's expectation as if she were his mother. The therapist incorporating a Kleinian view would address the deficits via the patient's projection. For example, the therapist might say: "You must be feeling pressured yourself, and feeling bad that you cannot face these expectations and sort out which ones seem realistic. Instead of relying on your own feelings, you are turning things around to make it seem that they are my or her expectations of you." The therapist following Wilfred Bion, with his effort to focus on "truth," might ask, "What's wrong with having an expectation?"

According to Brandchaft and Stolorow (1984), self psychology has added a significant new dimension to the understanding of negative therapeutic reactions and has contributed to the invaluable concept of self-object empathic failures as the prime cause of a negative transference. Self psychology and object relations can be intertwined, and both need to be used if the therapist is to be able to "wean" the patient from the defensive use of pathological, autistic objects, and to restore the patient's faith in the reparative functions.

I have concentrated here on the significance of addressing primarily the internal forces in a vigorous search of the self before turning to any external changes, that is, divorce. The focus for the borderline is more on the internal objects (projections, misperceptions, and distortions of reality), and for the narcissist on an exaggerated need for self objects, approval, and a tendency to quit or withdraw.

The major difference between these approaches is that in self psychology the patient's subjective experience is considered the patient's own reality, and not as a distortion (B. Brandchaft, personal communication, 1988) or, as Robert Langs (1989) refers to it, the "deep unconscious wisdom" (suggesting that the conscious mind can fool both the patient and the therapist). In object relations, the patient's "distortions" and "misperceptions" are considered to be aspects of the split-off parts and projections from within the internal world. Both of these methods must be examined within the scope of each pathology, while keeping in mind the specific theoretical functions of each method as an important source of analytic inquiry.

Self psychology, with its emphasis on mirroring, does not place much emphasis on the internal world. Recognition of splitting and projective identification are virtually nonexistent among self psychologists. Fear of giving therapists too much responsibility for the pathology can in fact take away from patients' responsibility to take the initiative and gain control over their own behavior, and to be responsible for the feelings coming from within the internal world. Caper, in the book *Immaterial Facts* (1988), saw psychic reality as a more important aspect than what occurs from the outside with external objects.

The description of the narcissist is derived from intensive review of self-psychology literature, and is discussed within the context of the theoretical and historical background presented in this volume.

Kohut

The term "narcissistic personality disorder" was first introduced into the literature by Heinz Kohut in 1968. Since then, Otto Kernberg and Kohut have been the major theoreticians examining the concept.

Kohut (1971, 1977), while acknowledging Freudian theory and Margaret Mahler's stages of separation-individuation, did not endorse either view theoretically. Kohut departed from intrapsychic structures of instinctual drive and defense theory of maturational forces. He claimed that affective experiences, and not instincts, affect the development of the self.

Kohut saw the self as an independent structure that evolved along its own line of development, and the narcissistic personality as a result of developmental arrest during the normal stage of narcissism, especially during the phase when the child was engaged in a normal state of grandiosity. Kohut considered the grandiose self typical of normal development, noting that in normal development this stage was followed by transmutual internalization and channeling of idealistic aims into more realistic goals. Kohut maintained that primary infantile narcissism is injured by maternal shortcomings, and that empathic responses are needed to modify excessive feelings of rage and guilt. Without these appropriate responses, early parental deficits will reactivate.

Kernberg

Otto Kernberg attempted to reach reality through interpretation of defense and resistance, pointing out oral rage and sadomasochistic destructive impulses. Kernberg (1975, 1980, 1989, 1990), in contrast to Kohut, described narcissistic personality disorder as a defense, and held that the narcissistic individual, as a child, was left emotionally hungry by a chronically cold, unempathic mother. Feeling unloved and bad, the child perceived the parents as sadistic instead of empathic, and the child took refuge in some valued aspect of the self as the only defense available. The resulting self-image defends against rage, envy, and the fantasized image of a loving mother. This pathology manifests itself in the inability to love others, a lack of empathy, emptiness, overdependence on acclaim, boredom, and an unremitting need to search for power, and makes the person unavailable to others.

Kernberg (1989, 1990) viewed all romantic love as having preoedipal components. In normal passionate love, the original rivals and other competitors of the same sex are overcome, and a triumphant identification with the oedipal rival is achieved. When Kernberg suggested that the polymorphous fusion of the quest to achieve oedipal victory has constituents of both pain and passion, I believe he was saying that, as painful as it is to be with an unavailable, narcissistic partner, it can also be a highly charged erotic experience. Kernberg's analysis is certainly in line with the theory that many patients with narcissistic disorders have never been in love. Kernberg's ideas regarding the narcissistic personality are compatible with the dance described in Chapter III of this book, in which the narcissist's withholding qualities are demonstrated.

Kernberg (1975) suggested not only that other people are attracted to certain qualities and attributes of the narcissist, but that narcissists tend to stir up certain unconscious feelings of envy and greed in others. Imagine what that does to the borderline partner?

Kernberg argued that if one allows another person's passion to dominate, as happens in narcissistic/borderline relationships, one becomes as a child, a victim, or a handicapped person, and this can severely impair healthy object relations (Kernberg, 1989, 1990). Kernberg seemed to have been saying that one can never be fulfilled by possessing the excitement found in another, but rather that it is only the true passions found within the self that can make a difference and can lead to eventual good personal relations.

Other Theorists

Both Herb Strean (1980, 1985) and Jurg Willi (1982) describe collusive patterns of couples derived from unresolved oedipal conflicts. Willi, who saw love as "oneness in narcissistic collusion" (p. 60), was certainly on the right track when he discovered particular kinds of couples forming narcissistic collusion. Although he didn't refer to a borderline partner, he did describe a certain kind of love relationship similar to the mother-child experience. Willi referred to one partner as the narcissist and to the other as the "complementary narcissist," to this dyadic relationship as the "narcissistic marriage," and to the dilemma as the "narcisistic couple conflict," which he considered the principal aspects of narcissistic collusion.

In the attempt to make a diagnostic profile of dysfunctional love relationships, Sharpe (1981) expands Willi's and Strean's theories and discusses two kinds of relationships, the "symbiotic" and the "oppositional." The "symbiotic" reflects the developmental themes of Mahler's symbiotic phase, and the "oppositional" reflects unresolved developmental disturbances of the separation-individuation phase. In a later work (in press), Sharpe defines the "oedipal couple" as more competitive in nature and requiring a different kind of therapeutic management than the symbiotic or oppositional couple.

According to the philosopher George Hegel (1821), "man does not desire an object. Man desires the object's desire." Isaacs (1943) supported the explanation that desire is always wanting and desirous of something. Many theorists describe desire differently. Klein argued that perceptions of others are merely a scaffolding of projections of the child's innate internal object images that dominate how others are perceived. The implication is that the experience of wanting is inherent in some image or fantasy. Pathogenic narcissism emanating from primary and secondary narcissism can then severely impair relating to other objects, particularly when these internal images are obscured by one's desiring a fantasy or an idealized image which, in reality, can never be acclaimed. I believe this corresponds to Kohut's "the gleam in the mother's eye" (the joy the parent receives while watching the child achieve and accomplish).

Wolstein (1987) portrayed Kohut's stress on self objects as an exaggerated emphasis on the outer social and interpersonal side of the self, as "insupportably one-sided," and as lacking in "dialectical tension" (p. 32). Wolstein asked, "How does a psychoanalyst accept this unusual counsel: to both become a self-object and remain capable of interfacing with a patient? How does a psychoanalyst, as self-object, follow the suggested agenda of being both empathic and confirming?" (p. 32). Wolstein proposed that this is difficult for the analyst to accomplish without feeling burdened by this stance.

Schain (1985) noted the differences between Klein's and Kohut's views about narcissism. In Kohut's theories, the responses of the narcissist are in direct response to the environment. Kohut indicated that Klein did not dispute environmental deficits and their effects, but rather emphasized patients' responsibility for their own dissatisfactions. Schain noted with appreciation that Kohutian techniques are particularly effective in relieving distress and in rebuilding the self; he proposed, however, that the Kleinian view enhances the patient's understanding of the internal life of an individual. It is my view that Klein's work is more appropriate to primitive disorders. Her theories will be described more fully during the discussion of the borderline syndrome in Chapter II.

Integrating many of these theoretical perspectives, one may surmise there are different kinds of narcissism. My empirical evidence suggests there is a "Kernbergian narcissist" and there is a "Kohutian narcissist." The former is the one who responds defensively, is more regressive in nature, and attempts to get back at the parental image for failing the child at a more primitive sadistic level, during the more normal phases of development. The Kohutian model of narcissism depicts the more highly developed narcissist, whose primary and normal narcissistic phases were virtually unattended to at the phase-appropriate time.

ROLES OF THE MOTHER AND FATHER: OEDIPAL ISSUES

Although Kohut stressed the importance of the mother's vital function in providing mirroring for the exhibitionistic side of the child during normal stages of the narcissistic line of development, he appeared to ignore the mother's role in terms of offering safety and protection. Kohut's emphasis tended to be on the importance of empathy in the mother-child mirroring process, and it appears that Kohut overlooked the vital role the mother plays in offering bonding and attachment experiences, a role described more clearly by object-relations theorists (namely, Klein, 1955; Fairbairn, 1954; Winnicott, 1965d; Bowlby, 1969; Grotstein, 1983). Masterson (1981) confirmed that Kohut's ideas exclude the mother and object relations.

Klein, more than any of her followers, understood the need for the mother and the breast. Klein maintains that once the infant recognizes the wholeness of the object (at about 6 months) and its relation to the self, the infant can begin to freely search out beyond the breast to the environment, usually first with the father.

The development of the Oedipus complex is strongly influenced by the special relationship with the mother, and when this relationship is disturbed, it results in a challenge or stirs up rivalry with father prematurely. One cannot leave the breast or turn to father until the infant first feels safe with mother. Somewhere besides mother, there is an innate preconception that beyond the breast there is an object more stimulating, challenging, and exciting. This is the place for the oedipal father.

Guilt, arrogance, and exhibitionism get in the way of ever overcoming oedipal strivings to compete with father for the desired mommy. That guilt turned inward leads to self-persecution and self-hatred, loss of curiosity, individuality, and thinking.

In the depressive position, one can begin to face and tolerate what one, in fact, does not know. To compete with a parent then becomes tantamount to killing the parent! If the child knows everything and is almighty, then the parents are either idealized as having everything, or they are devalued as having nothing because the child has it all. Unknown aspects of the self keep the narcissistic partner in a continual state of anxiety. Turning away from the self to others, by making excessive demands through arrogance and intolerance, is an expression of the narcissist's need to be the all-knowing, God-like, omniscient one; the provider, the protector, and often the one who takes over (including the treatment). Many narcissists who are striving to be successful are developmentally not ready for the challenge. Their preoedipal strivings are not contained because of the failure in the mother's capacity as a maternal container, to serve as a "holding mommy." For narcissists, the lack of a mirroring mommy to reflect the child's normal and healthy narcissist endowments, or to empathize with the child's excessive demands, can result in faulty reflections of the child's true talents, ambitions, goals, and aims.

Of all the theorists, I believe Grotstein provides a more in-depth understanding of the Oedipus complex. Grotstein (1980,

1981, 1983, 1984b) described the "prey/predator" instinct and his theories on bonding; Bowlby (1969) provided theories on bonding and attachment; and Mahler, Pine, and Bergman (1975) discussed separation-individuation phases. Before the infant is ready for father, argue these theorists, the infant must have some sense bonding with mother.

According to Grotstein (personal communication, 1985), the analyst/father Oedipus is not a real rival but a mock rival. Our patients are rehearsing with us in preparation for the "real" hunters of the "real predators." Grotstein (personal communication, 1983) recognized a social Oedipus rather than a sexual Oedipus in that mother provides safety, but father shows the way to challenge, to find truth, or to avoid truth, to seek out natural curiosity, or to avoid curiosity, and it is the father who prohibits. Father then challenges us to risk, to reach out to others, or to avoid new experiences, through denial, arrogance, fear, guilt, and other defenses.

The Oedipus myth, as perceived by Bion, provides a linkage to curiosity in harmony with the child's innate epistemophilic instinct to make discoveries leading to the quest for truth and knowledge. Bion's (1958) paper "On Arrogance" and Grotstein's publications (1981, 1983) offer profound insights, adding further dimensions in integrating Klein's concepts about the Oedipus complex into a more expansive view that transcends incest and parricide.

Freud's Oedipus may be misunderstood as a literal Oedipus. For Bion, the myth does not have to do so much with a sexual component. The oedipal myth within a Bionian frame of reference may be viewed as a precursor to knowledge of psychic reality, that is, to rely on one's own feelings and instincts as an essential part of the learning apparatus in the early stages of a child's development.

The Oedipus myth, and other myths such as the Garden of Eden, the Tower of Babel, and the riddle of the sphinx, suggests that finding truth leads to blindness, thus leading humans away from curiosity. Some individuals learn that curiosity leads to danger, whereas others learn that curiosity leads to passion, experience, and learning.

The blinding of Oedipus's eyes to truth rendered him a mental cripple, and this happened as a consequence of his epistemophilic curiosity to "know all." The warnings of his mother and the already blinded Tiresias were to no avail. By forfeiting his eyes, Oedipus became the paradigm of the lifelong mental invalid known as "every man."

The oedipal implication for the narcissist may be understood in terms of the child's grandiosity; that is, if the child wishes to have what daddy has and tries to take mommy away, what will he do with mommy once he gets her? The narcissist is never curious enough to acquire the tools daddy has to achieve realistically.

The implication in marital therapy is that the narcissist needs to achieve oedipal victory, the "real" way, in contrast to the "omnipotent" way. Unknown aspects of the self keep the narcissistic partner in a continual state of anxiety. The therapist plays the role of both of both "breast" and "mock rival."

CONCLUSION

The narcissist, preoccupied with self-regard and driven by an overwhelming desire to be appreciated, lives with the paradox of hatred turned inward to the self and distorted entitlement fantasies. The narcissist is constantly searching for a rejoining to a time when mommy and baby were one, a time of being mommy's special child.

The literature suggests that we tread carefully with the narcissist regarding oedipal conflicts to avoid narcissistic injury at all costs. If we take this approach, are we then, like Oedipus, blind? How then do we ever help the narcissist achieve oedipal victory? If we can wean these "kings" and "queens" who lie or sit before us away from guilt, exhibitionism, and arrogance to move toward a resurgence of natural curiosity, we can be assured that as clinicians we are doing our job.

CHAPTER II

The Borderline

CLINICAL DESCRIPTION

Persons who suffer from the borderline syndrome, referred to here as borderlines, do not have much sense of self, do not feel entitled, are subject to annihilation anxieties, and will do anything for others in order to feel a semblance of bonding, relatedness, or connectedness. The borderline often has a distorted self-image, suffers from poor boundaries, and needs a different kind of treatment than the narcissist. Having no earlier memory of entitlement, borderlines, not heavily rooted in their own experience, frequently misperceive who they are and become easily threatened and dominated by other people's views and opinions. The borderline does not develop a feeling of self-worth because needs and feelings are perceived internally as bad and persecutory, and the borderline is quick in finding impulsive ways to relieve anxiety. While the narcissist is trying to prove a special sense of existence, the borderline is trying to prove his/her existence as a thing in itself. With defective ego boundaries and an inability to hold on to needs, thoughts, or feelings, borderlines feel consistently internally impoverished.

Borderlines are overly invested in others, have shame and blame defenses, make use of magical thinking, and are dominated by abandonment anxiety (Case 5). They have moments of pervasive mindlessness and desolation, isolated mental states that are felt to be like bottomless pits or black holes, a phenomenon to be discussed later in this chapter. Borderlines evacuate parts of themselves onto others through projection to get rid of those aspects that are terrifying or that suggest potential danger to the self.

Many borderlines have been physically or emotionally abandoned by abusive or alcoholic parents or parents who are clinically depressed, absent, or psychologically unavailable. Mothers of borderline children, who lack reciprocity with the child's affective states, are unable to validate or confirm the child's experience. "How dare you say I never did anything for you? You know I had a little drinking problem, what did you expect me to do about it? It wasn't my fault! I couldn't help it!" The borderline often becomes the sacrificial object and compromises the self at any price. We see this phenomenon in child custody cases (Lachkar, 1986), as even when the marital bond is broken, primitive emotional, destructive ties remain as powerful forces in these battles.

In the attempt to defend against shame and embarrassment for having needs and desires, the borderline frequently turns to self-soothing modalities in the form of foreign objects, substance abuse, addictive relationships, promiscuity, deviant compulsive behaviors, suicide attempts, and other acts to ward off nameless dread.

Many borderlines experience need as shame. The borderline husband may confide to the therapist, "I'm so ashamed that I told you in front of my wife that I masturbate!" The therapist, who understands the need for detoxification and the techniques by which to accomplish this goal, might respond, "Yes, it is hard to ask your wife for what you need, so you can 'do it' all by yourself, then you don't really need anyone, and you do not have to ask for what you need."

Because borderlines lack maternal bonding experiences of the "good breast," they do not seek, as do narcissists, to reenact the drama of being the special child; this is a pattern the borderline has never experienced. Any reminder of separation or defects relating to these survival issues threatens the borderline's sense of existence, and will bring about such defenses as projection, splitting, denial, magical thinking, persecutory anxiety, and projective identification. Any hint of separation issues may arouse such retaliatory fantasies as to teach the other a lesson. Borderlines search for those with whom they can bond. If the promise of a bond is threatened, the borderline may lash out with a retaliatory response or with self-mutilation.

Borderlines suffer primarily from illusions, rather than delusions or hallucinations. They promise the world, but cannot live up to those promises because of uncontrollable rage as well as general lack of impulse control. For a short while, the borderline can playact at being the good self object and, when coupled with the narcissist, seems capable of mirroring the narcissist's grandiosity and omnipotent fantasies. However, the borderline's lack of impulse control, and inability to contain or hold on to the self, get in the way of ever following through. Inevitably this leads to the borderline's tendency to violent episodes and to intense conflict with his or her mate. Old experiences, as painful as they may be for the borderline, are "safe" because of their familiarity (Lachkar, 1983), and are preferred to new or different encounters.

Borderlines are often "as if" personalities, in Helene Deutsch's term (1942), or "false self" (see Case 4) personalities (Winnicott, 1953, 1965e), a term denoting a masked sense of self. The borderline person will say, "I'll be anything you want me to be, just don't leave me."

The borderline is like a chameleon, and is reminiscent of the character Woody Allen plays in his movie *Zelig*. Woody Allen, as Leonard Zelig, meets a Chinese man, and soon after becomes just like him, even to the point of speaking Chinese. Then he meets a rabbi and he becomes a rabbi, speaking Hebrew, wearing the traditional hat, black long coat, and payots. Then he meets a psychoanalyst, who asks what he does for a living. Woody responds, "Why me? I'm a psychoanalyst," and is glib and imaginative with the jargon.

For the borderline, then, the focus is primarily on bonding and attachment issues. Borderlines often form addictive love relationships (Case 11). Because they lack experience in forming healthy bonding relationships (including normal dependency), they form parasitic relationships, and project their needs in hostile, threatening ways. Because their defenses and demands are excessive, borderlines tend to remain in the dance, rarely achieving their aims.

OBJECT RELATIONS

Object relations is an intrapsychic approach to understanding the internal world, including the patient's "distortions" and "misperceptions." This is a technique whereby one's projections, fantasies, and split off parts of the self are studied in order to comprehend one's inability to have healthy interpersonal relations. Object relations theory provides us with an environmental mother, a background mother, a being/doing mother, a weaning mother, and a containing/sustaining mother, to help establish different kinds of bonding experiences. The importance of therapist/mother as the container becomes more vital in object relations, because the central issues revolve around persecutory anxiety, shame, guilt, confusion, and fantasies of separation.

From an object-relations point of view, the borderline patient is unable to use the self-object relationship. Feeling that needing is bad and shameful, the borderline has a defective capacity to learn from experience. Needs are disavowed and split off, rather than used to reach out to those who can be helpful. The borderline has really never been able to leave the mother's body, thus has difficulty with separateness, and lacks differentiation among reality, myth, self, and object.

The writings of Kernberg, Mahler, Grotstein, Klein, Tustin, Masterson, and Bion, among others, are excellent resources for understanding the borderline syndrome. Kernberg used object-relations theory to expand the concepts of Jacobson, Mahler, Freud, and Klein. The formulations of Masterson (1981), Adler (1985), and Mahler, Pine, and Bergman (1975) elucidated further the profound sense of internal emptiness typically experienced by persons suffering from these emotional deficits.

Kernberg

According to Otto Kernberg's developmental model (1975), the borderline is constantly searching for external organizations and groups with which to easily identify in an effort to overcome the lack of an integrated self-concept (splitting between good and bad objects). In Kernberg's borderline personality model (which is more pathological than Kohut's model of the borderline personality disorder), the borderline clearly shows defenses of splitting and projective identification, a marked impairment in reality testing, and an inability to tolerate frustration.

Adler

Gerald Adler (1985) described a continuum model in which patients with either disorder may flip back and forth or travel along a narcissist and borderline continuum. Adler (1985) viewed the borderline state as being a precursor to transference, and described the basic cause of anxiety as the threat of the loss of the self through disintegration, as a consequence of being abandoned. Adler (1985) described patients with borderline pathology as distinct from those with narcissistic disorders and therefore not amenable to the same kind of treatment. Borderline persons lack evocative memory, and so lack the ability to soothe and relieve their own anxieties.

Winnicott

D. W. Winnicott claimed that the borderline disorder develops from failure of maternal need fulfillment, and because of maternal preoccupation that conforms to the world of "false selves" (see Case 4). Winnicott described a painful inner world that craves to heal.

Winnicott has provided us with the concept of a "holding environment," and an environmental "being mommy," whose function is to help the child with the "being self" (as opposed to the "doing self"). The false self of Winnicott's theory is the doing self, who must conform to mother's wishes and demands.

The being mommy is the one available to the child's being self (through the mother's trying to understand how the child feels as opposed to what the child does). The baby doesn't know when the mother is absent, because the mother is available to anticipate the baby's needs. When there is no caring mother, the baby develops a premature false self or doing self in order to please mommy (see Case 10). Winnicott helps us understand why many borderlines want unconditional love, the love for the being rather than the doing self, the love for *who* rather than *what*; why the person who has missed out on the early attention of the mother now wants mother not part of the time, but all of the time. These patients have difficulty providing for themselves, engage in magical thinking ("If you love me, then you will know what I need without asking"), dress inappropriately, cannot find work, and cannot maintain relationships. In conjoint treatment, the borderline patient will often complain that a mate does not give unconditional love and finds it difficult to understand the therapist's response that unconditional love is for babies, not for adults; adults must come through with their commitments.

Winnicott's concepts of "ego relatedness," the being mommy versus the doing mommy (see Case 10), and the holding, facilitating, or environmental mommy add a new perspective, and provide a powerful approach to understanding the borderline's profound sense of isolation and loneliness.

Masterson

James Masterson has described the rewarding object relations part-unit (RORPU) as a state in which the pathological ego aligns itself to avoid abandonment depression, forming a kind of false adaptation to society, rather than a true or real self. This false self is based on the need to get approval at any cost. The difficulty of self-expression for the borderline was defined by Masterson (1981) as being the need to avoid identifying and activating individuating thoughts and wishes, in order to defend against the abandonment depression that such activation would trigger.

Masterson (1981) has provided us with another acronym, the WORU (withdrawing object relations unit), a situation in which the mother won't be there for the child; if the child has an opposing thought, the mother will withdraw. The need for approval is transformed into punishment from a mother who negates the child's separate views, opinions, and other wishes for self-expression. Masterson (1981) described a mother who appears to be totally absorbed in her child, overcaressing, completely in tune with every nuance of the child's needs and wishes, only to withdraw from the child suddenly, either by turning her attention to other interests, or by grossly misunderstanding the child's needs and wishes.

The borderline patient needs to know that someone will hear a complaint and will not provide them with a "quick fix" (Weiler, 1987). The doing mommy can be experienced as the withdrawing mommy. To fix something too quickly can be the same as getting rid of the child, leaving the child feeling abandoned. For example, if the child says, "I have a headache," and mother responds, "Well, go take a Tylenol!" the child may feel emotionally abandoned.

Grotstein

James Grotstein (1980, 1981, 1983b, 1984a, 1985) not only has made valuable contributions toward an understanding of the pathogenic personalities and primitive mental defenses of the borderline syndrome, but also has provided a meticulous review of the literature. Grotstein insisted that "there still exists unmined psychoanalytic gold in those primitive hills which is very worthwhile exploring" (1980, pp. 479–546), and his in-depth review of primitive mental disorders helps us to perceive how borderlines feel "a nothingness," rely on other objects and substances to deny their depression, and are in continual search for who they are. The depressed borderline person's will to live is disavowed, and appears to be replaced by a psychotic need for an afterlife. Grotstein maintained that borderlines have limited psychic vision lacking in fantasy life, and that their internal world is void of those images that might sooth or fill the empty void.

Borderlines have difficulty differentiating between wanting to do something and doing it. The distinction gets lost in the moment, and the individual does not seem to know the difference between the desire to harm someone and the actual act of doing it. It is one thing to say that you feel like hitting or killing someone, or chopping off his head, and another thing to do it!

When the infant does not develop the sense of confidence in the mother's capacity as a maternal container for psychic content, bonding does not take place. Grotstein (1987a) gives Bowlby credit for proposing that bonding and attachment is the fundamental model for both normal and abnormal personality development. Bonding is basic to all elements of human life, in that it encompasses all of "our attempts to regulate and be regulated and to establish meaningfulness for ourselves and others" (Grotstein, 1987a, p. 5). The treatment for the borderline (discussed in detail in Chapter VIII) must therefore address what gets in the way of bonding and relating, and must take into account the deficits, psychological or neurobiological, or psychical.

Klein

Melanie Klein, has contributed more than any other author to our understanding of the need for the mother and maternal attachment. Her ideas are also applicable to the treatment of couples exhibiting infantile persecutory anxiety and primitive defenses.

Klein developed the term "reparation" (a concept that will be addressed in more detail elsewhere in this book) out of a need to "repair" in her own personal life. Klein suffered the death of a sister with whom she had intense rivalry and all the attendant conflicts: ambivalence toward her mother; rejection from her father; and an oedipal triangle with her brother and her mother (Clayman-Cook, 1987) Grosskurth (1986) and Clayman-Cook (1987) put together the pieces of Klein's tragic life to demonstrate the impact her early experiences had on her life as a whole, and on her intimate experiences as an adult and as a psychoanalyst.

Klein, formulating her theories upon her own experience, has given us an unusual appreciation for the preoedipal struggles occurring within the early formative years of ego/self development. "Melanie was born to the apparent disappointment of her mother and father" (Clayman-Cook, 1987, p. 29), and reared in a nonloving environment (where she sensed that her parents valued her sister and other siblings more than herself). Klein had insight into the early stages of infantile development. She was the only sibling not breast fed by her mother; she was fed instead by a wet nurse. Perhaps because of the deprivation she suffered in her infantile years of envy and rivalry, Klein clearly understood the need for the mother and the breast. She believed that through the process of identification with the maternal object, the infant feels safe, for it is only then that it has "possession of the breast."

Klein's description of the fantasized attacks the infant makes upon the breast relates to the notion that the infant cannot tolerate any painful feelings (such as waiting), and therefore splits those painful feelings off, and projects them into the external world and eventually onto the analyst. The fear that someday these projected feelings will backfire forms a preponderance of destructive impulses to turn away from reality, and we see this occur with the borderline personality. The therapist must make a meticulous effort not to take in the negative projections the borderline has assigned and to avoid identifying with that which is being projected. The therapist must safeguard against "owning" a part of the projected destructive aspects of the personality.

Bion

It was Wilfred Bion who transformed Melanie Klein's ideas into practical conceptions. For Bion, as for Klein, a good breast becomes experiences such as warm empathic responses related to others, and not the breast as a thing in itself. Bion's profound contributions were based primarily on the philosophy of Immanuel Kant.

Bion's epigenetic developmental theory is used to help explain how couples and individuals learn or don't learn from experience; why individuals repeat the same mistake over and over again; and how and why they seek out or avoid truth, learn to think or to avoid thinking, and learn to think or not to think about the unthinkable thoughts. Bion teaches us how to think and to understand how thinking becomes distorted.

To understand Bion, it is important to know something about the special language used to describe his concepts.

The "K" Link

Bion's innovative construct uses the letter k (as in knowledge) to describe an emotional link between people. The "k" link typifies the individual who tries to find truth through introspection and psychoanalytic inquiry, and − k (minus k) suggests the reverse. The k link is based on the search for truth and knowledge, and the − k link represents the avoidance of truth and knowledge (Bion, 1963; Grinberg, Sor, & de Bianchedi, 1977).

Alpha and Beta Elements

Alpha elements are functions that can be used for verbal thoughts and expressions that are suitable for communication, learning, and thinking. Beta elements (or functions) are undigested facts; beta functions are not memories, but refer to intolerable affects that can be used only for evacuation, not for thinking or learning from experience.

Detoxification

Detoxification is the nullification of the poisonous substance that the child experiences when feeling bad inside. The process involves the therapist's ability to take the toxins or poisons out of the patient's internal world and transform them into a more digestible form, suitable for thinking and understanding.

Transformations

The transformation from beta elements to alpha function requires a container, a person who can make use of the projections and who is able to provide a good breast. If the good breast has not been experienced, one cannot possibly know of its existence ($-$ k). If you tell someone to think about snow and that person has never been in snow, there will be no reference for that experience. If you tell someone to think positive when he or she has had only negative experiences, the person will be unable to formulate positive thoughts.

The "Quick Fix"

According to Bion (1977), anxiety is useful in channeling painful affects into constructive avenues. Splitting off of important affective experiences can severely interfere with healthy object relations. Usually each partner is quick to relieve the other from anxiety by offering a quick solution or a "quick fix" because neither can hold onto painful thoughts, feelings, and affects long enough to work anything through.

Containment

Containment is a term employed by Wilfred Bion to describe the dynamic relationship between the mother and the infant. Bion's model of the "container and the contained" connotes the mother's capacity for transformation of incoherent emotional experience into meaningful feelings and thoughts. The mother's capacity to withstand the child's projections, anger, frustration, and intolerable feelings becomes the support base or "container" for these affects. This can occur if the mother can sustain intolerable behaviors long enough to decode or detoxify them. Bion believed that the therapist's/mother's capacity must be deep enough to hold the projections and not abandon the child.

Containment is needed because of the borderline's tendency to externalize and to blame others; therefore, it is difficult for the borderline to use others as self objects and to maintain them as a source of nurturance. The ability of the mother or therapist to withhold and withstand for the child the intolerable feelings long enough to understand those feelings is an aspect of containment.

Because needs are warded off by shame, borderlines have a pervasive tendency to force, intrude, or invade their objects. The tendency to evacuate is considered tantamount to getting rid of a crucial part of the self, namely, needs and feelings. For Bion (1977), all needed objects are bad objects; they are needed because they are not possessed. Many borderlines experience need as shame.

Thinking

According to Bion (Grinberg et al., 1977), thinking is a function of the personality. Bion presented the development of thought from (1) preconception, to (2) conception, to (3) concept.

These stages can be illustrated by the relation of the infant to the breast. A preconception occurs where the infant has an innate idea that somewhere there is a breast; but without ever having experienced the breast, the infant remains hungry and frustrated without knowing why. This is called a preconception. When the infant has an experience with the breast, a mating between the nipple and the mouth, this becomes a conception. When infants can realize they need the breast or realize what is missing, they start to develop thoughts about the breast, a concept. Borderlines tend to disregard preconceptions.

The therapist's use of "preconception" (an unborn thought, like intuition) is crucial in modeling that one is not afraid to trust one's own sensory perceptions as is typical of the borderline partner. Preconceptions, curiosity, thoughts, needs, and feelings terrorize and persecute the individual. Thinking never develops when psychic conflict is felt to be too threatening, as in, for example, "I can't stand to feel like a helpless little boy." The containing therapist might respond, "Yes, but if you can depend on me, then that little boy part of you can grow; if not, you will always feel little and small."

The therapist's avoidance of preconceptions may collude with the patient's own vagueness, aloofness, lack of clarity, confusion, and fear of risking, fear of sounding foolish, and hopelessness.

BLACK HOLES

There is much in current physics literature on the possible existence in the universe of black holes (Hawking, 1988). According to Hawking, the actual, physical black hole is an object of such density and such magnetism that it swallows up whatever comes into its path. It is called a black hole because it emits no light; that which has fallen into its abyss has forever disappeared. This, of course, is a gross oversimplification but, with apologies to the field of physics, serves the purpose for the analogy presented here.

The metaphorical, psychological black hole is defined by Silverman as follows: "The black hole is the experience of emptiness, the void governed by despair and disillusionment" (Silverman, 1988). Grotstein described the terror of the black hole as being the result of unknowable forces, the underlying elements influencing disruptive states, or as derivatives of catastrophic states. It is therefore the state of meaninglessness that epitomizes states of terror, rather than deprivation itself.

Grotstein characterized the human as being "meaning-obsessed," (1987a, p. 5). I believe Grotstein has validated my own hypothesis that it is not for the cure that one searches, but rather for meaning and understanding. Many borderlines suffer from endogenous depression and must defend themselves against the experience of being sucked into a black hole, the sensation of disappearing, falling, or vanishing. Black holes often represent the ultimate damage of dissolution (Silverman, 1988), and the ultimate of danger, falling into a bottomless pit, a vacuum without any ground or foundation to "hold." It is annihilation/disintegration of the self, the dissolution into a state of nothingness (Grotstein, 1984b), the disintegration of the self, and the lack of "evocative memory," which is defined by the loss of the capacity for object constancy (Adler, 1985). Bion (1962) called this syndrome "nameless dread." Tustin (1981) described the sense of emptiness as a result of premature rupture of primary oneness.

The appearance of black holes is very common in the artwork of borderline patients. According to Silverman (1988), the artwork of borderline patients is consistently dominated by black holes, empty spaces, voids, and a most profound experience of aloneness and emptiness (Silverman, 1988, p. 15). It is their attempt to communicate this experience that is beyond words (beyond verbal descriptions).

My visualization of the black hole within the internal mental space of the borderline is of a round circle with nothing inside. Imagine a blank circle, the blank part within the circle represents the void, the inability to hold thoughts as they relate to experiences. Then imagine what happens when the borderline learns that developed thoughts do not destroy. The empty circle image is replaced by the circle with little dots inside, dots that represent ideas, thoughts, and experiences that can now be useful, for thinking and decision making.

I propose that it is not so much deprivation that contributes to conflict with reality for the borderline as it is meaninglessness that constitutes the major modes of the borderline's mental state. Grotstein's explanation of the borderline's experiential state is that it is based on the "dialectic of the anxiety over the consequences of abandonment," the "terror of the unknown." He suggested that it is the "anxiety over predation or mutilation as the known or knowable terrors, but ultimately the terror is one of "nameless dread," of chaos, of entropy, of meaninglessness, of nothingness" (1987a, p. 4). The ultimate terror then is for the borderline to fall into the black hole.

When we deal with as complex an issue as the borderline personality, it may help to appeal to literature for an appropriate analogy, one that will help us define the implications of theories about the borderline personality with respect to therapy and the borderline syndrome. Franz Kafka's *Metamorphosis* gives a vivid depiction of the borderline personality, and reflects how the experience of needing can be a grotesque phenomenon (Eyton, 1986; Kafka, 1915). *Metamorphosis* presents a model for Kafka's own abandonment fears, anxiety, depression, and parasitic dependency needs. Kafka illuminated the borderline's general confusion of normal and healthy desires, wishes, and needs with something ugly and disdainful.

In the story, Gregor becomes transformed into an insect in a metamorphosis resulting from Gregor's mother's lack of attunement and empathy, and her inability to offer containment or reverie to Gregor's abandonment anxiety, feelings of betrayal, disavowal, shame, and self-compromise. Gregor's parents seem to have no regard for his individual needs, and his "needs" are reduced to those of the insect he has become, and reflect his despair and grotesqueness. Gregor becomes the little adult, feels indebted to his parents, and has to provide for them (borderlines tend to have a predisposition for this kind of self-subjugation, sacrifice, and self-compromise). The feeling of not existing as a human being, typical for borderlines, is of course also exemplified by Gregor.

Kafka has given us a sense of the overwhelming nature of the borderline syndrome, and of the complexity of the borderline personality.

CONCLUSION

In love relationships borderlines tend to distort and misperceive the good intentions of others. Because words can be used just as much for evacuation as they can for verbal thought, the experienced and sensitive clinical ear begins to pay more attention to what is projected rather than what is said.

Object relations has offered principles useful in understanding the borderline personality, has bestowed us with a wealth of concepts useful for conjoint treatment. Application of object-relations theory helps these patients to take more responsibility for feelings and behaviors. Patients are enabled to think more rationally, to make use of perceptions and experiences, and to take some control over their own destinies. In probing the primitive mind, Bion teaches us how to think, how to listen, how to experience, to "detox," "transform," "contain," and "sustain" powerful emotions that transcend ordinary human capacity. To paraphrase Freud, where shame was, thoughts shall be.

CHAPTER III

The Couple

The Dance, The Bond,
The Drama

The configurations of the narcissistic/borderline couple are conceptualized within the metaphor of the dance to describe the ongoing, circular, and never-ending movements. There is a dance between the partners, but there is also a dance between the psychodynamics (movements between the intrapsychic and the interpersonal). There is a dynamic flow in the interactions of the partners as they move between idealization and devaluation, projection and introjection, shame and guilt, manic defenses and helplessness, and envy and greed. The vacillation between processes keeps these partners in a state of unresolved tension and conflict.

An individual may have both borderline and narcissistic characteristics; since these can occur simultaneously (Cases 1 & 2), it may not be clear if the person is a borderline or a narcissist, or is just exhibiting certain features within a particular dyadic unit.

Previously we asked, which borderline are we talking about? Which narcissist are we talking about? The "drive and defense" (Kernbergian narcissist), the "libidinal" (Freudian narcissist), the "developmentally arrested self object" (Kohutian narcissist)? To add to the confusion of which borderline are we talking about?—there is the lower functioning, more disturbed Kernbergian borderline, and there is also a higher functioning Kohutian borderline. Also, to which object are we referring?

A Freudian object, a Kleinian internal object, a Kohutian mirroring self object? (Chapter IV explains this in further detail.)

Grotstein (1985) emphasized that many techniques are necessary in this couple therapy, but asserted that the narcissist is in need of a more empathic mode than the borderline, and suggested that empathy must be interwoven with interpretation about the dynamics of the primitive unconscious. Grotstein (1991) also maintains, "The narcissist is not only looking for perfection, but also seeks perfection to defend against internal persecutory anxiety whereas the borderline seems to give up on attaining perfection, and instead, projects the ideal into others imploring them to be their leader, an invitation which a narcissist cannot resist" (personal communication). Winnicott (1953) introduced the issue of management, indicating that management is the thing that patients lacked in the early developmental process. Kernberg (1975) suggested more confrontational, environmental interventions, or supportive psychotherapy for the borderline. Francis Tustin's (1981) notion of the "hard object" corresponds to this line of inquiry, in that the more disturbed child (encapsulated psychotic child) substantially needs hard objects to stand against in order to feel safe. The complexity of these entangled relationships and the borderline/narcissist defensive structures are viewed within a theoretical framework with the hope that this approach will prove useful to therapists.

It may prove helpful, before we address the major topic of this book, to spend a few moments with the psychoanalytic and therapeutic foundations of the ideas you will find here.

Freud

Sigmund Freud saw classical psychoanalysis as a medical science and competed with other physicians to prove a scientific foundation to his theories. Freud believed that humans were dominated by biology and were born with either a force toward life (Eros) or a force toward death (Thanatos).

Freud was destined, however, to develop a more object-relational approach. The movement away from the individual toward a more personal theory of relationships actually began with Freud's formulation of the Oedipus complex, his finale to the external struggles of human beings, and group psychology. Freud considered a man's ability to find a place in a civilized world to be contingent on his ability to live safely in father's house, tame his own sexual urges, find his own sexual mate, and live amicably, while allowing his father to have his own life.

Freudian treatment had to do mainly with love and hate feelings, and how those feelings lead to either happy, healthy experiences or destructive experiences, depending on the amount of libidinal or aggressive energy coming from the drives within the individual. Although his approach became somewhat more object relational, in general, Freud did not recognize the importance of relating to others. How does this suggest the therapist handle an overly aggressive partner? "Are you a bully because of your 'aggression' or are you a bully because there is not an other to help you contain your impulses?"

Ego Psychologists

Ego psychologists distinguish between ego, as an agency of the psyche, and self, leading to the perception of a self separate from a physiological ego. In ego psychology, the focus is primarily on the interpersonal.

Ego-psychology theories are the primary basis for object-relational thinking, and for determining how the elements of the ego are played out against the environment. Ego psychologists have weaned us from biology, replacing the medical model with an experiencing ego, suitable for adaptation. They have replaced the term "id" with the term "object."

There were a number of theorists who advanced the movement away from Freudian analysis to self psychology and object relations: The work of Harry Stack Sullivan (1953) is significant because of its emphasis on the interpersonal as it relates to development. Alfred Adler (1927), who saw a human being not as an isolated entity but as one who moves toward others, stressed the importance of social urges in the development of personality. A number of ego psychologists, including Sullivan, Heinz Hartmann, Erik Erikson, and Ronald Fairbairn, focused mainly on anthropology, sociology, and the social sciences.

Hartmann (1958) developed revolutionary ideas, including the notion of adaptation, distinguishing between self and ego. He distinguished between "ego function" and "id-theory." For Hartmann, the ego had two aspects: as an organ against the inner world, and as an organ of adaptation to the outer world.

Edith Jacobson (1964) followed Hartmann's elaboration of integrated experiences of self evolving the self in the context of love objects (cited in Hedges, 1983). Erikson lines up with Hartmann in the view that a human being is more a social being than a biological one (Erikson, 1950). His work on social development and ego identity is particularly enlightening.

D. W. Winnicott's basic premise was that the ability to relate well with others depends on the baby's capacity to internalize the mother as a "good enough mother," or the "being mother"; and the baby's distinguishing between being alone and aloneness, or privation and deprivation. Winnicott's concept of the holding environment represents baby's early stage of development where there is perfect reciprocity, attunement, and at-one-ness with the "being self." The baby who is deficient in these early modes of relating comes to expect others to make up for these deficiencies. Wanting unconditional love leaves one in constant search for the unattainable object, responding through either the "false" or the "doing" self, ultimately leading to destructive or antisocial behavior.

Fairbairn (1954), departing from the classical Freudian view, believed that the child is born whole, is not tainted by instincts, and needs good objects, and that the ultimate goal is toward integrating life's experiences as they influence development. According to Fairbairn and Winnicott, good maternal experience leads to good ego development and primary at-one-ness of the child with that child's primary caretakers, and is crucial to the development of good object relationships.

Object-Relations Theorists

Hartmann (1958) paid attention to the society and adaptation as a means of relatedness, while Melanie Klein attended to the conceptual apparatus of the internal world. Klein, without intending to do so, provided a major tie between psychoanalysis and systems thinking in her effort to view conflict, the unconscious provocation one object has on another. She based these reactions entirely upon early infantile fantasies emanating from within one's internal world: the world of fusion, introjects, projections, part objects, and splitting mechanisms. Heinz Kohut (1971, 1977), as a self psychologist rather than an object-relations theorist, created other modes of relatedness using such clinical concepts as mirroring, idealization, self-object formation ties, and narcissistic transferences.

It was Klein who made an actual breakthrough in object-relational thinking. While remaining loyal to Freud's structural paradigm, Klein developed her own unique concept of an internal psychic world of ego-object relationships, maintaining that the environment is secondary; hence the beginnings of object relations and the term "psychodynamic." That is to say, all internal objects are projected outward, and when experiences of the outer world are reintrojected from the environment, one's impressions and one's existing anxieties are magnified.

For Klein, the environment is merely a mirror reflecting the baby's already existing internal conflicts. Klein believed that the first form of anxiety is persecutory. As Segal (1964) stated, the environment confirms, but it does not originate, the baby's primary anxieties and inner conflicts. Klein developed the idea of pathological splitting of "good and bad" objects through the defensive processes of projection and introjection in relations ascribed to primitive anxiety of the death instinct. The death instinct gives rise to the fear of annihilation, and is the true and ultimate persecution.

Klein taught us how one can form an identification with others and even with parts of others (also known as whole and part objects).

Klein's notion that individuals are object seeking and object relational, not drive seeking, was her main shift from a Freudian orientation. Her views offer profound insights into primitive pathologies (e.g., perversions) and into how one can form an identification not only with another person, but with part objects (e.g., a breast, a penis, or even one's car, urine, or semen) as expressions of bodily experiences. Klein helps us understand how one either has to possess the breast or can allow the breast to feed and nurture. This phenomenon is similar to Meltzer's description of "zonal confusion" (1967). The contributions of Klein help us understand the more severe pathologies, such as those of the psychotic and the borderline personalities (the abused child, the battered wife), and how one can identify with another person through love, envy, or greed (part object functioning).

Klein helps us understand loss and abandonment as linked to the memory traces of the bad breast, the absent breast, or the unavailable breast, as opposed to the good breast. The bad breast may be perceived as a frightful destructive force (the "death instinct"), which, when introjected into the infant turns up not as an instinct, but as an object. Klein's emphasis was away from sexual tensions and psychosexual issues and to the dual nature of the instincts relating to the formation of identification with the mother and with parts of the mother's body. Although Klein did not dispute environmental deficits and their effects, she did emphasize patients' accountability for their own distortions, projections, and complaints. This point is significant in conjoint treatment.

I believe that many theoreticians today tend to take Klein too literally, and apply concrete meanings to Kleinian conceptualizations. In Mason's view, "Many do not read Klein carefully enough, but when they do can see that she explains quite extensively that 'breast' stands for 'mothering capacity,' which the baby relates to from birth in a very complex way" (personal communication, 1988).

Object relations were clarified by Mahler, Pine, and Bergman (1975). Mahler and colleagues described development phases beginning with an autistic phase, which gradually evolves to symbiosis followed by a practicing phase and culminating in a separation phase during which the children gradually differentiate and separate from their mother, and begin to establish an individual identity. It is during the last phase that the child becomes aware of the external environment.

Mahler and colleagues described splitting as a representation of mother into good and bad as a consequence of separation-individuation, a subphase of rapprochement, and as the core of the borderline pathology in children and adults.

Kernberg (1975, 1976, 1980) remained faithful to the concept of intrapsychic phenomena and excessive aggressive drive as motivating forces and to Freud's instinctual drive and defense theory. One's aggression, then, gets in the way of ever achieving success or object constancy. Mother is either perceived as all good or all bad, according to whether or not she gratifies the child.

Complementing Kernberg are Masterson (1975) and Rinsley (1978). These authors explained how these early experiences reinforce the child's tendency toward splitting.

Klein's views appear to have been different from Kernberg's in that Kernberg considered reality testing by interpreting resistance, defensive operations, and the negative transference. Kernberg attempted to reach "reality" through interpretation of defense and resistance, pointing out to the patient oral rage and aggression whereas Klein reached "reality" through primitive fantasy and persecutory anxiety. Klein, too, considered reality testing significant, but her emphasis was on psychic reality.

Self Psychologists

Self psychologists moved away from Freud's structural theory and instinctual drives toward an emphasis on self-mirroring objects.

Heinz Kohut was the psychoanalyst who introduced self psychology by expanding Heinz Hartmann's (1958) conceptual distinction between ego and self. Kohut and his followers—mainly Brandchaft, Stolorow, Lachmann—developed a set of organizing principles to understand certain kinds of persons exhibiting features that Kohut called narcissistic. Kohut's focus is on the rupture of the relationship and maintaining a bond through the ties to the analyst, Narcissistic pathology develops primarily, then, because of faulty mirroring and empathic failures with archaic objects.

In more recent years Kohut's ideas have been expanded to include the use of empathy—that is, the analyst's ability to become immersed in the patient's experience, in order to form a transference relationship.

Kohut did not feel that the more primitive states of narcissism were analyzable (Lachkar, 1985b, 1986). The authors who supported self psychology, including Atwood (1984), believed psychoanalytic origins must be sought in the subjective meaning emanating from the patient's experience.

Some of the confusion in discussing these pathogenic states stems from the complexity of the subject and the fact that Kohut's ideas are ever changing. At one time, Kohut found only certain forms of narcissistic disorders to be suitable for treatment, the patients with those disorders being those capable of developing a narcissistic transference relationship (Lachkar, 1984, 1985b).

Later Kohut began to conceptualize all disorders as disorders of the self, and viewed narcissism as part of a normal developmental phase. Stolorow and Lachmann (1980) modified Kohut's view on transference, stating that it is a conceptual error to consider the term "self-object transferences" as applicable to a type of individual, and that transference must be viewed as multidimensional.

In a dyadic relationship, whether through id, self, or "the other," the conjoint therapist has a new dimension in which to observe interpersonal intrapsychic conflict. All of this is significant to conjoint treatment.

THE DANCE

The metaphor of the dance has been used to describe interactions between narcissistic and borderline individuals (Lachkar, 1984, 1985b). For the narcissist, the movements of
the dance revolve around the major features of specialness,
adoration, and exaggerated entitlement fantasies. These are
accompanied by the defenses of isolation, withdrawal, omnipotence, guilt, and denial as protection against personal injury
to the self. Narcissists are higher on the continuum than
borderlines because they are dominated more by guilt than by
shame; tend to introject more than project; and have strong
punitive superegos that operate in terms of self-persecution,
self-hate, and guilt. In contrast, borderlines are not dominated
by superego demands, but instead respond to bodily sensations,
and are tormented by split-off affects and needs. Needs are
experienced as dangerous internal forces that are disruptive
and invasive. These forces are pronounced by shame, envy,
and persecutory anxiety. When the narcissist and the borderline
join, these dynamics initiate and engage these individuals in
an ongoing state of upheaval.

The Steps

"It's not the steps that count but it's how you do them."
Carmelita Marcacci (personal communication, 1977), master
ballet teacher, acknowledged as one of the world's greatest
dancers and choreographers, put it just that simply. Marcacci's
theatrical approach is applicable to the treatment of these
couples in understanding their dramatic interplay.

Every dancer knows about the importance of boundaries.
Dancers know the difference between spatial and emotional
boundaries. To invade another dancer's physical space leads
to a physical collision; the dancer knows how to protect
emotional space as well, and how not to allow others to intrude.
To search for approval of an audience or dance master, for
example, can lead to a loss of balance, a loss of timing, and a
loss of one's sense of center.

Psychoanalytic technique and theory are meaningless unless they are artistically, emotionally, and creatively executed. Every psychological movement, like every dance step interpretation, is poignantly expressed and has a purpose and a direct focus. Maracci emphasized that every step, movement, and gesture must be understood internally, processed, and related to a feeling state, or to a mode of experience before it is executed into the external experience. For instance, let us consider the parallel between intervention and interpretation. In a dance, if one performs an arm gesture, one must conjure up a thought, an image, or a feeling relating to the movement so as to give it meaning; otherwise, the gesture becomes empty and meaningless. In psychological parallel, it is appropriate for the couple to freely associate, argue, or battle; for the therapist, such behavior is inappropriate. What the therapist says and does must be conveyed with conviction and meaning. In interpretation, idle talk is not the same as words that are related to a feeling state. The therapist must convey a message with passion, focus, and conviction, and must not transmit what Bion referred to as idle whistling.

As with the dancer or the musician, playing the notes or doing the steps is not enough. Eye contact, tone of voice, gestures, phrasing, timing, and intonations cannot be taught, but come from within. I am not suggesting that all psychotherapists study some art form; I am, however, suggesting that we all try to be as sensitive and as spontaneous as possible, to allow ourselves to be unique, and to recognize that there is a carryover from other art forms to the art of psychoanalysis.

Hence, the pas de deux begins to unfold. For the soloist, the narcissist in the relationship (the one requiring center stage attention), the dance revolves around a different configuration of movements. The narcissist says to the borderline: "I'm here because I see my own needy child part in you, and if I leave, I leave behind an infantile part of myself that is yearning to become resolved and get worked through." The narcissist keeps returning to the narcissist/borderline relationship, in part out of disappointment and guilt. Feeling seduced by the borderline partner, the narcissist tends to fall for the false hopes and promises over and over again. The dance within the dyad is maintained through these unresolved parts.

Driven by the need to be desired and appreciated, the narcissist will be the one who most often tends to withdraw. Fearing a loss of specialness, this partner is easily injured or outraged when not properly mirrored or understood. The narcissist, with an exaggerated sense of entitlement, seeks out others to confirm and to justify these distortions, while the borderline feels left out, displaced, outcast, nondeserving, worthless, and empty.

In my view, typically it is disappointment in the outside world that draws the narcissist back to the borderline partner. The borderline, suffering from engulfment and abandonment anxiety, becomes an available "secure" object to return to. Because of faulty object relations, the narcissist becomes easily injured, and relationships are easily disjointed and disrupted. Disappointment occurs because narcissistic personalities act as though they are truly superior to others and devalue their objects. In treatment, the narcissists often are the ones who "know more" and are "always right." Greed, envy, grandiosity, and the flipping back and forth of the idealization and devaluation process interfere considerably with the continuity of the treatment. Many of these couples cannot stay in conjoint treatment. The narcissistic partner tends to dominate and take control (the inflated sense of self), as if to say, "We don't need anyone's help." They cannot tolerate hearing another person's point of view, and will often defend against it by engaging in battles or arguments.

For the borderline, then, the movements take on a different configuration. The borderline moves toward the object when there is hope of bonding, and away (through defenses of blaming, attacking, splitting, projection and projective identification, sadistic attacks, and evacuation) when there is a threat to that bond.

The borderline stays in the dance because of the need to work through feelings of unworthiness. Lack of conviction keeps the borderline plodding along on treacherous ground and from doing the steps to get out of the circle.

The borderline can playact at being the mirroring self object for the narcissist only for a short while. Then the narcissist's tendency to withdraw evokes profound abandonment anxiety within the borderline partner. The narcissist leaves, either physically or emotionally, but returns out of a pervasive sense of guilt-ridden anxiety and disappointment in the external world. The use of transitional objects for the borderline is limited, thereby making loneliness even more excruciatingly painful.

Many borderlines continue to live in impoverished and bankrupt inner states because they quickly give up parts of themselves much too soon. They fuse or align themselves with others to validate or justify that the "badness" is in the other. They get lost in the choreographic schemes of the narcissist and their own promises that they can never keep. Their inability to tolerate any of their own badness keeps them feeling empty and unfulfilled. The desire to believe in the other as the savior who will make things right keeps the borderline in the dance.

In order to maintain a semblance of specialness, narcissists are continually drawn to a tie with archaic objects. They turn to borderlines, believe in their promises; but borderlines, lacking evocative memory, cannot live up to their promises. The narcissist, whose idealization of others results in a state of constant yearning for approval from others, may leave or withdraw from the relationship, feeling disappointed and overwhelmed, or may respond through intellectualization or a defensive narcissistic rage. The tragedy is that a new ending to the pas de deux seems never to come.

Circular Behaviors

As the narcissist/borderline dance becomes apparent, so does a pattern emerge. The interactions are circular and are never ending. The dancers go round and round, and the observing therapist even begins to get dizzy. The therapist, unlike the couple, must maintain the focus, and teach the partners to "spot." The spot, as all dancers know, is crucial to maintaining one's balance and equilibrium.

As the drama unfolds in many of these relationships, there is the desire for a new ending. This circular, repetitive behavior becomes very intense, and since conflicts unfortunately do not get resolved through repetition, they often end in frustration and rage. Because of the intense need and desire to be at one with another, the inadequate sense of self-worth, and the desire to prove worthiness, borderlines seem to be always available. Narcissists, by contrast, withdraw and isolate themselves when not properly appreciated or mirrored. Such oppositions of movements often bring about a profound threat to one's sense of existence, which is always subject to predation and outside danger. For the narcissist, being stuck in the circle represents avoidance of the problem. To face a problem, from the narcissist's perspective, is tantamount to being less than perfect. For the borderline, to face one's problem is equivalent to being bad, and thereby not deserving to exist in the world.

In the following exchange in an individual session, the therapist could soon see the first indication of a potentially narcissistic wife, ready to engage in circular behavior:

THERAPIST: I understand that you are mad.
WIFE: I'm not mad, I'm, I'm angry.
THERAPIST: You're angry.
WIFE: I'm not angry, I'm frustrated!

The therapist was left feeling helpless, and it became clear that the patient might be a narcissist in need of perfect mirroring and responses. The patient was letting the therapist know how difficult it was for her to digest, or to be able to take inside, anything the therapist had to say. The patient appeared to need to be in charge of her own words, because she would not count on the therapist to understand her. The therapist responded, "You must get upset when I or others fail to understand you."

As the therapist in this case, I used my empathy and countertransference. I let the patient know that I understood what it feels like to be frustrated, and said, "I do not have the special words." The patient would not yet be told about her confusion, and how she evoked hostile and sadistic responses in others.

The same narcissistic wife was in a session with her borderline husband. In this case this led to sexual withdrawal on the part of the narcissistic wife, and feelings that he was nondeserving and bad for needing on the part of the borderline husband.

Other patients of mine, Mary and her husband, Joe, were having a sexual problem. In our conjoint session Mary began, "I asked him to rub my thigh and suddenly he pinches me!" Joe turned toward her and said, "I did not pinch you!" She insisted, "Yes you did!" He repeated, "I did not pinch you! You asked me to rub your thigh and that's what I did." She snapped back, "How can you say that? I am telling you, you pinched me and I don't like that!" Joe shook his head, "There you go again, you always have to have it your own way" (as his wife demonstrated the narcissist's need for perfect stroking). "Now I know what you're going to do. You're going to withdraw from me, and not have sex with me and not talk to me for several days." For a while Joe said nothing, but then he suddenly spoke: "OK, I'm sorry, I won't do that again!" (the borderline tendency to subjugate self).

The borderline husband becomes compliant and subjugates himself and his needs. Unable to take up an issue and sort out something that has been bothering him, he takes out his frustration by pinching his wife. Typically, borderlines perceive neediness as bad and cannot tolerate owning up to their needs, so they instead express needs in hostile, destructive ways. Aggression gets confused with real needs for love, affection, time, and attention, and the borderline husband pinches his narcissist wife.

When in a "pinch" the therapist must take the focus off the aggression and get to the legitimacy of needs and entitlement. We must get beyond the pinch, and try to consider the hurt feelings, because if we do not, we will all be in a fight or all going around in circles together, pinching one another.

The kind of sexual withdrawal that took place in this scenario is indicative of circular behavior. The couple needs a therapist who is willing to decode, and to pay attention to conflictual issues and safeguard each against defensive actions.

The question is not who is right and who is wrong. Each partner has a subjective experience of the truth. To engage in the fight—"Let's go find the faulty one, the enemy, the one to blame"—does not lead to a "feeding" therapeutic session of richness and understanding; instead it brings both partners to impoverishment and more emptiness because it perpetuates the dance. The need is for the therapist to understand each person's experience and the real underlying issue, to decode and detoxify empathically the complex communications and the unthinkable thoughts, and then to translate them into a tolerable language.

. The active involvement of the therapist through immersion into the couple's confusional distorted inner world can help to enhance the holding quality of the couple's circular interactions, enabling more understanding of their subjective experience. Couples often attempt to engage the therapist in fights. It is difficult for the therapist to maintain the roles of therapist, mediator, and mommy when immersed in the couple's quarrels and arguments. To help diminish circular communications, the therapist almost has to assume the role of a mommy with two children or siblings. By interpreting the wish to disavow the other person's subjective experience, or by interpreting the desire to engage us in an argument, we not only can provide a profound diminishment of primitive defenses, but can encourage the development of healthy ego functioning. In this modality, we can offer emotional relief to facilitate the formation of appropriate affects and feelings as they relate to real needs.

Individuals in narcissistic/borderline relationships are very bonded and connected. As uncomfortable as these couples may feel, the partners are joined together in spite of the discomforts. One partner evokes in the other some aspect of the self that needs to be worked through. My experience has taught me to understand these aspects not merely as symptoms of a sick relationship. The conflicts contribute to some invaluable developmental insights (e.g., the partner not being good enough, not deserving enough, not knowing how to mourn). The therapist might say: "You are trying to change your husband to be a special way with you, the way you always wished your father would be with you. The only problem is, if you keep trying to change either of them, then you can't see either of them as he truly is, or allow yourself to mourn, grieve, or deal with the loss, and ultimately experience the opportunity to repair the damage within yourself."

It is important to illustrate the difference between feeling like pinching someone and actually doing it. It is OK to wish it, to say it, or express it in another way, but it is not OK to do it! If there is someone to attack, there must be some good reason to protest. Bonding is difficult, especially for borderlines, because of the false self that continually aims to please. Often the borderline will project into the narcissist that the narcissist is too critical, while the borderline will assume the role of the innocent victim, and will act out repressed feelings by never complaining. Often these repressed desires are demonstrated in passive-aggressive ways (see Case 6). For a self that wishes desperately to comply, there is little or no awareness; instead there is a withdrawing into a wishful, dreamy, sleeplike state, frequently associated with the defenses of projection, evacuation, and massive denial of envy and greed. These passive-aggressive features, which tend to evoke intense reactions (feelings of betrayal, confusion, disappointment) in the narcissist, also leave the borderline feeling internally empty.

Because borderlines cannot tolerate needing, and cannot own up to their own inner badness, they need a bad object (such as a rejecting spouse) to project onto. In this way, they can hang on to the good and caring parts of themselves, and can say, "Look what they have done to me!" Because of shame, borderlines often resort to victimization.

The narcissist who needs perfect mirroring, perfect stroking, and perfect responses is seeking to be in control, and when personally injured, typically withdraws. Rather than focusing on the "real" issues, the area of anxiety, the narcissist turns away from the self and the frustrations of not always being the "special child." The narcissistic wife in our scenario was asking for unconditional love, and she needed desperately to understand that unconditional love is for babies and children and not for adults. She may not have realized her need for perfection, how her tone of voice affected the way she forced her needs upon others, and how this may actually have evoked responses such as pinching.

The circle continues; the dance goes on; the need of narcissists to bond and fuse makes them more likely to be with those who offer the promise to admire, confirm, and reaffirm the grandiose self. Narcissists find individuals to bond with who can affirm their view of the bad borderline daddy, husband, or mommy who mistreated or bankrupted them, giving further justification to the already existing omnipotent and virtuoso self. The narcissist usually returns to the borderline in the hope that the borderline's new promises will be fulfilled, only to find that it ends again and again with, "Look, there you go again." Continual withdrawal strips the narcissist of feelings, resources, thinking, and, most importantly, reality testing.

Excessive Entitlement Fantasies

In the dance, the narcissist, who needs mirroring and is dominated by omnipotent fantasies, is the one who most often withdraws, feeling a loss of specialness, the need for approval, and an excessive need for appreciation. A divorced borderline husband may withhold child support and custody payments in order to stir things up, and get even with the fantasized all-encompassing mother and spouse who betrayed him. The narcissist may withhold custody or visitation rights out of an exaggerated sense of entitlement: "It's mine. I worked hard for it all my life. Therefore, I am entitled to it." Borderlines never feel enough entitlement!

Yet the dance never gets completed. Instead of ending with a finale, it continues on like a rondo, always with the hope and yearning for the harmonious experience, the fantasy of togetherness achieved through the unification of mind and body, sacrifice of the self at any cost. Any disruption of this unity may be experienced as a profound danger. As couples, their dynamics and circular pattern may dramatically emphasize and exaggerate their current perspective of reality, whereas as individuals, these behaviors may appear as subtle nuances (Lachkar, 1985b).

It is important to recognize that, in spite of the pain and circular patterns, these behaviors are not purposeful; rather, they are unconscious reenactments of infantile longings and are attempts to work them through with a new reparative object. It is like a play, and the wish is for a new ending.

THE BOND

Bonding is not to be confused with going along with the pathology (collusion). Bonding between therapist and patient essentially entails the therapist's becoming a feeding mommy who can offer safety and protection; in bonding the therapist bonds with the needy parts of the personality, understanding the patient's vulnerability. Borderlines and narcissists have very different experiences in bonding. Borderlines need to prove they exist; narcissists need to prove a very special sense of existence.

The Borderline

Bion believed that the borderline had never established a bond, and Rinsley (1978) confirmed Bion's notion; Rinsley observed that borderline persons have difficulty learning from experience, have shortcomings in relationships, and commonly misperceive, distort reality, and misuse those who offer themselves willingly. Lacking in good mothering experiences, the borderline does not realize the need for the breast; until the borderline finds the breast to be a reliable source of nurturance, needs, desires, entitlement longing, and bonding needs appear as bizarre split-off objects (Lachkar, 1985b).

A suicidal borderline wife, a substance abuser who had recently stopped taking drugs, wasn't sure she wanted to see me as a therapist because I didn't hug her, as her other therapist did. Yet I had other qualities she thought were vital. Especially significant was that she found me emotionally available, an experience she had not had before. She felt she needed a hug because she had never experienced a holding environment. No one had "touched" her internal world with understanding. Words were not enough; unless she was hugged, she felt she was not being cared for. The hug was like a drug offering, a quick fix. This patient needed to understand that acting out a feeling is not the same as thinking and understanding something about the need for it. The therapist can still be a good mommy, even without offering the patient everything.

Only when the patient began to realize that thinking could lead to something meaningful and lasting (internal hugs, and eventually external hugs) was she able to be weaned from purely physical hugs and from other bodily sensations. She learned she had a mouth that could talk, and could get fed, if she could learn to ask for what she needed. Thinking, linking thoughts that lead to new ideas, verbal expression, containment, holding, patience, and understanding had never before been experienced by the borderline wife. "I've always thought I was the one who had to provide it all. And for the first time, I don't feel very guilty. I guess I don't always have to give in."

The therapist who understands the importance of bonding for the narcissist/borderline couple has an opportunity to become the new self-object/mommy/therapist, and to protect the borderline from the narcissistic partner's effort to reinforce the borderline's invincibility (repeating emotional abuses similar to those suffered in the past). The primary therapeutic task is the identification of feelings.

The transformation from nonverbal states to verbal states with the borderline comes about through channeling confusional affects of anger and rage into contact with feelings of helplessness, betrayal, insecurity, and neediness—in effect, to point out the fear and the terror associated with them. Often what this means is to rely on someone else.

The couple's honeymoon has the promise of mutuality and the fantasy of a special relationship or bond, but when one partner realizes the other partner is not part of the self, and has his or her own needs and individual strivings and uniqueness, there can be severe trauma. The wife might say, "He was never like this in the beginning of our relationship!" The therapist can facilitate further understanding by explaining the background to what has become the dance (the beginnings of all relationships have the semblance of a symbiotic merger). Narcissistic/borderline couples experience great trauma, similar to the archaic one, when there is a separation period; the birth of a new child or a new career can recreate old feelings of hurt and injury.

Brandchaft and Stolorow (1984) found bonding for the borderline patient to be the revival of an archaic merger, the transference of the longed for self-object bond to an idealized parental image. Stolorow and Lachmann (1980) suggested that a prestage to transference is the revival of a symbioticlike merger, apparently a reference to a primitive state of bonding. They said that if the therapist interprets the splitting and projections, the patient will respond in a hostile way, but if the therapist interprets the disruption of the bond, the patient can relate. Brandchaft and Stolorow (1984) stated that interpreting the splitting leads to empathic failure and to the inability to revive a bond. Stolorow contended that there is no such thing as borderline personality; the syndrome so labeled is to be understood in the same intrasubjective fields as other self disorders.

In my view, the borderline takes on a different configuration, moving toward the object when there is hope of bonding, and away when there is a threat to that bond. A patient might say at one time, "I'm afraid to depend on you and become too needy!" and then at another, "I'm not going to continue in the treatment because you make me feel helpless; although I did not feel angry this time, I felt in our last session you made me feel helpless."

The therapist here has an opportunity to bond with the healthy helpless and needy part of the borderline partner, and to say: "It sounds as though you are getting better; that you can tell me you felt helpless and not get enraged about it is a sign of progress. I wonder, why would you want to stop now?" The therapist must bond with the vulnerable and needy parts to facilitate integration, concurrently pointing out the dangerous parts that get in the way of ego functioning and relatedness.

In bonding with the borderline, the therapist relies mainly upon containing/sustaining functions and the therapist's own soothing and tension-relieving capacities; this allows the therapist to tap the undiscovered areas of the internal world by holding on tightly to the specific areas of anxiety. The therapist must make a meticulous effort not to bond with the borderline's false self, projections, or splitting. For example, a borderline spouse in conjoint therapy once heard me interpret some material to her husband, and was favorably impressed. "Maybe that's how I should talk to him," she said. It was important to point out to her how her false self now wanted to fuse with me to become me, act like me, and take over my role. The borderline patient needed to understand that if she were to become me, she would lose out on her own experience, and not be able to find her own voice or existence.

Therapeutic bonding occurs when the therapist can be viewed as a feeding and providing mommy, instead of an empty or absent or depriving mommy. The borderline personality exhibits characteristics beyond the level of awareness. Bion described a danger that presents itself in an unrecognizable form and that he called the "beta shield." A simple example of this is one's disregarding a parking ticket, and then being shocked to find out the car has been impounded. Since the borderline is unable to think ahead, plan for the future, or recognize that there are consequences for actions, the therapist must be able to plan certain events, prepare dialogues, encourage more contact, including telephone sessions, or do whatever it takes to help the borderline organize and put structure to a chaotic, fragmented state. Protection and safety for the borderline are provided through the therapist's emotional availability. This availability is in direct contrast to the danger of a narcissistic spouse who continually projects negative feelings into the borderline.

The Narcissist

Empathic interpretations that offer mirroring and the sustaining functions that offer containment are meaningless unless they connect to the person's immediate area of anxiety.

Eventually, the therapist may try to bond with some area of the narcissist's life that causes pain, and to connect this event with a current interpersonal one. I said to Matt, "If you cannot recognize how the 'everything' part of you feels overly entitled, then you will not be able to see how others may take advantage of you. Your boss, for instance, may make you work long, extended hours because he, like yourself, may have exaggerated, grandiose ideas about himself, and be unrealistic about how much he expects of you! Then there's your mother, who always made you out to be the one who could do everything, be everything!"

"I know everything! I don't need anyone to tell me what to do!" For the narcissist, the grandiose self gets in the way of bonding and of expressing needs in a healthy way, and the narcissist suffers great anxiety related to taking in knowledge "feeding" from others.

The difference in the bonding experiences for narcissists and borderlines goes to the roots of the etiologies of their disorders. The narcissist differs from the borderline in that the narcissist once had an early special experience with the good breast, and so has experienced bonding. During the symbiotic phase, and as long as there was mutuality of self-involvement, the self object was able to mirror the baby and to provide special attention to the child. The problem arose when the mother was unable to tolerate the baby's separateness when the baby started to separate-individuate, and so abruptly stopped giving the baby special attention.

This scenario creates a longing for a rejoining with the symbiotic mother, when mother and baby were one, and baby was mommy's special child. These longings and strivings remain in the memory traces of the special relationship, and stay stuck in omnipotence and idealistic fantasy. The borderline, never having been a special child, cannot seek to reenact that drama, and instead is preoccupied with survival issues. Without the memory of the good breast, needs become split off, suitable for projective identification. The borderline lacks this experience. In effect, the borderline has needs, but does not value these needs—indeed disavows needs and longings—because of not having sufficiently experienced the good breast.

Omnipotence tends to destroy; therefore bonding with the narcissist must relate to needs, and, at all costs, must not feed the grandiose part. Narcissists often feel injured when we focus on their deficits. Bonding with the narcissist may mean an uncomfortable emphasis on the omnipotent part of the self that wards off needs: "Because I am focusing on a part of you that causes you pain, you may feel that I am not appreciating the rest of you as I call attention to the part of you that is causing you difficulties. You may feel that I am not appreciating the part of you that is talented, bright, and creative. This may be the same thing that goes on in your relationship. You may also feel threatened here and need so much of my approval that it might make it difficult for us to explore the undeveloped parts of you that seem to create so much conflict."

This kind of directness and attunement may eventually lead to bonding with the painful, deficient part of the narcissist, the part that seeks constant approval and validation, and cannot tolerate negative responses. The therapist might say, "You may want my approval and the approval of others, but you already have received lots of approval and attention for your achievements and accomplishments. It hasn't lasted or really fed you, because the attention and approval are always coming from the outside and not from within. In fact, it is a paradox that the mere preoccupation with seeking approval can actually get in the way of ever attaining it because of the insecurity you project into others. Instead of getting the recognition you deserve, you may get devalued." The narcissistic defenses and attitudes may create an effect opposite to the one desired. The grandiose and omnipotent parts of the personality can actually turn against the self, and get in the way of ever attaining the desired goals.

To bond with the narcissist the therapist must diminish the patient's omnipotence. The grandiose self frequently takes on the role of the grand provider or the caretaker. A narcissistic wife claims she is upset because her breasts are too small. The clinical data and history of this patient indicate that she wishes that she could be the one to "provide it all." I interpret, "If you can have the biggest breasts, then you don't have to take in anything from me, any therapeutic milk, and I then have nothing to offer you because you then have it all. Instead, I am to be the one to admire you for all that you have to offer me. 'f you don't have it all, perhaps you feel you have nothing to offer, and then feel you are of no value with nothing left to give. This puts you in the position of needing something from me, a state which makes you feel very anxious and uncomfortable."

In essence, the therapist must bond with the vulnerable part of the personality to facilitate understanding the split parts from both ends of the spectrum; either of the split parts leads to gratification (to become the all-encompassing breast or to destroy and devour the breast).

It is not up to the therapist to praise or compliment the narcissistic partner, who cannot understand why he or she cannot reach attainable goals (no matter how talented or creative the person is). The need is rather for the therapist empathically to mirror the part of the conflict, by not relieving the conflict, by empathizing, and by understanding how destructive the grandiose part of the self is. The attempt is to demonstrate clearly the parts of the self that gets in the way of maintaining appropriate affective responses within an interpersonal world in order to achieve the desired goals.

It is not enough merely to interpret the grandiose self; it is the explanation of the cause and effect of what the behavior creates in self and others that leads to integration. "Knowing everything" or "having it all" can evoke intense anger, rage, sadistic attacks, and envy in others. The therapist might say, "Even if you are extremely qualified, you may not get what you want because of an attitude you unknowingly project."

Neither the "giver" nor the "provider" ever gets a chance to get what he or she needs because the provider never has a chance to be a baby or be a mouth that can take in, digest, and be fed (Weiler, personal communication, 1987). The one who can learn to face being confused, not knowing, and having to ask then has to take the chance in the therapeutic feedings (the available breast).

In the treatment of narcissistic/borderline couples, the significance of bonding becomes apparent when one partner realizes the other is not part of the self, but has a separate mind, ideas, and needs. To tolerate that the other can have an opposing idea that can exist while simultaneously interfacing with one's own needs is part of the therapeutic bonding process for the narcissist/borderline relationships. Separating the couple too soon in these early stages may disrupt the bonding process (see Chapter VIII).

Revival of the Bond

Because the borderline never had the bond that the narcissist counterpart once had, the bond cannot be "revived." The reference is to a more primitive idea of bonding. The borderline lacks any memory of the experience of being special, so is establishing, not reviving, a bond. For example, a therapist felt threatened by the borderline wife's continual suicidal threats. Whenever the patient felt injured by the therapist or felt undermined by her narcissistic husband, she would threaten to swallow pills. The therapist failed to recognize that this was the borderline's wife's attempt to bond. As soon as the therapist was able to recognize this, to distinguish between the healthy needs and the parasitic ones, and to help the wife understand that this was her need to bond, progress began. "Why couldn't you see that I really didn't want to kill myself? I only wanted love and approval." The therapist began to focus on bonding needs, and the patient's participation in the disruption of the bond. "No, it's not your 'neediness' that drives others away, it is the fear you project into them."

Suicide attempts are quite frightening, especially to a therapist who feels a sense of responsibility to you. "I think what

I'm going to do here is going to be a bit different. Quite the contrary, I will make myself as available as possible so that you have an opportunity to form an attachment. I hope you can begin to depend on me as a mommy/doctor/me who can help you sort out the feelings of confusion instead of trying to kill them" (as in projection). I reassured the patient that she was good, worthy, and deserving, who needed to know that killing off her needs is not the same as asking for help.

The experience in bonding was quite different for her narcissistic husband, whose effort was to revive a bond by attempting to be the "special child" (attend sessions whenever suitable for him, interrupt, cancel appointments), reenacting a time when he felt entitled to his mother's full reign of attention before his baby sister was born. The mother (or the good breast) was once able to be the all encompassing self object for the narcissist, but was available to mirror the child only as long as there was mutuality of self-involvement. The baby meant too much to mother too soon, then suddenly was outcast and displaced, perhaps by other siblings, career, friends or a new mate.

In one case, a narcissistic husband longed to rejoin with the borderline wife, the one who "used to be." There was a similarity to an archaic experience with his mother before his baby brother was born: "Before he was born I was really special!" He mistook his borderline wife's neediness as her love and appreciation for him in the early part of their relationship. "For a while she would do anything for me (the false self). I used to be the center of attention with her, but now I realize that it was because she was too dependent and too needy to give me what I thought I needed."

Bion reminded us that in order to have thoughts to think about a thought, one must first have an experience with the mother or analyst to realize something is missing. Just as the inexperienced infant does not have the realization of the need for the breast, or the thoughts to think about needing the breast (or the analyst or the spouse), to realize there is a missing link, so the borderline patient does not have the sense of being entitled to, longing for, bonding with, or idealizing until needing, desiring are first experienced (Lachkar, 1985b, p. 114). "If I am not hugged, I am not loved, therefore, I shall give up needing and wanting," the borderline might say. This attitude severely impairs one's ability to pursue, search, and relate.

Reviving of a bond for narcissists must incorporate understanding how hurt they feel when others have ideas different from their own, and how this is experienced as a personal injury to the self. Integration and bonding occurs when the narcissist begins to tolerate the notion that two or more ideas may coexist concomitantly without the threat of dethronement. The painful affect that accompanies this state is the reminder of not being the special child.

·THE DRAMA

The Feeding Mommy

The therapist must be available for the play in order for the drama to unfold; one must allow oneself to become the feeding mommy or the protective mommy by staying loyal to the role. The feeding mommy must pay attention to the feelings that are projected in order to help the couples integrate and put meaning to their affective experiences. According to Bion, projective identification is essential, not destructive, and helps put meaning into a chaotic, fragmented world, through the mother's (or therapist's) ability to transform, decode, and provide alpha function.

The patient may say, "I am stopping, I can't afford it any more, I'm going bankrupt. Conjoint treatment isn't working!" The feeding mommy must respond in such a way as to provide alpha function and movement toward reparation and integration. The response might be: "I think you are telling us that you feel coming here isn't going to lead to further growth and development, to more understanding, but instead will lead to more impoverishment, that it will take something away from you rather than add something. Maybe we need to look to see what is in the way of your taking in something from me to allow you to depend on me as a feeding mommy rather than a taking away mommy or as a bankrupting mommy."

The therapy is the rehearsal of a new play to add to the continually repeated repertoire of the narcissist/borderline couple. The therapist for this couple has a part in the performance that, if done well, may change the outcome considerably. The therapist must upstage the couple's repetitious behaviors by providing truth and understanding.

A Shared Couple Myth

The myth of these couples gives rise to many shared collective fantasies, causing the couple to play and replay their roles with powerful passions. (Case 5). The scenario is like a play, a drama that is repeated again and again, back and forth, through the idealization and devaluation process, with the actors always yearning for a new ending.

One's personal myth or the shared couple myth can distort one's perspective of current reality. "My neediness will destroy" or "I already know what he will say!" Can we diagnose a "couple mind" in terms of the individuals' collective defenses based on isolation, need to destroy, envy, splitting, and projective identification? Is it possible to understand that one partner, having been victimized by others, will inflict pain upon the other partner to dehumanize and destroy that person? Understanding group formation and group dynamics can help formulate a fresher outlook with which to view such psychopathology in couples as battery, assault, sacrifice of the self or other, and other forms of physical and emotional abuse. Group myths and shared fantasies can help the partners objectify and study the highly charged passions so difficult to face for many couples (see Chapter VII). There are six common myths:

1. All I need is your approval and unconditional love.
2. We don't need treatment, we don't need help, we can do it ourselves (grandiose self and magical thinking).
3. We can't afford treatment. We don't have any money! (too

costly to need, an expression of an internal bankrupted, impoverished state).
4. Things will just work out! (realm of magical thinking).
5. To know everything and/or to "do" is the cure.
6. If only the other would change, things would be fine.

For the narcissist, the myth is for approval and reassurance, to join with others who are idealized and who are highly cathected with narcissistic libido; if others will only approve, the grandiose self will be validated and given meaning. The problem is that when others do not validate narcissists, they are left feeling frustrated and insecure, only to return to the borderline for reassurance. According to Bion, seeking validation outside the relationship is not the same as having a personal experience—not the same, that is, as finding meaning; learning from experience; trusting one's own preconceptions; interacting with others; and facing uncertainty, truth, and reality. The paradox, in my view, is that the more validation narcissists receive, the more insecure they become, because it takes them further away from relying on their own experience. According to Bion, validation of the self can come only from one's own experience.

For borderlines, the personal myth is that if only the other will love them, be emotionally available, take care of survival needs, be self-sacrificing, and offer proof that the borderline does indeed exist, everything will be OK. The misconception that to need is being bad is exacerbated by the faulty ways in which needs are expressed and projected—for example, when one becomes greedy and wants more than one should have (entitlement fantasies or an outcome of being the "deprived child"), or when one invades or intrudes into the other's emotional or physical space (e.g., the borderline living inside another object). In the personal myth of the borderline, strivings and yearnings for closeness or intimacy are ironically perceived as wrong. The borderline's defenses are obstacles to intimacy and serve only to push others away. The personal myth transcends the thing in itself to things in themselves. Borderlines often become their loneliness, their neediness, their nonexistence, and their nothingness. Their mythology suggests that others can see through them; that is, the borderline feels like a nothing, therefore is a nothing.

The borderline confirms for the narcissist that it is OK to withdraw, to avoid and turn away from problems, essentially because borderlines abandon their own experiences (the tendency to spill out, project, or disavow). The narcissist validates the borderline's personal myth (confirming that the borderline is a nothing) by disregarding the borderline's razor-sharp attacks and ruthless projections. The borderline embellishes the narcissist's indulgent schemes (of being "an everything") and the neatly exaggerated explanations to possess things, to have it all, to run away from problems, reinforces the rationale to turn to others. Together the narcissist and the borderline form many shared couple fantasies based on one being "an everything" and the other being "a nothing." For example, in one case, the borderline wife (the nobody) felt betrayed by her narcissistic husband (the everything). No matter how attacking, insulting, or hurt she was, the borderline husband would take it as a compliment. "You're selfish!" "You're inconsiderate!" "You're greedy!" The narcissistic husband's response would normally be, "Yes, I know I am because I'm entitled! I'm entitled!"

Excessive entitlement fantasies are often shared myths that tie in unrealistic and delusional expectations, and need to be addressed in terms of each of these disorders. For the narcissist, grandiosity often relates to guilt, to not being able to give enough or to be the idealized ultimate provider, and the narcissist will react by giving too much, whereas for the borderline, grandiosity may be a form of projective identification to ward off any feelings of shame and helplessness. At neither end is the partner able to give anything. If the therapist colludes with the delusional aspects and tries to offer too much without interpreting these grandiose expectations, the therapist is then going along with the mythology, the idealization, and the projections of the couple.

To participate in the overt expectations that the therapist will solve the couple's problems and will put an end to their bickering and devastating fights is viewed as collusion with the couple myth and does not lead to any realistic treatment goals.

The therapist might enlighten the couple as follows: "I feel like a mother to two siblings, both deprived, needy, hurt, wounded, and so vulnerable. To think that when you are both in this state of profound deprivation you can give or provide for each other's needs is quite grandiose. You also expect me to give so much in one session and if I don't you feel disappointed, but if I do then I am grandiose because no one can do everything or be everything. Furthermore, it would be quite delusional on my part to think that in such a short time, I could solve the problem. If I make promises I cannot keep or if I try to do more than is possible, then I am being unrealistic, and we will all end up feeling helpless and deprived. However, if we could understand just this little bit, then we could feel the work we did in this session was successful."

In this case the therapist must illustrate that a nobody-nothing and somebody-everything cannot possibly have a meaningful relationship.

DIAGNOSTIC DISTINCTIONS

Many authors do not differentiate between narcissistic and borderline vulnerabilities (see Cases 1 & 2) and simply place both of these disorders in one category of self disorders, "narcissistic vulnerabilities in couples" (Lansky, 1981; Solomon, 1985, 1986), or label persons with both syndromes as self-object failures. The implication is that it is the primary task of the couple to provide self-object functions for one another. It is, in my view, an oversimplification to suggest that both of these partners have narcissistic vulnerabilities, especially when one of them, the borderline, may be suffering from primary deficits relating to survival issues. In other instances, patients may exhibit both narcissistic and borderline patterns.

It is unfortunate that to date we do not have a more systematic approach for diagnosing couples, but we can at least apply our current knowledge to see if we can provide a meaningful structure with which to further understand these couples.

THE PATIENT WITH BOTH NARCISSIST AND BORDERLINE PATTERNS

In one case I supervised, the therapist was not able to note the qualitative differences between the partner more inclined toward narcissistic pathology and the one more inclined toward borderline pathology; she treated both as if they had similar vulnerabilities. The couple initially came to treatment because the narcissistic husband was upset and felt injured by his wife's affairs. The therapist turned the focus to the "reason" the wife had the affairs, rather than to the present hurt, wounded feelings of the narcissistic husband. The therapist needed to communicate that each individual experiences pain differently; instead, she concentrated attention on the narcissistic wife's history, which included how she had been rejected and abandoned by her father, and moved on to how she now needed other men to approve of and to appreciate her, and to be her lovers (because she felt attacked by her husband, who reminded her of her father). The therapist went on to interpret how the wife's idealized, grandiose view of her father got in the way of allowing sexual feelings, how she felt that her husband was too good for her, and how she felt too threatened to have sex with him. Because the therapist failed to recognize the personal assault to the narcissistic husband's wounded self, he took the therapist's responses and line of inquiry as an attempt to justify his wife's behavior. To add insult to injury, the therapist then remarked upon her observation of certain behaviors of the narcissistic husband that might have contributed to his "driving" his wife to these affairs—for example, the husband's demanding ways of cutting off his wife when she spoke. Although the therapist may have correctly analyzed the relationship, the narcissistic husband understood the therapist's responses to mean that he was responsible for all that had happened, and felt he did not warrant any empathy for his pain (hate turned inward).

Had the therapist recognized that the first priority was to give immediate relief by bonding and assuming an empathic stance (first with the narcissistic spouse to alleviate his anxiety), this couple might have remained in treatment; as it was, they did not return. The therapist, in this case, lacked empathy, and did not have sufficient holding capacity to soothe. She needed to keep in mind the importance of bonding and empathy, and to understand that each of these patients was experiencing anxiety differently.

These personality disorders may exhibit both narcissistic and borderline features, states, and traits. As we study the narcissist/borderline couple, we find that self-psychology and object-relations theories are applicable in the following ways to these disorders:

- Object-relations theory is more applicable to the borderline syndrome, especially in relationship to conflict dealing with bonding and attachment.
- Mirroring techniques are more applicable for the narcissistic partner.
- Containment techniques are usually more suitable for the borderline partner (Lachkar, 1984, 1985b).
- Both self psychology and object relations need to be brought into play in instigating the partners' faith in the reparative power of dialogue, both internal and external.
- Each partner must be weaned from the defensive use of pathological autistic objects.
- Each partner needs to establish a sort of "mental gap," an "area of the immediate," in which experience and thinking about experience can take place.
- Each partner needs to establish a background subject of maternal identification (the primal self object) to achieve a sense of psychic safety before each can separate and individuate.

A narcissistic husband, George, complained that his border-line personality wife, Ellen, did not greet him anymore when he came home, but chose to spend her time practicing the piano. Self-psychological views might lead one to misperceive the wife's playing as reflecting her need for mirroring and appreciation of her special talents. I believe that, in this case, the piano is a healthy transitional use of a transitional object to facilitate separation and not to further exhibitionistic aims. The borderline wife claimed she was practicing the piano more because she felt left out: "He doesn't even know that I exist."

With the clinical material presented here, I attempt to illustrate narcissist/borderline marital discord, focusing on specific self-object functions that each marital partner fails to fulfill both in the self and in the other.

By using Adler's (1985) continuum model, we can clarify the process of change that occurs in conjoint therapy. The border-line is in a more fragmented state. Narcissists are considered higher on the continuum than borderlines (Adler, 1985). When borderline persons improve, they tend to become more narcissistic, and when narcissists fragment or regress, they then tend to become more borderline. In addition, within these complex dynamics, anxieties are stirred up in different relationships.

As elucidated in many of the cases presented in Chapter IX of this book, we must safeguard against too early a diagnosis, especially when there is considerable overlap and interfacing between the two sets of symptomatologies. We see many narcissistic and borderline elements in both of these personalities.

Before any clarification can be made to help understand the overlap of dynamics within the couple interaction, we need to understand more about the operant psychodynamics of the individuals within the various aspects of their pathologies. There are diagnostic differences between the narcissist and the borderline in the way affective emotional states are expressed.

The psychodynamics of the narcissist/borderline couple are at least as complex as those of the narcissist and borderline individually. Psychoanalysts who have criticized these ideas claim that it is difficult enough to make distinctions between narcissists and borderlines in diagnosing individuals, let alone as a couple. Psychoanalysis, after all, is intended for the individual. I believe, however, that this framework provides an important adjunct with which to view those pervasive forces within this kind of dyadic, marital, conflictual relationship.

CONCLUSION

Using object relations and self psychology, I have tried to shed some light on what it is that bonds these couples together, and to develop some understanding about their interactions. I have attempted to describe the dance, the bond that relates the borderline and the narcissist in symbiosis, and the drama that permeates the lives of these couples, and that involves the therapist as well.

Diagnostic distinctions have been pointed out as they exist between narcissist and borderline, including qualitative differences of each partner based upon how each experiences anxiety. The qualitative differences in which anxiety is subjectively experienced are indicative of the different kinds of treatment each patient needs.

Although there is considerable overlap between narcissistic and borderline disorders, there are still enough recognizable differences that these can be helpful in the treatment. I have tried to provide a more systematic approach in diagnosing these pathologies.

CHAPTER IV

The Psychodynamics of the Narcissistic/Borderline Couple

NEEDS

There are similarities between the narcissist and the borderline in terms of how needs are experienced. Both have difficulty in expressing their needs to others in clear and healthy ways, and both experience needing as something foreign. The differences lie in the way each experiences anxiety and defends against needing.

For the borderline, to need is an expression of shame. Needs relate to persecutory anxiety and envy, and are experienced internally as bad and dangerous. Because of the borderline's defensive structures, needs are often expressed as intrusive explosive forces invading another object. Borderlines impinge and impose their needs (different from entitlement). Needs are primitive modes to express feelings of hurt, discomfort, longing, and rejection.

Many borderline patients experience a depriving yet suffocating internal mother who persecutes them; it is as if she says, "Don't ask, don't need anything." Rather than face the abuse, many borderlines protect themselves by already "knowing" what others will say. Thus, why should they bother asking?

Borderlines might not get what they need because their needs are not expressed directly, but instead are indicated by a process of "magical thinking." For example: "If he really loved me he would know what I want for my birthday." The borderline lives in a state of martyrdom struggling to preserve a sense of self. "Pardon me for existing" is often the attitude.

For the narcissist, to need is an expression of guilt. Anxiety emanates from the superego and is not an outcome of persecutory anxiety, as it is for the borderline. Needs then are considered as subservient traders to a powerful superego that is omniscient and restrictive.

Narcissists develop manic defenses to guard against greed and envy. They want so much, and want so much all at one time. In treatment they have unrealistic expectations and place outrageous demands upon the therapist: "Give me a diagnosis! Tell me what the outcome is! I want to know!" Aggrandizement gets in the way of learning and taking in suggestions from the therapist. The therapist might say, "Your wife has no right to interrupt you; how is it you allow her to do this to you?" And a typical response might be, "What do you mean I allow her? I tried once to get her to stop, but it didn't work." The therapist may then state, "This problem has been going on for quite some time. It's delusional and unrealistic to think that trying something once will make things work. It takes several times of trying and even many mistakes, but if you give up your needs, then you will never have a chance."

Narcissists typically deny their "smallness" and project a sense of being bigger and better than others, since they cannot tolerate taking in and learning from others (to do so represents an injury to the image of perfection). The fear of rejection and hurt feelings covers up wanting, learning, needing, and desiring (Case 9.) "Need, what's a need?" they might say. "I don't know what you're talking about!"

These particular pathological disorders are entangled and symbiotically fused. They play off one another. Narcissistic partners have to avoid needs as they get in the way of their maintaining an "independent" facade. Feeling they have a divine right to their lavish desires and participation in their own self-indulgent schemes, narcissists are not empathic about the borderline's needs. Narcissists refuse to recognize either their own needs or those of the borderline, thus denying an equally shared relationship. "I don't know why I'm here!" they may say, "I don't need this relationship."

The balance of power shifts back and forth between the partners, with the other experiencing helplessness. Narcissists become intoxicated with their own "power" and demands from the superego and develop manic defenses to ward off facing their own legitimate needs. In essence, the narcissist is never narcissistic enough.

The borderline cannot be empathic toward the "needy" part in the narcissist because needs are perceived to be like malignant tumors or infestations of worms or bugs or toxic wastes. When asked to be empathic about needs, the borderline lashes out and becomes even more demanding, envious, and destructive.

The borderline has a need to control their objects, not for power, but rather for safety, as a barrier or a defense against needing. Other people's ideas, views, and opinions are felt as pervasive threats to the self. The borderline may express this as, "Don't tell me what to do." The therapist must help the borderline discover that needing is healthy, that wanting somebody is healthy.

The literature has not sufficiently addressed differences between narcissist and borderline needs. Conjoint therapy must validate a truth for each partner within the therapeutic bond.

APPROVAL

At the risk of redundancy, I need to emphasize that it is important for the therapist to understand differences between what approval means for the narcissist and what approval means for the borderline.

Narcissists need approval to make sure they are really talented and brilliant. They require mirroring responses from others, and validation from those who may not see them as they see themselves. Borderlines need approval because they have difficulty relying on their perceptual apparatus or their experiences, and they need others to offer their "testimony."

If differences are not noted, the result could be severe fragmentation, not only in personal development, but with the entire separation-individuation process. For the narcissist, the search for approval obstructs development of an observing ego, leading to a substitution of attention in lieu of achieving "real" attention. For the borderline, difficulties with approval relate to the inability to hold onto one's own experiences, whereas for the narcissistic partner, the search for approval is for validation for omnipotent control.

A borderline patient's need for approval had, in past therapy, been seen as part of the narcissistic, grandiose part of herself, demanding and requiring inordinate amounts of attention, when in fact she was desperately struggling around basic survival issues and dependency needs. Unlike her narcissistic husband, she was not looking for approval, rather she needed the confirmation, the living proof, that she existed. This patient had been treated as if her need for approval was the same as her narcissistic husband's (narcissistic vulnerabilities).

Her old therapist reactivated a part of herself that was shameful. The feelings of being excessively demanding were associated with the numerous telephone contacts made outside of session. Her need for contact, keeping communication lines open and available with me were, in this case, regarded as healthy and not as a need for excessive attention. Until these issues were clarified, she could not achieve a sense of her own identity.

Susan's need for approval represented the core of her self, the core of her existence and revolved around the realization that she was not bad. In a conjoint session, she shared with us a fantasy of being jailed for shoplifting. The experience of jail made her feel she was being swallowed up, disappearing into thin air.

Her feelings became associated around the "free" telephone contacts, and her concern about being a thief who was taking something that didn't belong to her. Was she entitled? Deserving of the breast? Was she entitled to have her own needs? In time we were able to sort out that the stealing/shoplifting aspects were the projected split-off parts of her internal world.

For her narcissistic husband, this was a revelation. He initially perceived his wife as "putting me down." He became outraged, and interjected, "That's what she does to me, always makes me feel bad, like a thief." "I don't feel insulted," I said, "I'm glad your wife can share with me her feelings of longing and loss."

The myth for this couple was that the world clearly owed them something. In the wife, it was a reliable breast. For the husband, it was to recapture his lost entitlement.

In another case, a borderline wife reported an intense and painful account of child abuse in her early years. Her father would make her obey; if she cried, she would be beaten and be hit with an iron. This patient could not let her husband know that she was coming in for treatment because she feared that having needs of her own was a reenactment of being a "disobedient child." When the couple fantasy was interpreted, it was clear there still remained a part of her that had to be obedient to this corporal father/husband. The consequence of disobedient behavior was a devaluation by her husband reviving her earlier abused role with her father. When she was able to tell the husband and to face him with this realization, she came to understand that she was no longer a helpless child who needed his approval, but was an adult with a voice and some resources.

I believe this illuminates the considerable confusion in understanding what approval means within the context of a narcissistic/borderline configuration.

The Quick Fix

One clue to recognizing narcissistic and borderline disorders in couples is that these couples are not looking for a cure; the emphasis is more on being understood or having a new experience. Remembering that pain is preferable to emptiness for these couples, the therapist can recognize that the couple may reject therapeutic advice until they feel the therapist is fully immersed in their pain and their drama. Conjoint treatment can offer a most valuable experience for these more primitive disorders, particularly if the therapist withstands the temptation to offer a quick solution or a quick fix (Weiler, 1987). Ironically, what appears to be the cure is often not the cure. The real cure is the new experience with a new self object.

For the borderline, pain can offer a false sense of aliveness; it is preferable to stir up highly charged feelings, even at the expense of others, than to face an empty black hole. The preoccupation with pain (no matter how intolerable the pain may be) is still better than having to deal with an impoverished internal world. Many borderlines, for this reason, become obsessed with drugs, alcohol, weight loss, abusive behavior, or almost anything to avoid the real state of emptiness. Narcissists may respond with the quick fix, not so much to relieve themselves of the pain as to relieve themselves of the demands of a harsh superego. The narcissist usually cannot get what the external world will provide. Internal introjects or internalized voices from the superego continually remind the narcissist of expectations and failures. The dilemma is a significant one, because when the narcissist threatens to leave the relationship, this threat evokes attacking responses from the borderline and guilt in the narcissist.

The Sturm und Drang of these couples, I believe, can best be understood as a form of what Melanie Klein (1957) called "projective identification." The infant's way of getting rid of bad affects is to project them onto the "bad breast," a concept similar to Brandchaft and Stolorow's (1984) term "intersubjectivity." In intersubjectivity, partially undifferentiated states are understood to be manifestations or revivals of earlier mental states. The archaic experiences, as painful as they are, are safe because of their familiarity (Lachkar, 1983). The major difference then between projective identification and subjectivity is that projective identification refers to the patient's desire to get rid of something painful by projecting quickly onto another object, whereas subjectivity refers to the therapist's capacity to understand what the patient is experiencing via one's own attunement and the empathic stance. The therapist who understands the dynamics of the narcissist/borderline couple will take the longer road, and avoid the quick fix.

QUALITY OF ENDANGERMENT

The way the therapist protects the borderline from intrusion is different from the way in which the therapist protects the narcissist because the quality of endangerment for the borderline is markedly different from that of the narcissist. Narcissistic partners, perhaps out of guilt and feelings of specialness, will either give too much of themselves or take too much. At either end of the spectrum, they may become too authoritarian or too controlling, too meek or too mellow. The narcissistic husband might say, "When she threatened me with divorce, it felt as though I was hit over the head with a brick! I used to be too rigid, tight, and controlling. Now I give her anything she wants, because I realize how hoarding I was, and now I feel so guilty." The therapist might say, "This deeply concerns me, because before you felt entitled to everything, but now, because of your guilt, you feel entitled to nothing. Either way is not healthy."

For the borderline, the danger centers around the tendency toward fusion and self-abrogation. The borderline might say: "I know I shouldn't take the job. I know the customer is taking advantage of me, but I can't help it. I feel so seduced by him. He reminds me of my alcoholic father." The therapist might respond: "Yes, there is an intoxicated daddy/customer who seduces you and takes over your mind as your father did. Then you can't protect yourself because you become the child. This concerns me because as this daddy/customer takes over your mind there is no danger and adult you, but only a baby or little boy you. You are not a little boy now; you are an accomplished, grown-up man." The therapist has to bond with the internal part of the patient to offer protection against external predators as well as internal saboteurs. The therapist can do this by helping the borderline become more in contact with the "baby part" or vulnerable part of the psyche that can feel, need, and get fed, to help the borderline to express a desire, rather than to join up, fuse, intrude, or invade. The danger centers around the patient's tendency to destroy the breast via the massive projections of invasiveness in lieu of facing loss, void, and one's own vulnerability. One patient said, "I told my husband that Friday we have an appointment with the bitch!" (the therapist). The therapist's response was, "If you can make me into something bad, then the little deprived child in you doesn't have to face needing me."

The therapist survives the attacks, and maintains a bond by staying in contact with the area of endangerment, the split off part of the psyche which is felt to be dangerous and destructive.

Fear of Disruption

As the couple improves, there is a dangerous time for the marriage. Beyond the defenses, there's the ubiquitous fear of disruption of the relationship. The borderline cannot tolerate the anxiety of waiting or not knowing, or any confusional states.

Many fears are expressed through nonverbal communication, as in body language, or through physical sensations, as in somatization. The emphasis on pain conveys that something deep within the unconscious is being expressed. Because of their splitting mechanisms, borderlines either become excessively demanding and intrusive, or despair and become helpless and hopeless. Divorce often occurs during these phases, and it needs to be emphasized that although these stages are important developmentally, they must also be regarded as temporary. The best safeguard for the relationship is the continual interpretation of feelings and defenses, rather than the encouraging of action. It is vital to help these couples understand that they are not foolish to stay in these relationships, but rather that therapy is a positive step that affords them the opportunity to understand something about themselves and to work through the relationship intrapsychically, developmentally, and interpersonally.

The narcissistic/borderline entity has to be understood in terms of the projections and introjections. Often, these partners will want to split up prematurely. It is vital for the therapist to help them see that if they run away without understanding or resolving their conflicts they can recur at a similar point with another partner. Also, it is not a good time to disrupt a bond when the individuals are enraged or extremely angry with one another (paranoid-schizoid position). Even though being angry and dissatisfied can be viewed as a healing affective experience, from both the developmental and phase-appropriate points of view, it is not the same as being in the depressive position, during which one can make more rational decisions.

Many patients, lacking the experience of object constancy, are fearful the therapist will leave them; these patients distort reality and project onto the therapist their destructive fantasies. These projections must be interpreted so that maintenance of the therapeutic tie relies more heavily upon the reparative functions than on the disruptive ones. If these projections are not interpreted sufficiently, further persecutory anxiety may continue to dominate, especially for the borderline. For narcissists, disruption occurs more commonly by the therapist joining in the collusive bond and failure to illustrate how readily available the narcissist is to take in the borderline's projections. For the borderline, disruption relates to acts triggered by a forceful and provocative primitive unconscious and the failure on the part of the therapist to offer protection by interpreting the danger; the part of the borderline that tends to project, demand, control, and intrude. The narcissist needs to be reassured that vulnerability is healthy, but that the excessive demands could lead to a disruption.

Bodily Sensations

For the borderline, anxiety is often expressed not by words, but through bodily sensations. We need to help the borderline partner pay attention to these internal signals. Nonverbal forms of communication are often conveyed through body language, somatization, suicidal ideation, and many forms of addictive behaviors. These include not only addiction to drugs, alcohol, and food, but also addictive relationships. These nonverbal forms of relating can preoccupy, consume, or control the other person. This preoccupation, self-absorption, and compulsiveness seem prevalent in the borderline personality disorder. In essence, self-sacrifice, subjugation of the self, and the establish-ment of a false self take over in the borderline's attempt to cover needing and facing the void, for which these compulsions tend to act as a substitution.

Emde, in an unpublished paper presented at the Interna-tional Psychoanalytic Congress in 1987 in Montreal, reflected Freud's views, while expressing a diversification based on his own findings in developmental biology and infant observation ("Development Terminable and Interminable, II. Recent Psy-choanalytic Theory and Therapeutic Considerations," Emde, 1987). Emde discussed the need for safety, and, although he did not imply diagnostic differences in borderlines and nar-cissists, the contention was that the former have more need for safety and tend to act out from their biological states. Emde did, I believe, infer that certain types of individuals respond more from their bodily states than from their thinking states. Emde (1987) stated that affects, thought of as composite states of feelings of both pleasure and unpleasure, are rooted in biology, and function unconsciously as well as consciously. He appeared to be taking into account certain aspects of biological theory, especially signal anxiety, to describe the regulatory role and automatic functions of affective experiences.

> Signal anxiety prevents one from becoming overwhelmed by states of helplessness which in turn are linked to specific, hierarchically arranged affective structures which were originally experienced in early development. Other psy-choanalytic theorists since Freud have also portrayed a developmental sequence involving signal depression or helplessness, analogous to Freud's original developmental sequence involving anxiety. [Emde, 1987, p. 3]

The composite view of Emde's work suggests that certain states of helplessness are affectively experienced as dangerous threats to the psyche; however, signal anxiety can prevent one from becoming overwhelmed only if one can pay attention to these signals as important. This view is in sharp contrast to that of Kohut, who saw affective states as not necessarily derivatives of drives (bodily experiences and sensations), but rather as continuous aspects of our lives in relation to self objects.

One important implication of Emde's (1987) work for chronic marital conflict appears to be the recognition that certain partners are not being intentionally destructive, for they lack awareness of motivational forces. It is these forces that may be felt internally as something foreign or bizarre and as intrusive and invading.

Schain, in an unpublished work, applied Emde's observations to group therapy, and discovered that when the mother's response on an affective level is greater than the infant's on a cognitive level, the affective development is enhanced (Schain, 1985). As her main thrust, Schain combined innate and motivational factors from infancy. Schain's view appears to be that the therapist must stay in contact with these bodily sites and that bodily experiences are worthy of considerable time and focus within the therapeutic process. The implication is that words are not enough. The therapist, like the dancer, must speak directly to these bodily parts with meaning and conviction.

Pain and Self-Sacrifice

I would like to preface the discussion of pain and sacrifice by referring the reader to Chapter VII, where the ideas of couple myth are expanded to the importance of understanding a group self. In order to get a clearer picture about what it is that makes one endure pain, one needs, I believe, to understand something about group formation, and to what extent or extremes the group will go in order to preserve a sense of group identity. What occurs in the group can help us understand further what occurs in the collective couple "self," or in the individual self. The preservation of self and the need to protect it at any cost become more pervasive than life itself. People in groups as well as individual persons will try to preserve the self or the collective group self even at the expense of themselves or their own children. The kamikaze suicide squads are an example of this kind of behavior. In order to preserve a national cause, a sense of pride, or a group self, the kamikaze fighters were willing to die for their country.

Pain stirs up unresolved issues that need to be worked through in order for the individual to grow, develop, and face new experiences. As we have noted, both borderlines and narcissists fear new experiences, and prefer to reexperience old ones, even if those are painful and destructive.

Self-sacrifice is a phenomenon that occurs within the individual as well as within the group in order to preserve a self or a group identity. If a patient continually threatens suicide or makes suicide attempts, we can clearly get a sense about self-sacrifice. In certain religious sects, the members will choose death over loss of a group self (Lachkar, 1991). When self-sacrifice becomes more subtle, however, it is more difficult to discern. For narcissists, the parts of themselves to be sacrificed will be anything that will preserve self-identity or egocentricity. The narcissistic child may become a piano player because mother is exhibitionistically involved with the arts and wants her child to play the piano (as a reflection of herself, and even at the expense of the child's needs and desires).

Borderlines will frequently sacrifice themselves, their family, or their children. In court custody cases, children become the sacrificial objects, are placed in the middle of arguments, and are deprived, made to be go-betweens, and treated as little adults playing the role of mediators, therapists, and saviors (Lachkar, 1985b).

It is in nonverbal language that borderlines communicate disappointment to the narcissist partners who have failed them. The borderline sees this unspoken language as providing a connection or merging that is really the wish for the holding environment that never existed. When the potential of this holding environment is threatened, as in divorce, intense fear and the desire to retaliate dominate. It is at this point that the borderline will sacrifice self and family, paradoxically to preserve a sense of self, a force more pervasive than life itself.

Court Custody

In court custody cases, the narcissist may withhold because of exaggerated entitlement fantasies, but the borderline may be the one to withhold custody payments, and not participate fairly in property division and child visitation, out of a desire to get back at or to teach the other a lesson (Lachkar, 1986). Because of the false self, the borderline (the one to promise the world) may fool others under the guise of being the perfect parent, the victim, or the hurt one. The split side of the wounded self emerges, turning the world into the bad breast. Unfortunately, although the betrayal is against the self, the children are the ones who become the sacrificial objects. I believe many court officials, including counselors, evaluators, mediators, judges, and lawyers, fail to recognize how these personality types tie up the court system, and fail to understand that there are bonds that unite these couples even years after the dissolution process.

Similar to the sadomasochistic one, one partner needs the other in order to play out the role. Both partners are object seeking, but never object obtaining.

Child Abuse

An important clinical implication of the information we now have about the narcissist/borderline couple is the relation of that union to child abuse. DeMause (1974) has presented a historical survey of parental attitudes toward children and the relationship of such attitudes to the occurrence of infanticide and child abuse. Whether parents loved and cared for their children or exploited them in early America or in Renaissance Italy, what parents said to children, what parents fantasized about children, and how these behaviors affected children growing up in society were reviewed by DeMause. DeMause questioned the progress made in understanding of children from yesterday to today, and examined the evolution in childhood history and the prospects of change. From a psychohistorical perspective, DeMause presented a fantasy analysis of child abuse, providing an overview of the history of infanticide, abandonment, nursing, swaddling, beating, and sexual abuse and then examined how widespread each practice was in each period. DeMause (1974) published a painstaking review of the history of childhood in America, one of the most complete studies of child rearing available in America during the past 150 years.

It is important to note that we have a significant lack of clinical knowledge in these issues, and that we have severely undermined our ability to understand the basic tenets of what contributes to the makings of a child abuser. In my view, it is the projected split-off part of one's own abused internal child that one seeks desperately to destroy. If these issues are avoided, and are not seen in the light of splitting, projection, and projective identification, I believe we are limiting our capacities to treat these types of dysfunctional individuals.

Narcissistic Rage vs. Borderline Rage

I suggest that there is a difference between narcissistic rage and borderline rage. From my own experience, narcissistic rage is a response to being misunderstood, ignored, or hurt, especially an injury to one's sense of specialness. This occurs when one's sense of pride or integrity has been wounded. Narcissistic rage is a response to personal injury and may sound like, "How dare you put me down in front of our friends!" or "You're always humiliating me and embarrassing me, you make me look like a fool!" or "Here I have tried so hard and you never appreciate all the things I've done. I'm leaving!"

Borderline rage is a sensory response to the threat to one's existence; this rage has acting-out qualities that run alongside persecutory anxiety. Borderline rage is a response to the fear of not existing, as opposed to a narcissistic rage, which is in response to a special sense of existence. Narcissistic rage is an emotional outburst to a threatened self, an outcome of guilt, from an indulgent self. Borderline rage is the attempt to destroy that which is envied in order to hold on to the good internal objects. Therapists treating patients who are borderlines know what it is to juggle back and forth, to be emotionally available while not allowing one's own needs to be ignored or destroyed.

Borderline rage may sound something like, "Don't give me your excuses. You are nothing, deserve nothing, and therefore you shall have nothing!" (projecting the state of nothingness onto the other), or "There you go again, going out with your friends. What's the matter with you? Aren't I good enough for you?" (abandonment anxiety). "You'll see when you get back, I won't be here waiting around for you!" (borderline tendency to want to get even). The momentary states of anger and rage are to be regarded as modes of communication expressing legitimate feelings, and need to be recognized as healthy. If one waits too long to deal with feelings, however, they escalate and develop into something intolerable, losing original meaning and intentions. Anger escalates when one lacks acknowledgment of the internal signifiers that bring on terror. Murderous rage and retaliatory fantasy can reenter the psyche via projective identification, or as Bion puts it, "grotesque objects" in a haunting but unrecognizable form. Using Bion's concepts on thinking, the therapist translates the language of rage and attacks in order to provide digestible meaning.

Grotstein (1987a, b) proposed that the "states of experience" for psychotic and borderline personalities constitute the most fundamental of all mental events, and that they represent the confluence of elements of meaningfulness and of meaninglessness. Applying Grotstein's ideas to rage and anger within these two pathologies, I believe one might conjecture that what terrorizes these individuals is not the rage itself, but the unknown elements, also called "nameless dread," or states of entropy or of nothingness, which Grotstein so eloquently described as the terror of circumventing the black hole.

An allergic borderline patient, who may be feeling very hurt and vulnerable, may distort the therapist's attempt to be kind, caring, and understanding, and may suddenly turn against the therapist. The risk of looking into the internal world can be misconstrued by the borderline as stirring up an "allergy attack." The therapist may interpret: "I think you feel there is a 'mommy me' attacking you, and when you feel I am calling attention to some aspect of your behavior, it's hard to know when I am being the loving 'feeding mommy,' the one who is trying to protect you from something you do that is dangerous to yourself."

Borderlines are lacking in self-regulation mechanisms; the internal signals, the signifiers and instincts that enable them to anticipate a hurtful event are disregarded. For narcissists, rage is expressed as a direct insult to their sense of entitlement resulting in either physical or emotional isolation. Both borderlines and narcissists feel they are the innocent victims, and end up complaining and protesting vehemently, each about the other, "Look what has been done to me!" (See case 7).

Narcissistic Withdrawal and Isolation

It has previously been mentioned that the main defense mechanisms of the narcissistic personality disorder are withdrawal and isolation. Narcissists will isolate themselves, leave their families, ignore others, do anything to preserve a special bond. The narcissist's isolation and resulting behaviors create all kinds of fantasies in the borderline partner. Narcissists are unaware of the mortifying responses that they evoke. The narcissists would rather die than face humiliation, embarrassment, or injury to the sense of self. They will withdraw, leave, or disrupt a relationship, even if it is at the expense of self or others.

It is important to note that the withdrawing self of the narcissist is distinct from the false self, or retaliatory self, of the borderline. The borderline may be destructive in order to stir things up and to punish, while the narcissist may be destructive because of preoccupation with self.

There are two kinds of withdrawals: emotional and physical. The more obvious one is physical withdrawal, in which the narcissist walks away when feeling personally injured or misunderstood. The other is emotional withdrawal, which is covert, subtle, virtually always more insidious in nature than physical withdrawal, and therefore more pervasive. Narcissistic withdrawal and isolation can have severe detrimental effects on certain individuals exhibiting emotional vulnerabilities. These states of isolation can create profound feelings of inadequacy and confusion, especially in children, who are particularly susceptible. Winnicott (1965c, d) talked about the "capacity to be alone" (pp. 29–36), of "omnipotent control" (pp. 37–55), and of the tendency to invade "parental intercourse" (metaphorically speaking) rather than accept the tensions of being an outsider, because the borderline has not internalized a good-enough parent. Borderlines who are inclined toward feeling left out and nondeserving tend to identify with these withdrawing aspects. Borderlines, because of their susceptibility to taking in the projections of others, are not heavily enough rooted in their experience to recognize these maladapative processes. The identification is usually with a split-off aspect of the self that is clouded amidst a mass of vast confusion. The therapist must help the partners sort out how much of the withdrawing aspect each is accountable for, how much is delusional, and how much is reality based.

How Borderlines and Narcissists Misperceive

Because of their tendency to fuse with their objects, borderlines in particular misperceive and distort reality, so it is crucial to interpret not only their splitting but how their behavior affects others. I believe object-relations theory best describes these dynamics within the borderline syndrome.

Borderlines often distort and misperceive who is abandoning whom. They unwittingly abandon both themselves and others, but then turn it around so that they are the victims. Fearful of being left by therapist and spouse, they hesitate to express their needs (Case 6).

Having poor boundaries, these partners get caught up in their own delusional systems, which affect perception, judgment, and reality. Upon receiving a monthly statement for treatment, a narcissistic husband asks, "What's this?" The therapist answers, "That's your bill!" Looking perplexed, the narcissistic husband questions, "What's this for?" The therapist replies, "For treatment." The narcissistic husband responds, "Oh, you call this treatment? Why are you giving it to me?" The therapist answers, "Because that's what we agreed to." The narcissistic husband responds, "Oh!"

Often the narcissist will become enraged with the therapist for making such demands as request for payment. One might respond, "The little boy in you feels entitled, entitled to have treatment without ever getting a bill. You act as though I'm not entitled. So I'm not entitled to anything, and you are entitled to it all. This attitude can severely impair your reasoning, your judgment, your reality, your memory, and your perceptions, and leave you confused about what you really are entitled to." The therapist who has interpreted this has modeled clear thinking by following through and by staying on the point.

Drive toward Death Instinct or Drive toward Bonding

To open our discussion about the elements of the death instinct and the drive toward bonding, we need to consider the universal nature of cruelty and the sadistic tendencies in human beings that drive them to inflict pain upon others.

Loewenberg (1985), who presented at a conference on violation of human rights (reported by Lachkar, 1985a), discussed the discoveries made by Sigmund Freud about the erotic nature of violence. He cited examples from the Rat Man and Dora cases to demonstrate Freud's initial insights. It was Freud's belief that "the history of human civilization shows beyond any doubt that there is an intimate connection between cruelty and the sexual instinct" (Freud, 1909/1955). Loewenberg agreed with Freud, and suggested we cannot easily get rid of violence because it has genetic roots in the anal zone, and it is immortal in the nature of human beings. Loewenberg stated that the psychodynamics of violence is that one desires to destroy the despised part of oneself as it is projected onto the victim. In contrast, we may also project onto others positive qualities that they do not have, making them into idealized figures.

At this point, it is also important to consider Klein's (1946) concept of the death instinct. In terms of marital conflict, the sensory, perceptual aspects are considered as painful invasions to ward off danger. The death instinct may be a response to the black hole, or other threatening life forces experienced as emptiness. The persecutory experience is, for Klein, a pervasive force that is felt by the infant as bad mommy, bad breast, or bad daddy. The couple may disrupt the treatment, thereby "killing off" the therapist or the treatment as a way of getting rid of something because of impending dangers.

In the mental pain generated by experience of separation from the object tie, the borderline reverts to the primitive experience of a no breast, which is intolerable. There is a preconception that somewhere in the future there is a breast, that some mystical savior will rescue the person from the dangerous other, and will lead the person along the pathway of happiness. Beyond the pain, I believe that for the borderline there is the desire for self-development, bonding, and attachment experiences with a good parental object. Borderlines often join with pain because of the inability to hold on to the feelings of loss, deprivation, and mourning, or to identify themselves with victims.

CHAPTER V

Dynamic Positions and Transference Formations

DYNAMIC POSITIONS

Separateness

Some clinicians regard separateness as being literally a physical state, rather than an intrapsychic quality. It is not enough nowadays merely to state that clinicians must help individuals separate and individuate. One must first understand the psychodynamics to differentiate between separation and individuation. When we speak of separation, we are clearly referring to a psychological separation and not simply a physical one. Mahler, Pine, and Bergman (1975) have helped us to differentiate among intrapsychic fusions that occur within the couple dyad.

According to Mahler and her colleagues (1975), there are four subphases, along two separate tracks, leading to intrapsychic awareness: One of them, separation, leads to intrapsychic awareness of separateness, and the other, individuation, leads to the acquisition of distinctiveness and uniqueness. Mahler and her colleagues proposed that one gains an increasing capacity to recognize mother as a special person, to cathect, to inspect, to move gradually into the nonmother world, and later to move quite deliberately away from mother.

I believe the significance of this for the couple is that running away or doing separate things is not the same as learning to differentiate between needs, longings, desires, and wishes, nor is it the same as learning to tolerate one's own differentness or unique ways. A couple may learn to do separate things; however, doing separate things is not the same as coping, tolerating, and appreciating one's differentness (the "me" and a "not me"). The phases of Mahler and her colleagues have significance within narcissistic/borderline configurations because in primitive relationships there is difficulty in distinguishing the "mother world" (sameness) from the "nonmother world" (differentness). To fuse, to intrude on, or to force the other to change is just as destructive as withdrawing, ignoring, or running away. Ironically, even when the persons are living apart, they still may have something that bonds them or ties them together.

These phases are certainly important, but since we are dealing with severe pathologies in couples, rather than individuals per se, we must attend to the unit and define clearly these unique intrapsychic differences before we can respond therapeutically. For instance, one might interpret as follows: "On the surface you are able to do separate things and live a separate life; however, internally you are still very much emotionally involved."

Paranoid Schizoid Position

Klein's notion (1946) of the movement from the paranoid-schizoid position to the depressive position is, I believe, one of the most helpful ideas in understanding the fragmentation that occurs in these regressed couples. The movement from paranoid-schizoid to depressive interfaces with Kohut's idea of transmutal internalization (1971, 1977), Mahler and colleagues' phases of separation-individuation (including the autistic, the symbiotic, the subphases of differentiation, practicing, rapprochement, and object constancy (Mahler et al., 1975), and Grotstein's "dual track theorem" (1980).

The paranoid-schizoid position is a fragmented position in which thoughts and feelings are split off and projected because the psyche cannot tolerate pain, loneliness, and humiliation. In the depressive position, one becomes more capable of containing one's own sadness, loneliness, and emptiness, and can take more responsibility for one's actions and needs.

The paranoid-schizoid position was demonstrated by Klein to be the earliest phase of development. "It is characterized by the relations to the part objects, the prevalence of splitting in the ego and in the object and paranoid anxiety" (Segal, 1964, p. 127). If, in time, the child is to be able to experience a predominantly good and nurturing environment, it is essential for the infant in the paranoid-schizoid position that good experiences predominate over the bad and that the baby be able to view the mother as the good breast.

Partners in couple treatment tend to move back and forth between the paranoid-schizoid position and the depressive position. They are constantly moving from states of fragmentation to wholeness. In the depressive position they have a chance to integrate and comprehend their behaviors and events that led to the damage. Before reparation occurs, one must be able to tolerate the frustration and impatience of the depressive position (which Kohut referred to as introspection).

Depressive Position

Grotstein's contribution postulating Klein's phases of adhesive identification and movement from the paranoid-schizoid position to the depressive position is more helpful in understanding the fusion that occurs in couples than are theories that parallel or interface with Freud's developmental sequence of oral, anal, and genital. The depressive position interfaces with Klein's phases. The major tenet of Klein's work is that guilt, and the manic defense against guilt, gives a level of anxiety higher than persecutory anxiety.

In the depressive position, there is the realization that there is a "no breast" or an "empty breast," and one begins to express mourning, sadness for not having the breast. As the verbal expression of thought increases, the person begins to rely more excessively on sensory perceptions on which thought is based.

The depressive position begins when the infant recognizes the mother as whole object. In this position, there is a process of integration of the dissociation associated with feelings of ambivalence, and not everything is seen in terms of all black or all white; couples find that there are gray areas and begin to learn to balance between extremes. Individuals in this state will develop two defenses: manic defenses (which drive one to an opposite extreme) and reparation (Klein, 1955). Both these defenses are considered by Klein as based on omnipotence and denial of reality, and to be characterized by mastery, control, and contempt. There is the realization, in this position, that things cannot change overnight, and an allowance is made for feelings of mourning.

These comments on the depressive position are applicable in treating these two disorders, insofar as both borderlines and narcissists want the quick fix, and neither realizes that by getting things quickly and impulsively one can actually take away from rather than add to, and this can deprive the couple even further.

In the depressive position, borderlines in particular have a hard time giving up their false selves, and starting to show their true feelings, so busy are they making things look all right. Narcissists have a hard time weaning themselves from those who quickly gratify them with immediate excitement and approval.

If one cannot mourn, one cannot contain pain. If one does not mourn, one fails to reach the depressive position. In this position the feelings are too painful to contain, and one will continue to split off feelings or find quick replacements in quick relief to ward off those intolerable affects. If one cannot hold on to the feelings of sadness-aloneness in the depressive position, one can never feel truly entitled, learn from one's experience, learn to be alone, and even find inner peace.

Manic Defenses

According to Klein,

Manic defenses are evolved in the depressive position as a defense against the experience of depressive anxiety, guilt and loss. They are based on an omnipotent denial of psychic reality and object relations as characterized by triumph, control and contempt. [Segal, 1964, p. 126]

Manic Defenses vs. Integration

I believe Klein was referring to behaviors that operate at the extreme sides of the split, where the aim is to ward off feelings of persecution, shame, humiliation, and danger. If one has been passive, then one becomes aggressive, or if one has been excessively submissive, then one becomes overly aggressive—as in, for example, "Never again shall I be taken advantage of!"

This is not the same as integration, which emerges from understanding or humility; rather it is a defense against something. For Klein (1948), the ability to mourn relies on a "working through" and sorting out of feelings, not on manic behaviors and defenses. In her paper "A Contribution to the Psychogenesis of Manic-Defenses," Klein (1975a) stressed the importance of the depressive position and reviewed the splitting mechanism in a new light. Splitting, in this stage, is a precursor for the unification of opposing forces, and in my opinion is an all-important process. The implication for marital treatment is that patients in the paranoid-schizoid position, who are not integrated enough to sort things out, might attempt to stand up for themselves in inappropriate and bizarre ways.

In the light of treatment, couples, as adumbrated in this book, learn that wanting retribution, doing to the other what has been done to one, keeps them going around in circles. Because of the borderline and narcissistic defenses, neither partner is able to break from the primitive bond, nor is either one able to make justifiable or rational decisions. Tit for tat solutions, based on manic defenses or persecutory anxiety, do not lead to a solid sense of self, let alone to any understanding of the entanglement of defenses.

In the depressive position, one partner may realize that one cannot punish the other for being emotionally unavailable. It is in this stage that the patient comes to terms with the disappointment and feelings of hopelessness and despair, and begins to seek out new friends, mentors, and other ways of repairing the damage.

For the narcissist, the expression of a manic defense initially may sound something like, "Never again will I do anything for you! You never appreciate anything I do!" Whereas for the borderline, it may sound something like, "I'll show her! How dare she treat me this way? Next time she does that to me I'll do the same thing back to her!" In the depressive position, the borderline partner might rephrase the wording as follows: "No, I'm not going anywhere with you until you and I sit down and talk this thing out. You have hurt me and let me down. Now I'm not punishing you by not going with you, but I need you to know that you have hurt me and I will not tolerate it!"

Projective Identification

There is a phenomenon that occurs in a conjoint treatment setting for which there is not an exact name; the closest description is projective identification. Perhaps it comes close to Klein's notion of "confusional states," in which there are blurred boundaries between what is coming from without the psyche and what is coming from within (projective and introjective processes). This phenomenon is something like a reversal of roles, whereby one partner wants to get rid of or destroy in the other, what the one partner does not like in the self and sees in the other (dependency needs). The partner then enables the other partner to glimpse his or her own intrapsychic world.

In order for treatment to be effective with narcissistic and borderline patients, it is important that the therapist understand the different forms of projective identification. Bion saw projective identification as essential and healthy; Melanie Klein saw it as destructive. In his "Attacks on Linking" (1959), Bion claimed that an infant needs a container to express intolerable pain, and needs an object onto which to project painful affects, transforming them into something useful. As we have noted earlier "projective identification" is a term that Klein used to describe certain communications between the mother and the infant. I am using the term "projective identification" to express feelings of helplessness within the couple, and the need to attack in order to show others how it feels to be misused, abused, or displaced.

Bion made clear the healthy use of projective identification as an expression of protest and outrage. He transformed Klein's theories, giving more meaning to an understanding relationship with the mother and the need for maternal bonding and attachment. For Bion, projective identification not only helps understand the pain and frustration, but is the element that can put a chaotic fragmented world in some structural order via the mother's ability to transform, decode, and provide alpha functions.

In couple therapy, an intervention might be: "You are trying to engage me in an argument, and if I get into an argument then I'm not going to be available to give you back something meaningful that can feed you. At least you are letting me know what it feels like to get lost and why there is so much confusion."

There are two projective identification processes involved in couple relationships. The first one I will call single projective identification, whereby one partner projects into the other and the other partner identifies with that projection. The second process is a phenomenon I refer to as dual projective identification. This occurs primarily when both partners are simultaneously projecting into one another. Both deny the projections, and both identify with those projections.

In single projective identification, the projections with which one identifies are felt to be part of the self, as if they are one's own characteristics. Suddenly, one may feel anger or rage, even though these affects may be vehemently denied.

I believe this differentiation between the single and the dual projective identification processes is crucial because we need to be able to discover from whence the area of anxiety emanates, and this is particularly difficult when couples are in collusion, are engulfed, and are doing the dance. For instance, if we discover that through the process of single projective identification the borderline partner is projecting feelings of deprivation, we then have an opportunity to explore the primary feelings of deprivation and their etiology. Eventually, this can lead patients to further toleration of their own anxiety and more control over their own destiny.

In dual projective identification, while one partner may be projecting feelings of deprivation onto the other, the other partner may be projecting guilt. If we allow continued projective identification, affects of vigor and vitality would become reduced to mere states of submission and compliance, and possibly guilt, withdrawal, and isolation. Typical comments might be: "I'll just die if you ever leave me! I just can't live without you!" Or, "You're putting too much pressure on me!"

In dual projective identification, we may find a narcissistic partner withdrawing from the borderline because of fear of intimacy and closeness. For the narcissist, closeness and dependency may represent the loss of a grandiose tie with a self object. The narcissist may want and crave the intimacy, but may also fear that closeness could impede or destroy the omnipotent fantasy of ever connecting with and preserving the symbiotic unit: "I do love you and want to be with you, but my work comes first, can't you understand that?" The borderline may experience the narcissist as not caring, and thus may respond with crippling defenses: "I feel paralyzed! I can't do anything! I wish I could be more like you and concentrate on my work, but I can't. All I can think about is being with you!" I call this process dual projective identification because both are doing the dance. We can help borderlines understand that, if they try to possess the breast through their envy (to devour, possess, or destroy the object), they will end up feeling more deprived and left out; however, if they can allow the breast to feed them, and can learn from the breast, they can learn to develop something of their own. We can help borderlines recognize their clinging, parasitic behavior and establish ways of staying within their own boundaries through the use of transitional objects.

Projection vs. Introjection

Klein has used external objects as means of giving concrete expression to theoretical constructs, and has brought to light the use of projection and introjection as defensive procedures. Underlying the borderline, in my view, is the defense mechanism of projection, while narcissistic individuals are more inclined toward introjection. I am deeply indebted to Klein because her theories help us understand persecutory anxiety, and, as I have noted, I believe these differences are of key importance in the treatment of marital conflicts. I suggest that the study of internal objects through the process of projection is most appropriate for the borderline, whereas it is more effective for the narcissist to conceptualize feelings of idealization and self-absorption through the process of introjection. The process of introjection is that which motivates the narcissist to compete for the starring role, to have the desire to live up to an internal idealized imago whose standards are almost impossible to meet. Narcissists are continually struggling to get the steps right, but no matter how hard they try, practice, or repeat the experience, the internalized imago is an impossible goal. Understanding the projective and introjective processes helps the therapist interpret how the partners, in their similar dynamics, glaringly reflect one another.

Reparation

Applicable to the innumerable concepts Klein has contributed to the treatment of dysfunctional couples is the idea of reparation that occurs in the depressive position. Reparation is an ego-involved attempt to heal depressive anxieties and guilt (Klein, in "Love, Guilt and Reparation," 1937/1975e; Segal, 1964). After one splits back and forth continually between extremes, one finally comes to the realization that these fragmented behaviors cause damage to the self and to others, and reparation can begin.

For the narcissist, the ability to repair is difficult mainly because of excessive guilt and the lack of empathy. Kernberg stated that excessive guilt impairs object relations, and that the capacity for lasting relationships has to do both with guilt and with the genuineness of the wish to repair. Winnicott (1965b) discussed the capacity for guilt and for concern, while Mahler and her colleagues (1975) focused on the capacity for object constancy. Murray Weiler's idea of the quick fix, described earlier in this chapter, can be related to splitting mechanisms and to the covering up of the vulnerable part of the personality (personal communication, 1987).

I believe Klein comes closest in helping us conceptualize capacity for reparation. She based it on the capacity for guilt, which Klein proposed occurs in the depressive position, as opposed to primitive superego anxiety, occurring in the para-noid-schizoid position. I believe this is important for both borderline and narcissistic partners, particularly in distinguishing manic defenses against guilt and envy. For the borderlines, the capacity to repair is difficult, because genuine wishes for reparation are often confused with shame or the false self. Saying one is sorry, for example, is not the same as facing pain, moving through a process of mourning, and understanding how one's own behaviors have truly contributed to the problem.

FORMS OF TRANSFERENCE

Transference

In couple treatment, there are three different transferences, all of which need to be interpreted. There are the transferences of the individual partners, and there is the couple relationship transference. Whatever is interpreted has to be demonstrated to the couple in terms of their relationship.

There is a certain group of patients Kohut refers to as being analyzable. Kohut (1977) distinguished between two aspects of the bipolar self of the narcissistic personality. They are known as the "grandiose self" and the "idealized parent imago." The grandiose self is expressed in the need for mirroring. Mirroring subsumes a variety of supportive, affirming, and validating responses for the person's mastery and accomplishments. It is the grandiose part of the self that develops in the transference as all invincible, invulnerable, and all knowing, as if one were above everyone else. In the unfolding "mirror-transference," Kohut suggested that these patients require primarily empathic, approving, echoing, and confirming responses, and if these are not forthcoming, become outraged.

In contrast, the idealized parent imago, whereby one experiences others as existing solely as an extension of one's own needs, extends to the external environment. The idealized parent imago provides a source of identification; the therapist, for instance, is to be available only as an extension of the patient's needs, and is not to have needs of his or her own. Often friends or marital partners exist only as a service to the excessive needs and demands of the narcissist, and they too are not to have needs of their own.

Vertical Split

There is a concept of the personality called the vertical split. The vertical split in the personality consists of two sectors. The first sector is the unbroken merger with the mother: The patient becomes the executor of the mother's grandiose wishes and the messenger of her superiority. The second sector is characterized by certain goals and idealized attitudes internalized by the father. Kohut called regression the yearning for the merger with the mirroring mother, and the vertical split is the part of the self without unique self-concept. For clarification, Kohut suggested that the admiring and mirroring functions be considered the traditional maternal aspects, and the idealizations as developing out of paternal functions. The bipolar self in the transference according to Kohut (1977) has a chance to restore when the patient can recognize that although we never outgrow the need for self objects, the types of self objects we need in life do change as we grow.

Borderline Transference

We know from Kohut that a narcissistic transference does exist. But is there such a thing as a borderline transference? The consensus is that the borderline personality does not adhere to classical patterns of transference. It is generally thought that in order to form a transference relationship, one has to be higher on the borderline/narcissist continuum. In the conceptual framework of the discussion of narcissistic/borderline couples, I suggest that many transferencelike phenomena do emerge. It appears likely that what occurs in the couple's relationship does indeed get replicated in the transference. I propose that there is a borderline transference. The difference is that the borderline massively projects feelings into the therapist in a way that is quite different from that of the narcissist. For instance, in a conjoint session a borderline patient is asked by the therapist to remember to discuss a particular issue with her husband during the week. As usual, the borderline wife forgot. The analyst and the husband are left feeling discounted and ignored. Is this transference? Can we regard the disavowel aspects of the borderline as a part of the self being transferred onto the therapist? If so, can we call this a "borderline transference"? Perhaps the discussion on countertransference can help us explore these concepts further.

Countertransference

A dramatic revision has occurred since the term countertransference was introduced into psychoanalytic theory during Freud's day. Freud viewed countertransference as resistance within the analyst getting in the way of understanding the patient. Countertransference was originally defined as the therapist's unconscious reaction, or the transference that the analyst had to the patient, based on the analyst's own unresolved conflictual wishes and unconscious fantasies (Freud, 1938/1940). D. W. Winnicott (1949, cited in Slipp, 1984) was the first psychoanalyst to expand the traditional definition of countertransference to encompass all the reactions the therapist had to the patient. Object-relations theorists, especially Klein, expanded these ideas even further to include even more primitive responses and reactions therapists were receiving from the patient's unconscious.

Samuel Slipp, who has done a very clear and concise review of the changes occurring in the countertransference phenomenon, acknowledged Klein, who developed a richer understanding of the use of this phenomenon. Slipp recognized Paula Heimann (1950) as one of the first to appreciate countertransference as a therapeutic tool, but it was Klein who first used the term projective identification. This term's use shifted countertransference from being related solely to the analyst's resistance to being viewed as an interactional analysis experience.

Narcissistic/borderline couples evoke reactions that convey the message that we must provide immediate cure and relief, immediate solutions, and that unless we do, we are disregarding the couple. In conjoint treatment as well as in individual work, this is an extremely crucial concept that must be handled skillfully to avoid severe acting out or premature disruption of the treatment.

The therapist who becomes confused with countertransference issues—for example, the therapist's own guilt, and feelings of worthlessness or of betrayal—may have a hard time sorting out the distortions. It is important to address the heart of the issues and to stay separate and to deal with the area of anxiety. Some possible interventions follow: "Yes, sometimes guilt is important. . . . There is appropriate guilt." Or, "Yes, it is OK to have expectations." Or, "What's wrong with having an expectation? What's wrong with feeling pressure? Discomfort? Anxiety? Maybe that's part of the problem, you both have a hard time tolerating any discomfort, so as soon as you get anxious you lose yourselves or blame each other. Sometimes it is appropriate to have these feelings."

Often the narcissist projects guilt feelings that the therapist is the cause of the narcissist's vulnerability and wounded self-image. Feeling that we do not appreciate them or that we are being too critical, narcissists respond with hurt feelings. The borderline, in contrast, may project into us that we are not doing enough; the borderline wants the quick fix, and often tries to make us feel ashamed and embarrassed for having needs of our own (payment, boundaries, schedules). This is particularly important, for many borderlines suffer from alexithymia (are split off from their feelings), and are not aware of what they are trying to express.

There are many countertransferential issues for the therapist, including feelings of being a failure, guilt, anxiety, not being good enough, and despair, but the most profound feeling is that of being abandoned. Patients will often disrupt the treatment to let the therapist know what it feels like to be left out, a form of projective identification. Many will not get well as a way of letting us know how difficult and frustrating waiting can be.

One of the most important and frequent countertransference issues in conjoint treatment is distancing, as in the following: "We decided to take a break. We don't need treatment anymore." There is often a notion that less contact is better, when in fact, one needs more closeness and more intimacy, not less. Often this is a collective couple fantasy, that now that they have had a little treatment, they are all well and can "do it themselves" and take a flight into mental health! In conjoint as well as individual treatment this countertransference issue is one that must be handled skillfully. The issue of stopping treatment must be dealt with by addressing the defenses in the couple transference and not by colluding with them.

If these defenses are not understood, or if the therapist colludes with or aligns with the pathogenic part of the relationship, the marriage can result in decompensation. An appropriate response from the therapist would be, "Now you are distancing yourself from me as you have from others." The patient is saying, "Look Mommy, I'm all well now, and now I can do it all by myself!"

Therapists who use a psychoanalytic approach to treating these couples must be meticulous in pursuit of understanding these defenses and how defenses contribute to our countertransference, playacting a recurring drama. More specifically, the therapist may feel guilty for "using" the couple, or may feel ashamed for needing them. The therapists can begin to feel like abusive, strict parents; punitive, harsh, noncaring parents; negligent parents; betraying, intrusive parents; and so on.

The issues around countertransference are difficult because there is no such thing as a perfect therapy or a perfect therapist. None of us can have perfect responses. The more skilled one is in handling the dynamics, however, the better chance one has in dealing with the ins and outs of these complex disorders.

Couple Transference

Transference interpretations must encompass the couple myth addressing the infantile aspects of the relationship. The therapist who uses a psychodynamic approach has a wonderful opportunity to make transference interpretations and to apply them to the couple mythology. I believe that many of the illustrative cases in Chapter IX not only highlight the splitting and projective aspects, but address the couple's shared collective ideology.

Individual transference must be directed toward the child's relationship to the parents, or other archaic experience. In conjoint treatment, transference must address the couple myth or the couple fantasy, similar to group psychotherapy, always keeping in mind what are the group dynamics and what are the group myths.

Therapist as Self Object

Couple therapy is a deep emotional experience of intense communication and feelings that occurs among three persons. Although vignettes can be described, and therapeutic sessions can be reported, it is impossible to teach a therapist a particular approach to conjoint therapy—what to do, how to do it, and what to say. The words that are not the therapist's own may come across as empty thoughts or empty theories, and if the therapist attempts imitation, there is a risk of mere mimicry, of the putting aside of one's unique way of viewing the material and of one's own beliefs, values, and theoretical framework. The techniques for couple therapy simply must be developed through the transference experience of the individual therapist.

Kohut told us that psychological disturbances are caused by faulty self objects, lack of attunement, empathic failures, and lack of mirroring from idealized objects, as the primary focus of the couples' feelings of dismay. These certainly are important; however, to ignore the internal world may lead to a form of collusion with or joining in on the pathology. Environmental or external forces are important, but if the primary focus is on the external, we are in danger of undermining the internal conflict. Furthermore, because of the tendency in couples to blame, failure to face the internal object world can be perceived as avoiding responsibility for one's behavior or as collusion. Object relations helps patients face these internal deficits, enabling one to take more responsibility for one's own behavior. The primary focus of the therapist as a self object must not be misconstrued as going along with the pathology. Self-object functions may shift from bonding and mirroring to containing and weaning as changes occur throughout various treatment phases.

Object-relations theory provides us with an environmental mother, a background mother, a being/doing mother, a weaning mother, and a containing/sustaining mother to help establish different kinds of bonding and self-object experiences. The importance of the therapist/mother as the container becomes more vital in a conjoint setting because the central issues revolve around persecutory anxiety, shame, guilt, confusion, and fantasies of separation. The empathic mode can be most valuable in conjoint therapy as an important source of exploration, particularly in the attempt to bond and form a healthy object tie.

The internal world or internal deficits are not emphasized in self psychology. In my view, if we turn to faulty self objects or to the patient's "subjective reality" as the primary focus of the couple's failing or dismay, and ignore the internal world of projections and introjections, then we may join in the pathology—that is, the tendency to assign blame or find the outside enemy responsible for all the couple's shortcomings in the relationship—and we may fail to see the projections from the perspective of internal "enemies." I believe it is not one over the other, but rather both faulty self objects and the structural ego defects that must be considered.

In sorting confusional and tangential modes of relating, the therapist should understand that although the mirroring mother certainly is crucial, she does not have the same impact as the containing and holding one. Unfortunately, many therapists misunderstand the notion of empathy and introspection, and misplace the emphasis upon external circumstances (the self-object tie), and tend to ignore the destructive parts of the personality. Sometimes the empathic mode is not enough and the therapist needs to turn to a more holding/containing/ sustaining/hard object mode and may, for example, assertively state: "Of course there is an external betrayer. Now you say it's your wife; before you said it was your brother. You need to know that there is also an internal betrayer. This internal betrayer keeps you feeling helpless and seriously impairs your judgment and the way you relate to your wife and to others." This kind of response usually feels good to the borderline because it gives a sense of having something inside, and can lead to deeper emotional experiences.

The most important function, according to Grotstein, is the analyst's "detoxification" of the banished elements of self that have been exiled into unconsciousness. The use of empathy is crucial to conjoint treatment, but there is also another technique, which comes from the classic Kleinian psychoanalytic school and from British object relations, the "weaning" of infantile, childlike aspects of the patient into more mature states of development. Application of Bion's work can help the therapist understand the couple's experience, which can lead the therapist to a valid interpretation of what is really happening in the relationship.

These theories overlap and can be suitable for various stages within the conjoint setting. Many authors have written of these methods, but I wish to add that it is important to keep in mind that the more primitive the couple, the more emphasis should be focused on the mirroring and bonding needs (self-object functions). Timing and listening, as in playing a musical instrument, are the very essence of successful therapy.

"Teaching" Others to Become Self Objects

Rather than to teach how to be self objects, it is the job of the therapist to become the self object. We cannot teach empathy and mirroring; rather we need to become the mirroring object. These steps must be accomplished before anything is to be achieved, before an emotional separation must occur.

Many therapists treating couples are so influenced by Kohut and the movement toward self psychology that there is an unfortunate emphasis on the position that we teach the partners to become self objects or to become unduly understanding. Because of their defenses, neither the borderline nor the narcissist knows how to serve as a self object or how to perform self-object functions for the other. On the contrary, the focus must be on affective experiences and the various feeling states.

In conjoint treatment, just as in individual treatment, the narcissist cannot serve as a self object, because first the borderline must be weaned from an internally unsafe world and the narcissist weaned from overinvolvement with the self.

Although teaching partners in a fragmented relationship to empathize with one another is certainly a laudable aim, in most instances it is an unworkable one. While these couples are in the initial phase of conjoint treatment, empathy is an unknown entity. It seems to be a more realistic goal, then, to help these couples slowly make a transition from pathological dependence to healthy dependency to separation. The being mommy allows the patient to feel, to be, and to experience, not to do and to act. The major thrust of the treatment is to help one relate, rather than to "teach" self-object functions.

"Understanding" can often be a block or defense against taking action, standing up for oneself, holding on to one's own thoughts and beliefs, or moving toward separating oneself from the confusional states (see Case 3, Dana and Bob). Many partners will say, "Yes, I understand, I understand," without really understanding anything. One cannot have understanding without having experiences with a good, available, containing, and sustaining breast (see Bion, 1977). To paraphrase Bion, without experience there can be no understanding. Taking something quickly from the therapist and imitating is not the same as knowing—it is fusion! To be empathic or understanding can come across as mere mimicry or imitation, and to encourage the patient to be empathic can only replicate a false self or lead to a premature development, removing one even further from one's own emotional experience. The therapist, when serving as the self object and modeling self-object functions, also provides the containing and sustaining functions. Words then become empty thoughts, or thoughts without a thinker. Bion reminded us how important it is to allow one to have one's own experience. Paradoxically, "understanding" or "knowing" can be a defense against ever really understanding or knowing. Real understanding is introspective.

Transitional, Confusional, and Diversional Objects

Transitional objects. Grotstein (1984a, b, 1987) observed that the borderline adheres to the mother's body, has poor skin definition, and escapes to a state of mindlessness. Tustin (1981), Meltzer (1967), and Bion (1965, 1967) supported these ideas, and added that borderlines misuse "transitional objects" as "confusional objects," make poor use of "thinking apparatus," and invade their interpersonal objects so as to become fused with those objects.

Winnicott (1953) suggests the infant learns to wait and to control his impulsivity. It is suggested that wanting unconditional love can severely interfere with relating to others. According to Winnicott, the infant assumes rights over the object. The therapist can be used as a transitional object through the therapist's capacity to "hold" from regression to dependency. The more disturbed one is, the more one uses others as transitional objects.

The concept of the transitional object was first introduced by Winnicott (1953) to designate a symbolic inanimate object that represents a momentary absence of mother objects. The transitional object serves as a familiar source of comfort and soothing as it revives the mother's image, familiarity, and touch. Often these objects are blankets, soft toys, pillows, or articles of clothing; and in adult life, they can become quite sophisticated—for example, writing, computers, dance, music, clothes, as well as teddy bears (Case 9).

Borderlines have difficulty making sufficient use of transitional objects; the borderline may not have been able to separate from the mother's body long enough to seek self-soothing devices. When they are within primitive, preoedipal relationships, patients frequently may turn to other objects to work through internal conflict. Many borderlines cannot use inanimate objects as transitional, and instead use other persons as part objects. When the borderline is able to use them, transitional objects hold the borderline together during periods of separation, and help fill the empty spaces and the black holes, especially when the breast is not available (Case 9).

Transitional objects may be regarded as healthy only when the behavior is understood in relation to needs. Francis Tustin (1981) associated a transitional object with a web of ever-changing fantasies, used in a healthy way, to help the infant make a transition away from the mother. Tustin described the "bibby" and the first treasured possession with the idea that the baby had something good inside. These transitional objects make up for what is missing. Tustin made a profound distinction between the healthy use of a transitional object and a confusional object. According to Tustin, the autistic or "confusional" child needs hard, indestructible objects in order to achieve a sense of differentiation. "Such a child never experiences 'missing.' In his concretized experience, absence of a needed person is experienced as a 'hole,' which can be filled immediately with an autistic object" (Tustin, 1981, p. 107). My experience with couples has brought me to the view that, as bizarre as it might sound, affairs, alcoholism, substance abuse, or compulsive shopping or spending may be healthy if the motivation behind these behaviors is to soothe or to make up for the missing object.

Confusional and diversional objects. Tustin (1981) performed pioneering work on pathological autism, which she showed as leading to childhood psychosis. She discussed the differences between children in the encapsulated state and children who are in the confusional state. In this text, I borrow from Tustin's work on confusional states to apply it to the couple.

Tustin (1981) referred to the child's use of the confusional object as a way of hiding, rather than for soothing; of avoiding, and not as a object to enable the child to move to and fro. In my experience with couples, the use of cars, friends, affairs, drugs, alcohol, tears, shopping, computers, or treatment may be viewed as either transitional or confusional, depending on the motivation. I believe that most patients in marital treatment fit the "confusional" category more than the "encapsulated" one. The confusional states of the "me" and the "not-me" need to be transformed, out of the biological realm and into the mind, where the patient can think about and then understand the confusion.

In this work, I have used the terms "confusional object" and "diversional object" interchangeably to describe behaviors that occur in a conjoint setting, where the primary motivation is to block or to avoid intimacy and human contact. With confusional (or diversional) objects, there is no clear evidence of what is missing or needed (as there is with transitional objects), but rather we find vagueness and illusionary images. For instance, an affair might be an attempt to get even (confusional), rather than an attempt to rejoin or to bond with another for need gratification. Needs are not based on memories or desire, but are experienced as vague, obscure, and abstract. Alcohol or substance abuse, money, affairs, telephones, cars, or friends may be regarded as transitional or as diversional, once again, depending on whether the motivations behind involvement with these objects are for rejoining with the longed-for object, or for use as mere magical amulets to ward off dangers and to obstruct intimacy. Unlike transitional objects, confusional objects do not revive memories of previous good experiences.

Language can be used in a transitional or diversional manner, depending on whether it is a vehicle to enhance communication, to convey thoughts, or to interrupt thoughts. Patients who interrupt excessively, speak quickly, speak either loudly or inaudibly, and make jokes, are using language in a diversional manner. The person who uses language as transitional is one who digests thoughts and ideas, and is able to communicate and to engage in a meaningful interchange. Bion (1970) stated, "Sometimes the function of speech is to communicate experience to another; sometimes it is to miscommunicate experience to another" (p. 1). "The psycho-analyst," according to Bion, "must employ the language of achievement, but he must remember that the language was elaborated as much for the achievement of deception and evasion as for truth" (p. 3).

A simple example of a diversional/confusional object is a telephone answering machine. Sometimes an answering machine is a device that takes messages so that the receiver of the call may return the call at a later time. The receiver of the call, however, may never return the call; in this case, the machine may be viewed as a diversional object, whose purpose is only to confuse the caller, not to enhance communication. A borderline wife called the therapist following a conjoint session, and left a 45-minute message on the answering machine. At the end of the message, she thanked the therapist for "listening," and said that this was a "good session," and that the therapist should charge her for the time. The machine, in this context, may be viewed as a transitional object, taking the place of the mommy/therapist between sessions. The machine becomes the blanket, taking the place of the absent breast. Incidentally, borderlines need to know that this is a healthy way to manage because it can lead to bonding and to better relations with others.

Another example of a diversional/confusional object is an automobile. A family car with only one extra seat conveys a message of being a rejecting object, suitable for only two persons, rather than for the entire family.

Tears may be confusional when they block communication, as opposed to tears that convey pain, feelings of hurt, and meaningful sentiments. Dreams may be confusional when they block or intrude on feelings, or when used to detract from, rather than to enhance, understanding. Money may be confusional and diversional when used to withhold, rather than as functional in sharing and management. Medication may be viewed as a confusional object when used to cover up an existing problem. Sometimes it can be used as transitional, if it offers relief from anxiety enough to bridge the gap and establish a link of understanding and introspection. Friends may be transitional or diversional, depending on whether they are used to enhance communication, intimacy, and understanding, or whether they are used as status symbols or to block intimacy with others.

CONCLUSION

Among the innumerable concepts presented in this chapter, I have attempted to expand the usage of the transitional object to facilitate a more in-depth understanding of the primitive regressive structures of narcissistic/borderline couples.

CHAPTER VI

Primitive Defense Mechanisms and Psychodynamics

Theoretical Implications and Qualitative Differences

Many authors have contributed theories and constructs helpful in analyzing the narcissist/borderline relationship. Most prominent among these are Melanie Klein, Otto Kernberg, and Wilfred Bion, but others also have provided insights into the dynamics of these bonds. Klein's innovative ideas help us to understand why in some dyadic relationships, one partner (the borderline) continually acts out the destructive impulses (primitive superego), while the other partner (the narcissist) holds back because of an internal voice (superego) that reprimands, admonishes, and offers punishment and exile if one does not obey.

SUPEREGO

The literature refers to many different superegos. The Freudian view depicts an introjected whole figure, parental image that operates at the level of the superego. Klein believed that the infant first introjects part objects: the breast or the penis. Klein described a physiological experience of bodily sensations that affects the infant from birth. Often these affects evoke unidentified sensations of persecution, retaliation, and danger. Many theorists have confirmed the precursors of Freud's superego formation as coexisting with the "dos, don'ts, oughts and shoulds" representing compliance with strong parental demands during toilet training stages.

Like Klein, Freud's superego does not concretely refer to a little harsh man inside, but rather is a fantasy of an introjected parental figure. The distinction between Freud's internal object, and Klein's internal object helps one understand guilt at the level of the superego. Freud's concern about what others shall think is opposed to Klein's superego which is persecutory, the shame and concern about having needs (preoccupation that one's needs, thoughts, and desires can destroy or invade another person).

Mason, in his review of the literature, differentiated between Freud's superego, which follows the shadows of the Oedipus complex, and Klein's, which is more primitive, persecutory, and hostile because it contains the child's own primitive nature and impulses, which have been projected into it. Freud's superego is responsible for morals, conscience, ethics, and religion. It is the internalized image that continues to live inside the child's life, controlling, threatening, or punishing the child whenever the child's oedipal wishes attempt to make themselves known (Mason, 1981, p. 141). Mason contended the literature contains many papers that describe the severe, harsh, murderous nature of the superego, suggesting that the primitive superego (the fear of being destroyed, or the "death instinct") begins at birth. In his literature review, Mason considered Meltzer's (1964–1965) description of paranoid anxiety in association with terror (because of "dead objects" or "dead babies") being internalized. The significance of this work is that it implies that the kind of anxiety emanating from the primitive superego is of an explosive nature and different from the more developed superego formation.

ENVY

Klein, whose own internal object was her own mother (Clayman-Cook, 1987), either loved or hated the members of her family, and experienced profound, ambivalent feelings for them, including envy, jealousy, guilt, and greed. Klein made a distinction between envy and jealousy. According to Segal (1964),

"She considers envy to be the earlier of the two, and shows that envy is one of the most primitive and fundamental emotions" (p. 40).

The infant experiences envy in relation to the feeding breast. When the infant feels intense anxiety and this anxiety is experienced as innate badness, the breast becomes the source of the projections. The absolute supply of nourishment and soothing, the breast is also that which is envied and attacked when not readily available. In dyadic relationships, if the other person's attributes become the source of nourishment to compensate for one's own internal deficits, then the other concomitantly becomes the source of attack and envy. However, according to Segal, "envy does not stop at exhausting the external objects" (p. 41). Regardless of the consequence, envy seeks to destroy. The metaphor of the infant and the breast coincides with the adult relationship or the analytic couple: When one sees the other partner as the breast (or the source of all the goodness), it is envy associated with being unable to possess that spoils the relationship. In these couples one partner tends to make the other an everything and to devalue the self as a nothing (see Case 12). For instance, a borderline husband may say he's lonely and try to force his wife to quit her job as a nurse. Instead of filling his life with his own work, friends, or sports as sources of nourishment, he turns to his wife to supply the "nursing" for him. He then attacks his wife rather than using her for nourishment, or learning from her.

JEALOUSY

Jealousy, according to Klein, has an oedipal component, and is based on love. It is a triangular relationship, in which one seeks the possession of the loved object and the removal of the rival. Jealousy is a two-part process, in "which the subject embodies the other object for some possession or quality; no other live object need enter into it" (Segal, 1964, p. 40). Daddy is often the intruder between the feeding symbiotic couple. Segal believed that "jealousy is a whole-object relationship while envy is essentially experienced in terms of part-objects, though it persists in whole-object relationships" (p. 40).

GREED

Greed can fuse with envy, making for the wish to exhaust the other entirely, in order not only to own all goodness, but to deplete the other so that that person no longer contains anything enviable. The narcissist is frequently greedy, wanting it all.

GUILT VS. SHAME

Borderlines are dominated more by shame than by guilt; narcissists are dominated more by guilt. Klein initially felt that guilt occurs in the depressive position (see Case 8). In later writing, she stated that guilt can be experienced transiently earlier. In *Envy and Gratitude* (1957), Klein described both the envious superego and premature guilt as outcomes of early envy. Klein amended her view that guilt occurs only in the depressive position, and added that it can occur in the paranoid-schizoid position as well.

These ideas can be most helpful to the couple. Shame relates to needs, particularly for the borderline ("Pardon me for my needing love, sex, attention. Pardon me for my existence!"). Guilt is a higher form of development. The narcissist tends to use guilt to turn inward and against the self.

We need to know the difference between valid guilt and invalid guilt. Valid guilt has to do with commitment, and failure to meet one's obligations, while invalid guilt comes from the punitive part of the superego conveying harsh restrictive punitive messages that are internalized into the patient's un-conscious. One could label as invalid guilt that suffered by the narcissistic wife who could not have a close sexual relationship with her husband. Whenever she undressed, she heard the voice of her mother say, "Don't let yourself go; nice girls don't do things like that!" Hedges (1983) proposed that without guilt there could be no development of an autonomous self. The implication is that "guilt need not be looked upon as some troublesome affect to be eliminated but rather as one of the continuous driving forces in the organization of the self" (p. 30).

A wife called at the last minute and told me she would be unable to make the conjoint appointment. As the therapist, I let her know that her husband and I had been waiting for her and reminded her that she had cancelled at the last minute for the past three sessions. In a loud, attacking voice she yelled, "What are you trying to do, make me feel guilty?" My immediate defensive response was to want to say, "Oh, no, of course not!" I caught myself, and said instead, "Well, what's wrong with guilt? Sometimes guilt is appropriate and valid, and other times it is not."

DUAL-TRACK THEOREM

We have observed that narcissistic/borderline states and traits vacillate back and forth, so that it is difficult to tell within the relationship if one of the partners is narcissistic or borderline. Grotstein's dual-track theorem (1981) is similar to Klein's theory of movement between the paranoid-schizoid and the depressive positions. Grotstein suggested that the paranoid-schizoid and depressive positions occur simultaneously, and that throughout life, one tends to move back and forth between states of wholeness and fragmentation.

The concept of the dual track allows for interaction. Fantasies and reality occupy equal footing. Grotstein viewed interaction experiences as dialectical forces that continue throughout the lifetime between one's fantasy life and one's own ability to view life more realistically, and felt that the dual-track theory is of special importance as the mediator reconciling the growing disparity between classical and Kleinian analysts.

We now think of normal maturation as continuing perma- nent states that exist side by side with states of separation-individuation throughout life, so that no matter what the state of development or the chronological age of the individual, maturation still continues. This is important because therapy takes place in a dynamic state; the couple interaction continues to flow from one state to another, in spite of the structure of the stages of development.

SELF OBJECTS VS. INTERNAL OBJECTS

There is considerable overlap between the narcissist and the borderline disorders, and working in a conjoint setting requires considerable insight to focus on their dynamic interplay, including when to use internal and external interventions, the movements back and forth between the intrapsychic and interpersonal processes (introjective and projective), and understanding the motivations behind these forces.

Do we interpret the projective, attacking-internal persecutory mother? Or do we try first to understand something about this attacking internal mother, and why she is the way she is? All are important; however, to ignore the internal world, its projections, misperceptions, and distortions, may lead to a form of collusion—for example, the tendency to evacuate or blame others for all shortcomings in the relationship. I am not suggesting that environmental or external forces are to be disregarded, but if the primary focus is on the external, we are then in danger of undermining the seriousness of the internal conflict as a vigorous source of analytic investigation.

Self objects refer to an interpersonal relationship whereby the self object functions solely to provide for the child's omnipotent and grandiose needs. Kohut reminds us that psychological disturbances are not a result of drives, but are caused by faulty self objects, lack of attunement with the archaic objects, empathic failures, lack of mirroring from idealized objects, and is the primary cause of conflict. According to Kohut, there is a time in the child's life when these grandiose desires are normal. In couple therapy, any threat or disruption to the symbiotic merger can get distorted or exaggerated, can become the primary focus of the couples' failings or dismay. On the one hand, the self object is thought to be a separate object, but on the other, it is felt to be part of the self forming a collusive bond.

Internal objects refer to an intrapsychic process whereby unconscious fantasies are split off and projected. Klein's elaborations on unconscious fantasies surpass Freud's in that they are ubiquitous, always active, and ever present. Klein believed that the infant can perceive the world as a good breast, which can provide the infant with food and nurturance or an attacking bad breast, which can deprive the infant.

Particularly in marital treatment, helping couples understand and take responsibility for their own behaviors can best be accomplished by noting the differences between self and internal object functions, and how they specifically apply to the narcissist and borderline disorders. Because of persecutory anxiety and the borderline tendency to split and project, it appears to be tention on internal objects for the priate to make use of self objects ⁿelming feelings of anger and rag ne and attack one another. Addr nables one to feel more in contro d, more structured and grounded. used and misinterpreted as collu eatment, we try to wean patients away from blaming others.

To distinguish when it is more efficient to make use of internal objects and when to use self-object responses, we need to make reference again to the term projective identification. According to Brandchaft and Stolorow (1984), the application of the theory of projective identification connotes the real danger of depriving patients of means to defend themselves. These authors feel that to fall back on interpretations of projection is to the detriment of the subjective experience of the patient. Self psychologists are doubtful if projective defense mechanisms truly exist. Self psychologists tend not to believe that a person deliberately tries to evoke a negative reaction in another person and continually fight against assuming they know the "objective truth" (Lindon & Gabbard, 1991, p. 35). Of course these individuals have their own subjective experiences, but they also need to know that these experiences also may be destructive and harmful to them. The self psychologist might question, "Who are we to decide that the analyst's view is better?" The Kleinian might respond, "Because I'm the 'mommy' and I'm the breast that feeds you, and you're the 'baby'!"

To help clarify the difference between self and internal objects, Brandchaft and Stolorow (1984) proposed that self-object functions suggest a state of recapturing normal functioning that had been traumatically and phase-inappropriately ruptured during the patient's formative years. From a Kleinian perspective, there are states of fusion or partial fusion with interpersonal objects. Structures within the self's ego are formed by projective identification aspects of self that are projected onto interpersonal objects.

A battered wife as victim, for example, can keep changing spouses, but will repeat similar experiences within each new situation, and will keep feeling abused unless the internal "beater" or saboteur is interpreted as part of the internal world. The therapist might interpret, "Yes, there is an external abuser, but now there is also an internal one who beats you up." Unless this is interpreted and worked through, no matter how often one changes the environment, the same configuration occurs again and again. While external circumstances are important considerations, they can also support one's delusions, and, in turn, one's projections.

Let us take the example of the narcissistic husband who has fantasies about other women because he is craving excitement (See case 5). What needs to be addressed is the internal dullness, and to discover what's in the way of finding the real excitement or the real passion! Narcissists often lose contact with the self and thereby with the passion from within the self. The borderline makes a good projection for this fantasy. What needs to be interpreted to the narcissist is the internal mother who says, "Why bother, look away, you're too good to even bother with such a person," but by avoiding confrontation one is also avoiding passion and creativity! "I can't tell my wife she's boring!" Getting rid of something by turning to "passion" or mania paradoxically diminishes the passion and creates further disappointment and narcissistic injury to the self. The narcissist's needs for self objects, the formation of positive ties, and the need to turn to a variety of external sources can help explain what that person's real self-object needs are. The formation of healthy object ties provides for both the narcissist and the borderline a vital function, and is not to be confused with fusion or immersion. Often such individuals who are partners in couples turn to the wrong self objects, keeping the partners in a circle, reinforcing their delusions, boredom, confusion, anxiety, dullness, and emptiness. While I suggest that both internal and external object functions are vital, it needs to be emphasized that both need to be explored in light of these two specific disorders.

Internal objects have been found to be associated with psychosomatic illness, claustrophobic anxiety, panic attacks, alexithymia, and asthma in borderline and psychotic personalities. Mason (1981) believed that the fragmentation leading to psychosis can be the result of an anxiety that is a psychic equivalent of a powerful internal enemy (as described in his paper entitled "The Suffocating Superego"). Grotstein (1981) confirmed this position from another perspective; Grotstein noted that an internal object is characterized by qualities of projective identification and of the epistemophilic instinct from the patient, which casts a rich clinical light on a powerful internal persecutory force.

I have combined an explanation of a Freudian description of an internal object, a Kleinian view of an internal object, and a self-psychological view of an external object to add a further dimension in explaining how narcissist/borderline couples intertwine. It is important to understand the various motives behind the introjective process versus the projective process.

Klein described the process of introjection and projection as a dynamic interplay of forces relating to projective identification. In love relationships, one internalizes (often the narcissist) the loved object and idealizes it. When the person is disappointed, the love is gone, and feelings are turned inward to become self-hate and self-persecution (Lachkar, 1983). The motives are often persecutory to ward off annihilation, and when borderlines are endangered they try to get rid of the internal hostile object by splitting off and projecting. Klein, in her paper "On Identification" (1975d), suggested that the internalization of the breast as the first good object includes a considerable amount of narcissistic libido. When the breast is experienced as hostile, it is destructive and becomes, metaphorically speaking, an adjunct to the death instinct.

Why are these theoretical perspectives important in conjoint treatment? Why is the knowledge of both object relation and self psychology important? We need to know these differences in order to be sure that we are addressing the internal conflicts and deficits and not being seduced merely by the external deprivations. A borderline partner may decide to quit therapy because the partner does not have enough money. The therapist must be able to address the "needs" as they relate to the internal world and not focus on what the patient can "afford" (external). To focus on how to make money can lead to disaster, whereas to focus on the internal feelings of bankruptcy can lead to containment. "I don't know about the external bank, but if the internal one is felt to be so empty, so without resources, then it would be very hard to see what could be done" (the black hole).

I believe that in conjoint treatment it is important to understand why borderlines are not capable of making use of self-object functions as are their narcissistic partners. The internal world for the borderline ranges from giving one a sense of internal gratification, pleasure, wholeness, and safety to the other extreme of confusion, persecution, anxiety, discomfort, and danger.

FANTASY LIFE OF NARCISSIST VS.
FANTASY LIFE OF BORDERLINE

Narcissists tend to turn toward the world of fantasy rather than the world of reality. One might speculate at this point that narcissists in general have a greater capacity to make use of fantasies than do their borderline counterparts. The narcissist has richer, more vivid earlier memories than those of the borderline; and, unlike the borderline, who disavows or splits off the experience, the narcissist has the ability to recall early experiences. The narcissist, therefore, seems more inclined to turn to an internal fantasy life.

The rich fantasy life of the narcissist can certainly be exciting, intriguing, and creative, and the therapist must take care not to destroy these qualities. Narcissists respond negatively when we infringe on their creative fantasy life. "It is not your creativity that is in question, but it is your attitude at any alternate suggestion that we must address," the therapist might say. The therapist must expand on the creative aspects of the narcissist's personality in order to bond with the narcissist. "For a short while others will make you feel unique and special, but this cannot be sustained because you haven't expanded your mind to encompass the fresh ideas that we are trying to develop. You close the doors when you push these ideas away."

The narcissist's fantasied grandiose self is reactivated and is reinvested with excessive libidinal energy, enabling a richer fantasy life to emerge. In sharp contrast, the borderline's inability to conjure up these internal images results in the individual being forced to resort to acting out impulses instead of fantasizing about them. I remember a colleague on a television talk show responding to a call about a woman who was concerned about her husband's admitting to being a transvestite. The therapist's response was, "Tell him not to wear the panties, but to fantasize about wearing them." Although it is not clear if the husband was borderline or not, this questions the borderline's capacity to make use of a fantasy life.

Kohut's theory of the etiology of perversions (1971) stimulates consideration of the possibility that narcissists may internalize a self object, and that borderlines, who cannot form a narcissistic transference, cannot draw up rich internal images, or fantasies.

To expand this notion further, let us review Loewenberg's (1985) account of Jacobo Timerman, who had been an Argentinian newspaper publisher, and became a victim of persecution, and an upholder of human rights, and who was tortured in an Argentinian jail. Timerman explained what happened to his mental life while he was incarcerated. Speaking of his surroundings, he described a "conversion from a dark, gloomy place to that of a universe of spontaneous innovation and institutional beauty" (p. 20). One of the most important conclusions to be drawn from Timerman's experience is the notion that the cell became a microcosm and that the fantasy of the peephole in Timerman's cell became an "inner world," or an "eye" looking from his cell into another world. According to Loewenberg, the role fantasy plays in the emotional life of such individuals as Timerman can be a vital force in one's survival.

Applying this notion of fantasy life to the couples described in this book may provide further insight as to why a borderline often feels hurt and left out when in a relationship with a narcissist. Is it that the narcissist is likely to be able to conjure up the image of the other partner, and is more apt to fantasize and keep the image in mind? Is it also that the borderline cannot use imagery or symbolization, and is bound by the dictum "Out of sight out of mind"?

ENTITLEMENT FANTASIES

Within the dance of the narcissistic/borderline configuration, reality often gets distorted because the borderline can be lured into the narcissist's delusional world of entitlement fantasies (Case 7) and grandiose expectations, and can be seduced. Compromise is difficult and often ignored, ending in a no-win situation. The borderline often gets lost in endless confusion when the partner does unfair things (the borderline's tendency to comply, (see Case 4). Together, the partners form a folie à deux, a collusive bond. This behavior can exacerbate an already existing condition of a "no self" for the borderline, and further activate a "grand self" for the narcissist. "Why do you get to have things your way all the time?" asks the borderline. "Why?" responds the narcissist, "It's because I'm entitled, that's why!" Paradoxically, narcissists never feel entitled enough. Narcissists have difficulty in getting the real help that they need because of the converse side part of the personality that splits off needs into their borderline counterpart that says, "You're just too demanding!"

The psychodynamic process brings out the pathologies with respect to entitlement more clearly than any other form of therapy. With respect to entitlement, the narcissist has to face the inevitable fate of greed, and to recognize that one cannot have it all, and that when one tries to get it all, one ultimately ends up getting very little, hurt, and let down. Unlike the borderline, the narcissist has to learn to tolerate frustration in order to develop a healthy dependency relationship with the therapist. The delusional fantasies surrounding the narcissist's excessive entitlement wishes must be continually addressed, and the therapist must be constant in interpreting how greed can destroy any interpersonal relationship. Because both the narcissist and the borderline have blurred boundaries, real entitlement needs get lost. The psychodynamic therapist must remind these partners of what is rightfully theirs. Narcissists have a right to their needs just as borderlines deserve to be responded to.

TECHNIQUES

Bonding and Weaning

The concept of the technique of "weaning" of infantile, childlike aspects of the patient into more mature states of development comes from the classic Kleinian psychoanalytic school (also called the British object-relations school).

I view the self-psychological approach as the bonding school, and object relations as the weaning school. Self psychology with its mirroring function is applicable in the early phases of treatment, when interpretations addressing internal deficits may be perceived as attacking. In the later phases, however, object relations provides a wider range of techniques in helping us wean patients from their destructive behaviors through understanding these behaviors within themselves.

The therapist cannot make up for early loss, but can help the patient learn to tolerate and to contain the loss, and can describe what is needed. Therapists need to bond and wean according to the developmental needs of the partners. A systematic arrangement of special boundaries that are limited, but comfortable enough for both patients and therapist must be developed; for instance, a borderline patient may need to make spontaneous contact with the therapist, as with instantaneous response to telephone calls (instantaneous "feedings"). This connection to the therapist can be as vital as medical intravenous feedings in early weaning. The patient can gradually be weaned to more structured calls with definite boundaries, then further weaned as the patient is able to internalize the therapist as a good object (see Case #9). The patient may feel threatened and may exhibit concern that the therapist will stop allowing the calls abruptly, or will cut the patient off, which would leave the patient with the notion that having needs is bad. Needing can become tantamount to, and synonymous with, abandonment.

During this weaning process the therapist has an opportunity to bond with the healthy part of the patient by interpreting that living inside somebody (intruding into mommy's private life) is like hiding, or like taking something that doesn't belong to one. There is never a chance to get fed if one lives inside another object; furthermore, one never gets the real feeding that is needed (the breast) because the breast is outside, not inside. To paraphrase Mason, inside are the guts, blood, and other unpleasant parts, suitable only for unborn infants (personal communication, 1988). "This baby part of you that was so demanding before is now able to wait and have regular arranged telephone sessions with me. This is a definite step forward, and shows us that you are making progress!" If something urgent were to come up and the patient could not wait, then one could always go back to "demand feeding" calls; however, it must be explained within the context of the therapy and with interpretation that there has been a set back, and that something is in the way of progress (developmentally this may correspond to Mahler's "practicing phase"). Borderline patients need to know that making contact is the healthy part of them, that it is not their needs that make others turn away, but rather their uncontrollable demands. In conjoint treatment the process is to wean patients from blaming and attacking defenses, and demanding behaviors (the infantile part of themselves), and slowly to enable them to contain their own anxieties by facing their internal deficits. The therapist might say, "If you act like a baby then you will get treated like one and end up feeling more abandoned and left out."

Weaning in conjoint therapy is done in order to transform intolerable affects into containment via intrapsychic and introspective processes; it is the gradual pulling away from acting and doing something, to thinking about and understanding something. "You want your wife to have sex with you, but she is letting you know she doesn't want to have sex with a demanding baby. Instead of facing what your wife is telling you, you are trying to force her to be different. If you do that, you will end up feeling more rejected."

During the latter part of the first year, the infant makes some fundamental steps toward working through the depressive position. The paranoid-schizoid position, however, is still in force. Klein believed that as individuals we go back and forth between these two positions. If persecutory anxiety is not too prevalent during the first stage, the infant will become more interested in the environment than in the preoccupation with the availability of the breast (Klein, 1946). Klein viewed weaning as a trauma that inaugurates the Oedipus complex: frustration imposed by the feeding mother, causing the infant to turn away from the mother and to move toward the father. Later Klein changed this concept to a new view on weaning in which she saw it as the escalation of the weaning process that begins in the depressive position (Klein, 1975c). Klein equated the Oedipus complex with the depressive position, when persecutory anxiety diminishes and love feelings emerge. The realization that the child cannot possess the mother causes the child to turn away from the breast and to be propelled forward to seek new libidinal objects (Klein, 1975c).

Object-relations theory provides us with an environmental mother, a background mother, a being/doing mother, a weaning mother, and a containing/sustaining mother to help establish different kinds of weaning and bonding experiences. The importance of therapist/mother as the container becomes more vital in a conjoint setting because we're dealing with very primitive disorders. The central issues revolve around persecutory anxiety, shame, guilt, confusion, and fantasies of separation.

Mirroring vs. Containment

Bion's (1962) conception of the container and the contained is perhaps the most useful and all-inclusive concept of countertransference phenomena for borderlines, psychotics, narcissists, and even neurotic and normal conditions. It has been my experience that the notion of the container and contained is one of the most useful in conjoint treatment.

Bion believed all psychological phenomena, whether normal or pathological, universally dissolve when the mind acts as receiver of communicative content, which the mother does in the state of reverie by using her own alpha function (Bion, 1962). This notion of alpha function is one of Bion's more mysterious terms for Freud's primary process period. It connotes the capacity for transformation of the data of emotional experience into meaningful feelings and thoughts.

Containment

Differences between the empathic interpretations, offering mirroring, and the sustaining functions, offering containment, are remarkable contributions to conjoint treatment. How does a psychotherapist treating couples become a self object to both partners, yet remain capable of interacting as a self object to both? Being empathic by reaffirming the patients' subjective experiences alone does not distinguish between true empathic resonance and collusion.

The mother, who is able to withstand the child's anger, frustrations, intolerable feelings, and unknown feelings, and who is able to translate and detoxify bad feelings, becomes the container for these intolerable affects. Through her reverie, and her ability to understand, sustain, and contain, the mother can feed back into the infant something that the child can take inside and hold on to. The therapist must contain these intolerable behaviors, and be able to decode or detoxify things into more digestible forms. The most important function of the analyst, according to Grotstein, is the detoxification of the banished elements of self that have been exiled into unconsciousness. Empathy is a crucial concept in conjoint treatment, but must be used alongside the concept of weaning. Weaning away from blaming and attacking defenses slowly enables contact with intrapsychical difficulties and deficits.

There is a step-by-step process for the partners in the couple through which they begin to see each other as real individuals, with separate needs and desires, who can coexist each with the other's needs. Cohesiveness represents an idealized parenting model, one that includes containment, mirroring, and providing optimal frustration (e.g., analytic boundaries and limitations), but one in which the "parent" is still warm enough and sufficiently emotionally available to work through hurt feelings and old injuries.

Mirroring

Mirroring is a term devised by Heinz Kohut that describes the gleam in mother's eye that mirrors the child's exhibitionistic display. Mirroring is a specific response to the child's narcissistic-exhibitionistic enjoyment, confirming the child's self-esteem. Eventually, these responses begin to channel into more realistic aims, and the child is able to validate and confirm which accomplishments were made, and is able to self-evaluate progress and abilities.

Concepts of mirroring and the empathic mode can be most valuable in conjoint therapy as a vigorous source of exploration, particularly in the attempt to bond and form a healthy self-object tie.

Empathy addresses the painful feelings, but containment transcends feelings to reach the depths and magnitude of the bottomless pit, annihilation anxiety, or the black hole, where lie the internal persecutors. One may continually disregard one's own needs because anxiety gets in the way of learning from experience.

No matter how insulting the borderline wife was the narcissistic husband would take it as a compliment. "You're selfish!" "You're inconsiderate!" "You're greedy!" "You're a pig!" The narcissistic husband's normal response to these insults would be, "Yes, I know I am. I'm entitled! I'm entitled!"

In sorting confusional and tangential modes of relating, the mirroring mother, although certainly crucial, does not have the same impact as the containing and holding one. Unfortunately, many therapists misunderstand the notion of empathy and mirroring, misplace the emphasis upon external circumstances (the self-object tie), and tend to ignore the destructive parts of the personality.

Confrontation vs. Empathy

Masterson (1981) suggested that borderlines respond more to confrontation, whereas narcissists respond more to interpretation, which is compatible with the notion that the object-relational approach is appropriate for the borderline, and self psychology for the narcissist. Masterson, more than any other author, has clarified for us that the narcissist needs an appeal to intellectualization, and seems to respond to interpretation and explanation. Masterson felt that the borderline, in contrast, responds more to confrontation. While the narcissist could take confrontation to mean attacking, a personal assault or injury to the integrity of self, the borderline will tend to experience a direct statement as involvement and caring. In narcissistic and borderline pathogenesis, both approaches are important and may elicit significant responses.

Many borderline patients become confused by empathic interpretations because they misperceive them as colluding with their mythology or their own persecutory delusions. These patients need clear boundary distinctions between chaos and confusion and order and structure. A borderline wife, for example, began to feel I was continually blaming her for everything that went wrong. I tried to clarify that sometimes she was responsible for certain things she had created from her behaviors, but often there were situations having nothing to do with her.

The therapist must be able to speak directly to the heart of the issues. Some years ago a couple came to therapy in great distress because the husband, Brian, had procured a gun, and while in a drunken state had tried to kill their eldest son. Brian and his wife, Catherine, entered the consulting room, and within a few minutes, Catherine was berating Brian, insisting that he get a thorough psychiatric evaluation, including testing, because she lived in terror that someday he might do it again. Brian turned to me, "Tell her to stop badgering me. It's over, done with, and I'll never do it again." In the first session I said, "What you did to your son was terrible. You must feel terrible; you must have some feelings about it yourself that you'd like to discuss."

In conjoint treatment I use interpretation similarly, to help understand feelings and to mirror feelings, but I use confrontation to focus on the destructive or crazy behavior because the feelings around that behavior are disavowed.

In another case, the narcissist wife reported that her husband has recently lost the mortgage to the house that she owned from a previous marriage. The borderline husband claimed that the reason he lost the house was because the wife did not contribute to making any of the house payments. He felt let down, and now would get even with her, to teach her a lesson. He distorted matters and turned the situation around to make it appear that it was all her fault. He would now show her what it feels like to be in a bankrupted state or to live in an impoverished empty house.

The therapist confronted the borderline husband with his distortion of the situation to make it appear to be his wife's fault. In this way he did not have to face his own fears and deficits. The therapist offered containment by indicating that if the therapist joined in on trying to find the one to blame, the session would get into a mess and all participants would all be in a bankrupt state. Confrontation, then, allowed the therapist to become a hard-enough object to push against the defenses when mirroring and empathy were not enough.

The Being Mommy vs. the Doing Mommy

One of Winnicott's (1953) most vital contributions, and one that I believe can be most helpful in blending being and doing mommy (Case 10) approaches is the idea of the "environmental mother," "the background mother," the "holding mother." These mommies are not the ones who speak or tell their children what to do. Their function is in being. As long as the child knows that somewhere there is a mother emotionally available, the child feels safe. The being mother does not do anything but merely is there and exists. It is her very essence that soothes, understands, and provides meaning for the child's existence. The infant is safe by simply being in the presence of the mother, and the infant has the right to the mother's total preoccupation. Often patients just need to know we are there in the kitchen or the office, even when they are not with us. Borderlines in particular need the environmental or subject-background mother who can tolerate and accept the child's various states of mind. For the narcissist, the focus is more upon the beaming mother who enjoys the child for who the child is, and for what the child can do or can accomplish. The being mother never tells the child what to do.

The doing mother is the mother who facilitates action and who tells the child what to expect and what is expected of the child. The doing mother takes pleasure and great delight in the child's accomplishments and basks in the acclaim of the delight of them. In the treatment of primitive mental disorders, these two states of existence must be applied depending on the affective experience of the moment. To become the doing mommy for the borderline may in fact recreate further abandonment sufferings. For instance, if the borderline says, "I have a headache," and the doing mommy responds, "Well, take an aspirin," this can be experienced as further rejection. I believe these two approaches offer invaluable insights into the various listening perspectives needed by each of these overlapping and ever-changing modes of relatedness within the depth and scope of these two disorders.

Winnicott (1965e) provided us with a holding environment and environmental mother who helps the child with the being self as opposed to the doing self (that is, the false self that must perform) through mother's preoccupation with the child. This preoccupation of the child is what borderlines have missed. Winnicott talked about the differences between privation and deprivation. For example, the mother of the little girl in a ballet studio dressing room is totally preoccupied with dressing and fussing with her. This is what the borderline missed out on: mother's total, not partial, preoccupation. In some of these relationships it is important to actually say, "You are not ready to do anything yet until you understand what you are feeling." One narcissistic wife told the therapist that her mother and father waited 10 years to have her, and when they finally did, they "couldn't do enough for me. I feel so guilty because I have had everything and my parents gave me so much." This information provides a clue for the therapist to quickly become the being mommy, not the one who gives advice, but the one to be available to hear the pain and mirror the grief and frustration.

Facing Deficits

Self psychology does not help patients face their deficits directly because facing deficits might induce disruption, empathic failures, or disregard the patient's subjective experience. In object relations, however, through various techniques (including those of containment and reverie) attempts are made to help the patient face anxiety and tolerate or confront internal shortcomings. This enables the patient to reduce anxiety and the tendencies to avoid feelings and to blame others for all external failings, and facilitates the development of the thinking apparatus and ego strength necessary for conjoint treatment. The main differences between a self-psychological approach and an object-relational one with respect to deficits is that in self psychology, one strives to understand the subjective experience of the patient, putting aside one's own preconceptions, whereas, in object relations, the therapist addresses the patient's distortions and misperceptions more at face value.

Containment, empathy, and mirroring not only provide a model but show that the therapist is not afraid to face issues and stand up to issues directly. If the therapist cannot stand up to patients' distortions, those patients cannot be helped to stand up to others and to face their own conflictual issues with their own partners. Interpretations must not be crude, callous, and uncaring, but need to be interfaced with deeper understanding of pathologies. An example would be, "You must be feeling very frightened or feeling very anxious and attacked because right now you are blaming your wife." This offers a holding and sustaining environment, enabling the patient to form an alliance or proper identification with the therapist as a self object.

These ego defects must be kept in mind, particularly for the borderline who may regard either the therapist or the aspects of the treatment as an intrusive or bizarre object, interfering in the couple's relationship (i.e., costing money, taking time, and so forth). The therapist sometimes tends to make premature genetic transference interpretations. Flicker's (1988) connotation is that the therapist, often too uncomfortable to handle the assault or the attacks, then tries to get relief by putting the onus into the patient's external objects. To expand this notion further, one may speculate that to make a genetic interpretation too soon may be misperceived by the borderline as a massive projection.

CONCLUSION

In this chapter, we have illustrated the wide range and variety of pathologies that go on from the narcissist end of the spectrum to the borderline end. Many of these couples go on and on, never able to resolve the intensity of their complex situations. Those of us treating these couples cannot ignore these significant differences (envy, guilt, shame, etc.), nor can we see these disorders as similar in depth and scope; that is, we can no longer view these couples from the perspective of "narcissist vulnerabilities" but from their distinctive and qualitative differences. Ignoring these key differences can present serious problems for the clinician seeing both disorders simultaneously, for there is endless confusion in the drift back and forth between these two states, not only in the developmental levels and intrapsychic structures, but with respect to the differences in the therapeutic techniques required to treat them.

CHAPTER VII

Group Psychology and the Narcissistic/Borderline Couple

The Tavistock Institute of Human Relations of London, where research and training with a model of group behaviors originated about 20 years ago, employs a systematic approach, concepts from group dynamics, psychoanalytic principles, and systems theory. A. K. Rice (1965) and Wilfred Bion (1959) believed that helping members decode and identify individual and group covert messages can be of great value. Interest in the Tavistock model is increasing, as more therapists become familiar with the basic premises, behaviors that are not easy to explain, as they are deep-rooted and complex. I share the view that couple myths are similar to shared group myths. Group myths, a concept adumbrated by Wilfred Bion (1959), are powerful ideas that dominate and intoxicate the minds of individuals when within a group setting. Group thinking is not motivated by rational thought, individual thinking, but rather by dogma, pedagogy, and primitive ideas. In primitive groups, poisonous pedagogy, split-off emotional feelings, physical weakness, and vulnerabilities project onto others certain aspects which cannot be tolerated within the group (making others the victim/scapegoat). The interaction between the victim and a terrorist is an illustration of this, whereby the group cannot tolerate certain aspects within itself, and attempts to destroy that which is seen in the victim.

According to Bion, in a group setting many individuals will give way to one's own thoughts, one's own mind, ideas, values, and principles and allow the group's ideology to prevail.

Similarly, a couple may form a shared couple myth, corresponding to the classical notion of "folie à deux," whereby rational thought concedes to joining up to the ideas of others. An example of a shared couple myth is when the couple uses the child as a "toilet," a term De Mause (1974) refers to as the abused child or as the "toilet child." The child becomes the receptacle for the projected, split-off, or unwanted aspects of the parents as they project into the child the intolerable parts of themselves. "It's all the child's fault! If it weren't for that demanding child, we'd be happy." In this instance the child becomes the scapegoat or "toilet" for all the adults' frailties, a method of relieving anxiety by not facing the realistic aspects of the conflict.

I have found both that group formation can be particularly helpful in working with couples and that the principles of group psychology can be applied to relationship therapies. Two kinds of groups described in the seminal work of Wilfred Bion (1959), the work group and the basic assumption group, are illuminated to expand our view of the primitive aspects of preoedipal relationships. I use Bion's theories along with my own concepts of the real relationship versus fantasized relationships (Lachkar, 1984, 1985b) to describe the idiosyncratic nature of the dyad as it arouses many distorted views surrounding archaic longings, yearnings, unfulfilled wishes, and fantasies.

Many theorists, including Freud (1921), Kernberg, (1976, 1980), Dicks (1967), Willi (1982), and Lachkar (1984, 1985b, 1986) share the view that group psychology can offer insights into understanding how individuals behave in a group setting. Some hold that marital relationships share similar properties to those that exist in group dynamics.

In his monograph on group psychology, Freud (1921/1955) showed that the ego ideal is the vehicle for group formation. In *Totem and Taboo* (1912-13/1955), Freud recognized the existence of a collective mind. I am extending this to the "couple mind." Groups, like the couple, use aggression and primitive defenses to guard against painful affects. Scapegoating is a common phenomonen to avoid the "enemy" (real or fantasized). Kernberg (1980) implied that the group guards against painful awareness of aggression. In small groups, it is hard to avoid the "enemy" because the fantasized enemy is right in the midst of the group itself. The relation to an imagined enemy is a crucial factor that binds the group's ideology. In scapegoating, the "real" enemy does not exist, but is a split-off part of the internal enemies. In the dyad the "enemy," real or fantasized, can be the affair, the mother-in-law, the friends, the money, and so forth.

Henry Dicks (1967) applied psychoanalytic object relations to the diagnosis and treatment of marital conflicts. Jurg Willi (1982) expanded Dick's (1967) view of marriage; Dicks felt that unresolved object relations fosters conflict between marriage and parent-child relationships. Willi (1982) took into account Dicks, Bion, and object relations theory when he found the central term "collusion." In his book *Couples in Collusion*, his basic theme was group dynamics.

I view the couple as similar in many ways to a group. I use group phenomena to understand the regressive/primitive nature in couples. The more regressed the couple is, the more they live in fear of an external enemy, and the more they tend to collude in each other's delusional fantasies. Similar to the group, something ties and bonds the couple together (as a form of a group). I believe my ideas correspond closely to those of Wilfred Bion (1959).

According to Bion (1959), every individual has an impact upon the group's functioning (much like a family system). Groups share collective myths, dreams, ideologies, and fantasies that distort their current perspective of reality. The couple, like the group, needs a leader (therapist) who can put words and concretize the mythology that provides justification and gives meaning to the couple.

Bion (1959) discussed two basic groups: (1) the work group, whose rational-thinking group members are task/reality oriented, and (2) the basic assumption group, whose members function on the basis of blame/shame, fight/flight, parasitic bonds, and who rely heavily upon magical thinking, and other primitive defenses (omnipotent denial, splitting, projection, and projective identification). In an earlier work (Lachkar 1984, 1985b), I refer to the real relationship versus the fantasized relationship. These designations are extrapolated from Bion's groups to provide further understanding of the regressive behaviors in couples.

The Work Group

Task orientation. According to Bion (1959), the work group has thinking, task-oriented members, whose primary concern is the achievement of goals. The group members are rational, are dominated by individuality, creative forces, and situational learning; and rely more on individual thinking than on dogma or group ideology. The work group does not oppose new ideas, and its members can operate through the mature functioning part of the ego; that is, work group members can tolerate frustration long enough to learn from experience and be able to stand up for beliefs and ideas.

The "real" relationship. Like the work group, the real relationship operates through the mature, observing part of the ego through which reality can be experienced in the sensory motor apparatus. Persons in the real relationship pay attention to instincts, signal anxiety, can learn from experience, search out truth and knowledge, and take the necessary steps to problem solve. They are not willing to take in the projections of others, and can tolerate a reasonable amount of frustration and unknown elements. The real relationship focuses on what is, not on what ought to be. In lieu of evacuation, anxiety is contained, feelings are expressed rather than spilled out.

Joseph Campbell (1988), the late mythologist, provided one view of the real relationship. He suggested myths help put one's mind in touch with the experience of being alive. The myth tells one what the experience is. For example, what marriage is.

> The myth tells you what it is. It is the reunion of the separated dyad. Originally you were one. You are now

two in the world, but the recognition of the spiritual identity is what marriage is. It's different from a love affair. It has nothing to do with that. It's another mythological plane of experience. When people get married because they think it's a long-time love affair, they'll be divorced very soon, because all love affairs end in disappointment. But marriage is the recognition of a spiritual identity. If we live in a proper life, if our minds are on the right qualities in regarding the person of the opposite sex, we will find our proper male or female counterpart. But if we are distracted by certain sensuous interest, we'll marry the wrong person. By marrying the right person, we reconstruct the image of the incarnate God, and that's what marriage is. [p. 6]

To expand even further on Campbells' ideas, I believe he was saying that when one considers the realistic aspects of marriage, one has to face that marriage is a sacrifice, not only each to the other, but to the unity in a relationship. Campbell saw a realistic relationship as existing in two phases.

First is the youthful marriage following the wonderful impulse that nature has given us in the interplay of the sexes biologically in order to produce children. But there comes a time when the child graduates from the family and the couple is left. I've been amazed at the number of my friends who in their forties or fifties grow apart. They have had a perfectly decent life together with the child, but they interpreted their union in terms of the relationship through the child. They did not interpret it in terms of their own personal relationship to each other. [p. 7]

Basic Assumption Groups

The basic assumption group opposes new ideas, demonstrates primitive behaviors, and uses unconscious defense mechanisms to get rid of anxiety and to discourage change. They are dominated by irrational, delusional thinking, group myths, and group fantasies. A basic assumption couple fantasizes that repetition of painful experiences or finding fault in the projected "enemy" will lead to conflict resolution. A basic assumption couple may, for example, try to force change through trying to force the other to change or other primitive modes of expression, rather than through acceptance of reality.

There is a tendency for members of the basic assumption group to depend on the leader and not to challenge what the leader says, which provides a false sense of safety. Group psychology explains why individuals who adhere to certain mythic origins need to form an identification with a leader who can concretize their mythology. Somewhere in the group lies an enemy who is to blame, and the leader is the messiah, the one who will save the group from calamity. There is always the wish for a new ending, however, the savior never comes, and the therapist is often the last hope (Bion, 1959, 1962; Lachkar, 1984).

Scapegoating. A familiar scenario is that the group leader singles out someone to be the group's scapegoat, and the group members go along because they need an object to project into, or because they idealize the leader, and are afraid to challenge or confront. The group then isolates the "enemy," splitting the person off as the bad object. The problem quickly augments into a vicious circle. The more outcast the scapegoat becomes, the more negative the scapegoat's behavior. The magnification of the bad elements serves to preserve the group fantasy that the group is good, and that any badness must lie in the outcast, isolated member. Scapegoats and victims feed the delusional system by taking in the projections and thereby identifying with them.

Fantasized relationships

Persons in fantasized relationships cannot learn from experience, and cannot tolerate pain or frustration. They lose sight of the task at hand, adhere to "quick fixes," and confuse their healthy dependency needs with parasitic ones. They pair off with others who justify their psychopathologies, and they form collusive bonds to those who offer testimony to the "other's" craziness. A diminution of reality testing and judgment occurs because couples in fantasized relationship are in constant search of approval. The narcissistic partner may seek to pair up with others who collude with exaggerated entitlement fantasies, whereas the borderline may seek justification in attacking and blaming impulses. The collective fantasized image of the relationship then becomes prey to disintegration because neither partner has a strong enough sense of self.

Understanding group formation helps in discerning why regressive couples stay in the "dance" or engage in circular behaviors. In conjoint treatment, our task must focus on helping these couples face the realistic aspects of their relationships, and continually remind them of why they have entered treatment.

The Affair: Real or Fantasized?

No book about conjoint treatment can be complete without addressing the proverbial affair; questions about this arise at every seminar or course on couples treatment.

It is my belief that the issue is not the affair, but rather the betrayal. If one betrays the other or oneself, it is likely that self-betrayal will be a theme that will recur in the couple transference, one that may manifest itself in such ways as in coming late to sessions, nonpayment, unfulfilled promises, forgetfulness, and guilt.

Group dynamics theories can further our understanding of relationships occurring outside the marital unit. The affair, viewed within the context of the basic assumption group, is a collusion of betrayal with another person, stimulating such primitive defenses as wishful thinking, splitting, projection, and envy. The affair is often manifested as the split-off part of the self to ward off persecutory anxiety and envy. It may be considered a form of "pairing off" or flight/fight (terms described by Bion as a form of joining with others who share common myths and distortions of reality).

An affair is a fantasy and is not based on reality. In some instances, it is also the highest form of betrayal, not only because of the lies and deceit to the partner, but also because of those to the self. The act indicates a lack of commitment, not only to a legal document, but to that which is considered by most as a sacred oath. Although this realization may evoke great guilt or shame, patients need to face this.

The notion of the affair can create considerable anxiety both for the couple and, because betrayal and abandonment tend to be projected, for the therapist. Patients often feel very embarrassed and very anxious upon admitting they have been unfaithful. One does not have to be an analyst or psychotherapist to recognize the destructive nature of the act of having an affair. The affair is not indicative of a whole object relationship, but a part object one. That feelings and conflictual issues get stirred up may sometimes be viewed as constructive, though only if understood in relation to the development of the self.

These comments are not moral judgments; they are not intended either to condone or to criticize, but rather to enhance understanding of individuals who engage in such betrayals. These external relationships need to be examined to determine what internal issues get stirred up within the context of narcissistic and borderline disorders. In my view, narcissistic and borderline individuals who engage in outside relationships often do so for reasons connected to their specific disorders and qualitative differences.

According to Scarf (1987),

> The discovery, by one partner, that the other is involved in an affair is a disaster, like a death—which, in an important sense, it actually is. It is the death of that marriage's innocence, the death of trust, the death of naive understanding of what the relationship itself is all about. [p. 128]

Scarf's research corroborates the views expressed here, that affairs are often a product of internal conflict and guilt feelings on the part of the one engaging in such acts. Getting caught can vary from being infuriating to being a disruption of one's whole life if the deceived partner discovers the "truth." The trauma upon discovery of the partner's infidelity can be an earth-shattering experience, one that leaves the other partner finding it extremely difficult to think, to work, or to function at all. The betrayed person's mind begins to wander; the person feels split off, confused, empty, depressed, and even suicidal when not in the presence of the deceiving lover. "They ruminate and get distracted by thoughts of the affair and the betrayal" (Scarf, 1987, p. 129).

A borderline husband who discovered his wife's faithlessness became so confused and disoriented he was unable to concentrate at work. He felt fragmented, unable to get up in the morning to attend to business, and when walking into his office, he experienced the floor and walls spinning around. He would gaze at people with blank stares. This kind of devastation not only is overwhelming for the innocent partner, but can be equally as tormenting for the guilty one. The borderline husband's feelings of shame, emptiness, and unworthiness became more pronounced in the light of this devastation.

A borderline wife was so emotionally demolished upon the breakup of the relationship with her lover that she described her experience as totally paralyzing. "I could not function, I would sit home all day, stare out the window or gaze at the answering machine just waiting for him to call. He decided to stay with his wife. I feel so hurt and rejected, as if I don't even exist or that I don't count" (borderline vulnerability).

A narcissistic husband described the experience as so unbelievably upsetting, that he kept driving by his exlover's house just to get a glimpse of her. "She represents all the excitement in the world. She possesses all the qualities I have ever dreamed up. When I am with her, I feel passion! I feel that I am truly alive! She makes me feel so good about myself! She appreciates me, and makes me feel that I am the most wonderful man in the world!" (narcissistic vulnerability).

It is clear that taking into account narcissistic and borderline diagnostic distinctions and the qualitative differences of these individuals' needs can be helpful in viewing these complex and often varied situational circumstances. For instance, the narcissistic partner may enter the affair to seek out others for approval and admiration, and to stir up excitement and passion, as a stimulus to evoke the "real passion" yearning within the self, while the borderline may seek an outside relationship to get back at or to retaliate against the narcissistic partner. In addition, the envious qualities of the loved partner may stir up deficits lacking in both partners; however, for the borderline these deficits evoke the need to possess and control, while for the narcissist they may evoke the need to get excitement from an external force.

In short, the affair has elements similar to those in basic assumption groups. The therapist must be careful not to join up with the collusional part of the affair because in the attempt to hold on to the secret the therapist becomes the betrayer. A patient's making it appear that the therapist is the betrayer can take away from the real issues and focus of the conflict (see Case 12).

Intimacy and Closeness: An Emotional Distancer?

Many authors have described the affair as an emotional distancer, or a vehicle through which couples play games back and forth between closeness and distancing. A partner might say, "I wait at least 2 days after he calls and then I call him because I don't want him to think I am overly anxious or needy."

To view the issues as merely a process of intimacy and closeness or separateness and distancing is, in my view, an oversimplification of the dynamic process. Rather, the emphasis must focus more specifically upon the deficiencies within the personality seeking to emerge. It is not the affair that is the issue, but it is the affair that stirs up the issues, the desires and fears, and brings them to the individual's attention in such a manner that they cannot be ignored.

Narcissistic and borderline patients often resort to playacting or game playing because they are not truly grounded in their own senses of themselves. For instance, a borderline lover may playact at being busy when the lover or admirer calls, as an expression of a wish to have a more fulfilling life: "I distance myself from him because when he doesn't call, I feel so left out. I feel awful, as if there is no me, or as if I don't count, so I'd rather be the one to avoid seeing him than have him rejecting me." The feeling of not counting is typical for borderlines, and affair relationships with narcissistic partners, perpetuating the feelings of not existing, are quite common.

In other instances, the affair can stir up issues of control: "I feel so frustrated, I never know where she is or what she is doing. I wonder if she is making love to her husband, if she would betray me when she tells me I am the one she really cares about." This borderline patient is trying to resolve old issues of being controlled or dominated by his mother, and now is wishing magically to control his lover, a situation seen frequently with borderline patients. In the case of this affair, the therapist might interpret, "Yes, now you are wishing to live in someone else's house, rather than developing your own internal house. No matter how limited you may feel your own house is, it is still yours, and you have an opportunity to develop it; however, if you do as you did with your mother, if you are always living inside someone else's house, then you will never have a chance to face what belongs to you and what belongs to someone else."

A borderline unmarried woman involved with a narcissistic married man states, "He possesses all the qualities I have always wanted in a man. When I am not with him, I feel like a nothing, as if I'm going to die." Upon further investigation, this person is unconsciously seeking the lover's qualities for herself; however, the borderline defense of not feeling worthy gets in the way of fulfilling her need. The desire to attain must be viewed, in this case, as the healthy part of the relationship, and not as the destructive part.

Things are different for the narcissist, who will cling to the loved object in order to revive the fantasy of being the admired one and to gain approval. Admiration temporarily distracts the person from facing the distorted view of what he or she is truly entitled to, and from acquiring the ability to attain admirable traits of one's own. Through the idealization process, the narcissistic partner attributes to the other the role of the provider of passion and excitement. Viewing the affair in this way helps repair the split between the good and bad internal objects. Not feeling deserving enough to attain then forces the narcissist to join up, fuse, or become engulfed with another who possesses these admirable qualities. It is, then, the split-off parts of the self that experience desire through the painful bodily sensations associated with envy, annihilation anxiety, and primitive superego functioning. These split-off parts of the personality then get reintrojected back into the psyche as the external enemy, as persecutory and retaliatory anxiety, resulting in such responses as, "Someone out there is out to get me; I'm too needy!"

Neither the intimacy nor the distancing aspects of the affair are as related to the fear of closeness as to the parasitic bond. The affair is a flight into fantasy, an escape, or a joining up with a messiah, with someone to rescue one from facing one's shattered world. The real fears of the affair are related to such concepts as boundary confusion, as intrusiveness into the space of another's persecutory anxiety, a state in which one becomes overwhelmed with feelings of envy, greed, and jealousy, and primitive defenses of sadistic rage, shame, guilt, magical thinking, denial, idealization, and devaluation.

The fear of loss of the lover, then, is not so much the fear of the actual loss of the other as of the more important loss of contact with the defective parts of the undeveloped self, and both closeness and distancing are used in the affair to avoid this loss.

ROLE OF SOCIETY

The role played by society in the drama of the couple as a function of the group is perhaps best shown as the couple comes to litigation and the courts. Florence Bienenfeld (1980, 1983, 1986, 1987) has interviewed thousands of families during her 10 years as senior marriage and family counselor/mediation for the Conciliation Court of Los Angeles County.

Bienenfeld observed that many divorcing couples who litigate child custody and financial issues through the court systems were shockingly similar to the paradigm of the narcissistic/borderline couple.

> Mediators are very accustomed to working with difficult problems and disputes and with upset divorcing and divorced parents. There are, however, some parents who continually sabotage the possibility of ever reaching an agreement or of getting things settled. It is both fascinating and often frustrating to observe the way these parents see the other parent as causing all the problems. Both parents appear blind to how they themselves made the situation worse and how they each sabotage their own children. [Bienenfeld, 1986]
>
> The saddest part about these intensely emotional, non-ending parental conflicts is the way their children are hopelessly trapped in the middle. [Bienenfeld, 1986]

When asked why there are so many divorces, Bienenfeld responded as follows:

> Statistically there are over one million marriages in California alone and at least one out of two get divorced. There are many reasons: People get married for the wrong reason. They feel pressured that it is time to get married, or that no one else came along. . . . They bring in old unresolved issues from the past or they live with the idea that someone else will fulfill them or make them happy and when this fails they feel disappointed and blame the other. . . . Frequently, one partner will put the other partner on hold (often the narcissist), while working or raising children. . . . People cannot be put on hold. The best thing is to help couples be accountable for their lives, even victims or abusers. [Bienenfeld, personal communication, 1987]

Dr. Bienenfeld suggested that society should take more responsibility, that "there is not enough support from extended family, or neighbors, nor is there enough education from an early age teaching people how to communicate, how to settle disputes, how to mediate, how to get along with other people" (Bienenfeld, personal communication, 1987a.)

In these days, most children are reared by single parents and working mothers, left with baby sitters from an early age. In addition, one-third of children of divorce lose one of their parents after divorce, as a result of the divorce. Divorces are detrimental to family life, but are not nearly as destructive as the procedure the family must endure during and after the dissolution process. In short, the implication is that children are never able to mourn the loss of the parent. Without being able to mourn, the child then tends to get rid of the parent, and thereby is unable to introject the parent as an important and meaningful internal representation.

CONCLUSION

Within narcissistic and borderline relationships, the shared couple myth needs to be understood in terms of each one's delusions, distortions, and projections. Can we diagnose a "couple mind" in terms of the individuals' collective defenses? Is it possible to understand that one partner will inflict pain upon the other to dehumanize and destroy that person? Understanding group myths and couples' shared emotional fantasies can help objectify for study the highly charged passions so difficult for many couples to face. Both individual and couple transferences need to be dealt with in terms of the relationship.

Combining the Tavistock model with ideas from psychoanalysis and systems theory, one can expand and provide depth for the vision of the defensive aspects of what transpires when two individuals bring together their families of origin and their family myths and behaviors from the past.

CHAPTER VIII

Model of Treatment

OVERVIEW

Conjoint therapy is viewed as a precursor to individual psychotherapy or psychoanalysis. Conjoint therapy is accepted by many as an important adjunct to individual psychoanalysis or psychodynamic psychotherapy.

A systematic approach has long been needed to treat the preoedipal relationships of the narcissistic/borderline couple.

I have reviewed recent developmental theories and divided them into theories based on fusion, separation, or interaction. The movement from three developmental phases in conjoint treatment is interfaced with many concepts and various theories.

Bion (1970) postulated three types of interactions: one, commensural; two, parasitic; and three, symbiotic (healthy dependency). These concepts have been interwoven in the treatment phases.

The five-point treatment procedure, presented in my earlier contributions (Lachkar, 1984, 1985b), is based on these developmental phases: Phase 1, a state of oneness; Phase 2, a state of twoness; and Phase 3, the emergence of separateness. These sequences are outlined to illustrate movement from a state where self and other are indistinguishable, where boundaries are blurred and fused, to a state of more clarity, and finally to an awareness of separateness.

THE INITIAL INTERVIEW

Structure

The therapist using a psychodynamic or psychoanalytic approach tries to understand not only how the problem arose, but what the problem is. Some of these discoveries may begin in the waiting room.

The Waiting Room

The first face-to-face contact is made in the waiting room. It is here where the boundaries are established. Some therapists allow one partner to enter the consultation room and begin the session even though the other partner has not arrived; others insist that one should not begin until both parties are present. The decision depends largely upon the outlook and the "containing" capacity of the therapist. In my view, the couple coming for conjoint therapy must be treated as a couple, and not as individuals (except in the case where one has dropped out). I recommend that the therapist wait for both parties to arrive, explaining to the waiting one that it is best to do so. The therapeutic task is not to be manipulated into seeing one partner without the other if one is late or does not show up. Sometimes not doing therapy may be the best therapy! The therapist has an opportunity to hold on to the therapeutic frame by withstanding the anxiety of waiting and the tolerance of not knowing, and by not quickly relieving the problem.

The therapist needs to show empathy for the waiting partner, but to clarify at the onset that both partners are coming here as a couple because of a marital problem, and not for individual therapy. The therapist might say, "We all have to tolerate a certain amount of frustration and uncertainty, including myself. Before you came, we weren't even sure if there was to be a session, because your presence is of great importance here and we couldn't start without you" (bonding with the narcissist via the grandiose self).

If the therapist colludes with or relieves the frustrated

partner of the problem too quickly, then the problem can be neither seen nor addressed. The partner who behaves in the relationship as the waiting one, the placating one, again goes along with the absent or late partner. The therapist might say, "We need to let your husband know that his presence is very important, and it would not be the same without him. Now, if I see you alone, then you are no longer coming for conjoint therapy, but for individual help, and that is something you need to think about" (addressing the borderline tendency to act impulsively). "You can take your time in deciding what kind of help you would like from me, and I will be more than happy to wait until you decide." Usually this clarification takes only a few minutes in the waiting room, but it does require the therapist to risk, and an opportunity to reschedule needs to be offered.

The dynamics that occur in the waiting room are often very subtle, and the therapist's own sense of attunement will be a guide in the various problematic issues that arise. No matter what creative route the therapist chooses to manage these various difficulties, more important than what the therapist does is what the therapist understands. The therapist who understands how a commitment has been broken and others have been let down or kept waiting is in a better position to begin the work. The therapist and the patient(s) have now had an experience together, one that will most likely become the main thrust of the treatment.

Case History

Ideally, the first sessions should be aimed at getting as detailed a history as possible. The first session offers a unique opportunity to get a fairly structured family background. The history should include, basically, any suicidal ideation, drug or substance abuse (including alcohol abuse), child abuse, psychotic episodes, head injuries, organicity, and hospitalizations. Not to get a history is, I believe, a technical mistake. With more regressive couples, or with couples whose partners have less impulse control, an initial history may be difficult to obtain, and will have to be teased out in later sessions.

If I decide to take a history, and if during the history the partners continually interrupt, then I interpret how difficult it is to wait (as it was in the waiting room), and ask if this happens in the relationship, whereby nothing gets completed and no one ever gets fed. The purpose of taking a history is threefold. First, it is not the history per se that is of ultimate importance, but rather the process itself. One gets a chance to see who initiates, who takes control, who interrupts, and so on. Second, it further helps to establish the boundaries, and to make clear who the doctor is and who the patients are. It makes the patient feel safe and secure (because it indicates to the patient that there is a therapist there who is thorough, solid, and complete) just as one does when a medical doctor asks pertinent questions. Third, the information patients reveal helps the therapist to understand something about their backgrounds, and how they happened to meet and come together. Some of the more general questions I use are:

1. What is your full name?
2. Are your parents still alive? If not, what were the causes of death?
3. Do you have siblings? Where did you stand in the family? (Eldest? Youngest?)
4. How long have you been married? Have you had any previous marriages?
5. Do you have children? Boys or girls? How old are they?
6. Where did you meet your spouse?
7. What attracted you to her or him?
8. What qualities does your spouse have that you value and appreciate?
9. I'm going to ask you a very specific question. Now before you answer, I'd like you to think carefully about it. Don't rush, take your time. Why are you here?
10. What does it feel like to be here?
11. What is it that I do that you think can be helpful to you?

Often couples will ramble on in the attempt to answer the questions. Commonly they interrupt one another. Given the appropriate circumstance, I might say to the borderline wife, "Do you always interrupt your husband when he is speaking? Ooops! You're doing it to me now!" In a loving and caring way, I might add, "I know it's so hard to wait your turn. We just had an experience in the waiting room together, didn't we?" (bonding through our mutual experience of the moment).

Initially the responses tend to be free-associative and tangential. I try to focus on only one point. Question 10 is usually the most baffling. At this point I require very specific responses. I will say, "Let me ask the question again; perhaps you did not understand." In a very caring way I will ask, "What does it feel like to be here?" One partner may tell of being coerced into coming. "That may be so," I might say, "but that is not answering the question about what it feels like to be here." I may have to say several times and in an increasingly authoritarian manner, "Ah, you have not answered my question, 'What does it feel like to be here?' " The other partner may interrupt with a comment such as, "That's the same thing that happens at home, I can't get a response. We have this same kind of communication problem at home." I then acknowledge how valuable that information and insight is. "Already," I tell the couple," we are getting to see that what happens at home is happening here and this can be very helpful for us" (beginning of couple transference). I then take the opportunity to remind the partners how important it is to wait and to tolerate some frustration, because if we do that, something valuable does eventually develop. "Now we can see we are already beginning to get somewhere, and that feeling forced or being left out can, in fact, interfere with knowing how we are *feeling*" (undifferentiated feeling states). This process models how important it is to stay with one point, to maintain a focus, and not to get lost in "the dance." "If a partner gets angry," I respond, "but I don't focus, then we all get lost, and go round and round in a circle and never get anywhere. If that happens there won't be a 'me' here to help us focus. Perhaps why you are here is that you are not sure what you are feeling, and if you lose contact

with your feelings, it is impossible to relate to one another."
 It is important to focus more on the process itself than on the question. Commonly, one or both will get angry, suggesting that we go on (wanting the quick fix). This discussion frequently leads to the exposure of the difficulty the partners experience in holding on to their own feelings, and ideas within themselves or their relationship. A partner might say, "I can't hold on when he pressures me. I do give up too soon!" If the therapist gives up too soon, then the therapist is colluding with the couple, and with the partners' tendency to go along without ever achieving any understanding—that is, to engage in the dance or the circle.

Educating the Couple

A well-organized therapist has the responsibility of informing the couple about the expectations of treatment. The therapist must make sure that the couple is comfortable with the therapist. The idea that the therapist may have some special skills or experience that the partners don't have can be useful and effective: "If I were to go to you for legal counsel or investment counseling, I would assume that you would have some skills that I don't have, and I would have to rely on you and your experience. Now you are here to rely on my experience; you are assuming that I have some skills that you don't have. While you are here, you are going to have an opportunity to have a new experience" (preparing the couple for the "drama"). Part of educating the couple is allowing the "mess" to unfold. "Initially you may feel confused and uncertain about what is going on here, but in time things will get clearer. So right now it might be hard for you to be aware of what you need, simply because you are both going around in circles" (living in the "mess" through blaming, projecting, and evacuating instead of thinking) "and have been for quite some time." The therapist must educate the couple by indicating that, "for now, it is OK for us to stay in the mess together, at least for a while, so that all three of us may have an experience together. Meanwhile, I'll have to tolerate some waiting, some confusion, and some uncertainty until I get the information I need." (The information the therapist needs is the history.)

I ask the couple to feel free to ask me questions.

Example of the "Mess": the Swindler and the Spender

A husband said, "All I get is full of shit. The other day my wife phoned me and called me an asshole. She screamed at me for not taking her shopping. Then I found out that she was using the credit card up to the max. I can't stand it anymore! When this happens all I want to do is walk away." To this husband, I might respond: "Yes, it does seem like a terrible thing to see a mess. I don't mind seeing the mess or the shit here" (couple transference) "because I know that if I can see it, then we have a chance to correct it. Already, I'm beginning to see why nothing ever gets cleaned up or dealt with. There does seem to be some avoidance when there is a problem to face. This keeps things from ever getting accomplished (an 'asshole' is not the same as a mind that can think and understand something). I believe you feel it is such a terrible thing to look at a problem you and your wife are having, but if we don't look at it we won't be able to see the healthy side, and all you'll see is the failed, 'shit' part."

The omnipotent and submissive features in narcissistic and borderline couples must be addressed from the onset. Since the grandiose self within the narcissist frequently cannot tolerate needing anything, the narcissist will feel put down by the therapist's "needs." Common responses are to experience the therapist as controlling, needy, greedy, and "money hungry." Part of educating the couple might be as follows: "Yes, I am taking care of my needs, but I think there is some confusion here. You may be worried that if I take care of my needs, I'm not going to be available to help you take care of your needs, when in fact, it is the other way around. If I don't take care of my needs, there wouldn't be a 'me' here to take care of yours, because I wouldn't know how. Again, I think that's precisely why you are here—it's perfectly normal and natural to have needs and expectations" (responding by interpretation).

To the submissive part of the borderline I might say, "It's interesting how you didn't respond to my requests, how you didn't ask me any questions, and how you depended upon your husband to supply all the information. Do you always go along with what others say or wish?" (responding by entering the internal world).

When I ask each partner specific questions at the initial interview, frequently one will try to take over or take control. In the case of Vera and Jeffrey, for instance, a borderline wife waited until her husband was in the bathroom to ask if she could tape the session. Part of educating the couple is to help them learn that this is a conjoint session, and in this case we needed to wait for her husband to return so that she could pose the question directly to him. Within the context of educating the couple, I then had an opportunity to discover why the wife was not able to ask for her needs in the presence of her husband.

Ground Rules

The structure and formation of the conjoint treatment setting varies from therapist to therapist. One therapist may provide an open structure, allowing free association and open expression, while another may feel more comfortable providing a more closely structured methodology. As far as I know, there are no data as to which approach is more effective, but I have found that for me a systematic approach is necessary and is effective in establishing the appropriate boundaries from the onset while creating a solid therapeutic framework.

Typically, couples with primitive pathological mental defenses and disorders have life-styles that are chaotic and fragmented, and the partners are desperately seeking out some kind of order and structure. I have found that a systematic method is needed in order to set a solid therapeutic framework. There must be, I believe, an organized, efficient "mommy" who is warm, practical, and understanding and who does not appear sloppy or disorganized. These patients respond more readily to a sturdy, empathic therapist who is both sustaining and containing and who can withstand complaints. This setting can further facilitate the capacity to provide a safe holding environment in which to work.

The importance of the therapist/mother as the container becomes more vital in a conjoint setting because the control issues revolve around persecutory anxiety, shame, guilt, confusion, and fantasies of separation.

Here is an example of setting the ground rules:

"We must recognize that coming here is a commitment and a big responsibility for all of us. I will be committing myself to you and to this relationship, but in order for us to work together I must tell you about the ground rules. I request that you come here at least once a week in the beginning, until we see if we are able to work together, for at least the next 6 sessions. I require at least 2 weeks' notice if you cannot make the session. Also, if I go away I will give you plenty of notice. If there is an emergency, or something urgent comes up, of course I will take that into consideration, but ultimately it will be up to my discretion as to what an 'emergency' is. If you need to change the hour and if there is time available so that I can do that, I will be happy to do so, but you must know that this time will be set aside just for you, and you are both responsible. After 6 weeks, we will have an opportunity to reevaluate. How does that sound?"

I also let the partners know about one more important ground rule concerning telephoning me in between sessions, and confidentiality. "If either of you needs to call me, you may feel free to do so; however, I do need to let you know that this is a joint experience and whatever happens here is to be known among all of us, and that any information you disclose to me is subject to be shared, at my discretion. I think this is an important thing for you to know."

Ordinarily, along with addressing issues of commitment, I set ground rules for payment, insurance, and other housekeeping matters, but I may wait until another time to deal with these details; I use my sensitivity and attunement to decide what is appropriate in each situation.

When the initial interview is drawing to a close, it is helpful to all to recapitulate and sum up what has transpired. Keep it clear and simple. Couples with primitive disorders and defenses have difficulty holding on, and need absolute clarity. For example: "In this session I have had a chance to get a glimpse of part of the difficulty you are having. You are having difficulty waiting, and if you can't wait, then you can never get the feeding that you need. I'm concerned that you may get so impatient here that you may not be able to wait. It's going to take some time to see why you berate yourself and put yourself down. The healthy parts of you were able to come here and ask for help, and you should be acknowledged for that. The unhealthy you wants it all right away. We also discussed the ground rules, and I hope you understand that we have all made a very important commitment. Are there any questions?"

Generally, cases will be presented in Chapter IX; however, for purposes of illustrating the primary interview, and to demonstrate ways of getting to the issues and coming to closure, I will describe my first session with Vera and Jeffrey.

Case Example of Initial Session

Presenting Issues

Vera and Jeffrey had been involved in an ongoing relationship for 3 years. Vera had two teenage children from her previous marriage who were currently living with her exspouse. In this session I attempted to stay in contact at all times with the partners' affective interactional states.

The first session was less structured for the couple than later sessions, primarily because I sensed that both partners needed to vent their feelings and that to be overly structured would divert the expression of pent-up rage and anger. The need in this session was to evacuate, using the therapist as the "toilet breast." My attunement represented the instantaneous choice to be a being mommy rather than a doing mommy.

Three emerging themes are depicted in this case: (1) blurred boundaries regarding the lack of clarity as to who is responsible for what, (2) the issue of the "bullshit" session (in which "shit" is tossed around instead of ideas usable or suitable for thinking and developing understanding) versus a productive "feeding session," and (3) circular behaviors; that is, the partners are in a circle from which they can't extricate themselves.

I tentatively diagnosed Vera as the borderline, and Jeffrey as the narcissist. Although Jeffrey had many borderline features (inclination toward violence, drinking, drugs), his primary anxiety seemed to center around his strong need for recognition and appreciation. His primary defenses when faced with narcissistic injury to the nascent self were guilt, introjection, and withdrawal. Vera, although she attempted to struggle with her entitlement wishes, was still too split off from her needs to be considered narcissistic. Her primary defenses were attacking, blaming, splitting, projection, and projective identification.

Jeffrey called to tell us he was going to be late, and Vera was asked to wait. He finally arrived. As soon as they entered the consultation room, where I greeted them, Jeffrey needed to use the bathroom. My first thought was that Jeffrey possibly needed to evacuate (the therapist's preconception), but I was cautious not to formulate an idea.

Vera (the borderline wife) was seated while Jeffrey (the narcissistic husband), indicating that he was having a "male problem" and needed to urinate quite frequently, went to the bathroom. While Jeffrey was in the bathroom, Vera asked me if I would mind if she recorded the session. I let her know that if this were an individual session, the choice would be between her and me, but that since this was a conjoint session, we would have to take this up with her husband. She responded that she wanted to tape the session because it was hard for her to remember things (borderlines' lack of evocative memory). Jeffrey returned and seated himself in the chair next to Vera. I turned to Vera and asked her if she would like to ask Jeffrey if he would mind if she taped the session.

VERA: Do you mind if I tape the session?
JEFFREY: Well, I guess it's all right. No, maybe not!
THERAPIST: Sounds like you have some mixed feelings about it.

JEFFREY: I do.
THERAPIST: We may have to pay attention to that.
JEFFREY: No, I decided not to allow you to tape it.
THERAPIST: Sounds like you made a wise choice—you paid
    attention to something inside of you.
VERA: That's OK, we don't need to.

I noted with some suspicion how easily Vera gave up her needs.

I asked each partner the questions I outlined in the case
history section of this chapter, questions about their previous
marriages, expectations, and so on, and I watched each individual very carefully. I observed Jeffrey become very impatient
with Vera, and when it was Jeffrey's turn to respond, Vera
looked very uncomfortable, as if she couldn't stand waiting for
her turn. Jeffrey, although he seemed to have an easier time
waiting for his turn, looked very angry and very annoyed.
Both looked suspicious of me.

Vera complained that although she loved Jeffrey's warmth
and friendly ways, she resented his drinking and violent temper.
Jeffrey's complaint was that Vera was too bossy and picked on
him, didn't listen to him, and didn't value or appreciate him.
Vera declared that just as soon as she brought up an issue or
something that bothered her, Jeffrey would bring up issues of
his own (the narcissist's disregard for others and excessive
feelings of entitlement). Each partner felt invaded and intruded
upon.

Vera free-associated to a time when they met in front of a
revolving door. I didn't say anything, but thought how the
revolving door was like the dance, the circle from which these
persons were unable to extricate themselves. No wonder Vera
needed the tape recorder; this couple was trying to deal with
too many issues. Perhaps this was why they were unable to get
out of the circle. I realized that she was telling us something
about their dynamics, that their way of relating still felt like
being caught in a revolving door.

I allowed a certain amount of freedom, interchange, and
going back and forth, but when I tried to focus on one issue,
Jeffrey suddenly turned on me accusingly. "Wait a minute!

That's very unfair of you. I was talking and you interrupted me!" My countertransference reaction was as though I had been hit over the head, attacked, and reduced to a very small child who had done something very naughty. I immediately got a sense of the violent and abusive side to Jeffrey to which Vera had earlier made reference. Jeffrey bitterly complained about how rude I was, as if to say: "How dare you, don't you realize how special I am?"

THERAPIST: I'm terribly sorry, I certainly didn't intend to interrupt.

JEFFREY: That's what's happened my whole life. Even when I was a child, my mother interrupted me as if what I had to say wasn't important (this indicated some of the source of Jeffrey's narcissistic injury).

THERAPIST: Well, unlike your mother, I do find that what you have to say is very important, and you're right that no one has a right to interrupt you (this was my response as a therapist becoming a mirroring self object).

JEFFREY: That's what happens a lot between Vera and me. Vera acts as if she's responsible for me.

THERAPIST: (to Vera, with an empathic and knowing look) Now I know what it feels like to be attacked, but if we both get into the battle, this session will become a terrible 'mess,' good enough for the 'garbage' or the 'toilet' (I used their words or association) and this would not be a productive session.

Just then Jeffrey interrupted me.

THERAPIST: (looking at Jeffrey) That's the very thing you got mad at me for. (Jeffrey caught himself.) You are both entitled to have real and legitimate needs. For you, Jeffrey, no one is allowed to interrupt you when you are speaking—not Vera, not me, not anyone—and if I did I certainly do apologize. (I did not interpret at this point that the reason people interrupt him is because he never stops talking.) Now that's what you are entitled to, but you are not entitled to become physically violent or abusive with your wife.

I turned to Vera.

THERAPIST: Yes, you are also entitled to get your needs met. I think it is very difficult for you to get them met at this point, because you want it all now, like a demanding little girl who wants so much, but is never heard. You too, Vera, have a right to your needs, and no one is allowed to hit you or use any form of physical force. Even if you do "push buttons" you still have to realize that no one has a right to touch or get violent. You are responsible to hold on to your own mind and your own "tape."

Closure

In closing with Jeffrey and Vera, I said: "I will feel we have accomplished something, and that I have earned my fee today, if only we can understand something about how important your needs are, and that this is an area where we need to work. Speaking of needs and the fee, I would like to know which one of you is going to be responsible for the payment of this session."

These comments and the partners' responses closed the session: "When would you like to meet again? I recommend we meet for six sessions, to see how we work together, and to at least sort out some of these issues. How does that sound to you? Would next week at this time work out? Yes, good, I will have a chance to explain more about this procedure, and you will have a chance to think about some of these ideas and we will review some of the ground rules. Please, if you have any questions next time, feel free to ask. Remember, if you call me to speak to me out of session, that anything you say, at my discretion, will be open for discussion, so you might want to think about that for the next week. Goodbye."

Thus the curtain opened, the drama has begun.

SIX-POINT TREATMENT PROCEDURE

In an earlier contribution (Lachkar, 1984, 1985b) I suggested the following five steps:

1. Conjoint treatment may be viewed as a prestage to individual psychotherapy or analysis. The therapist must see the couple together before transition into individual therapy, to form a safe bond, and to caution the partners not to move into individual work until the couple is ready (too early a separation can induce a "rapproachement crisis").
2. The therapist needs to be aware that the couple interaction may diminish individuality, to safeguard against this through provision of boundaries and limitations, and to assure both entitlement to their own subjective experience.
3. The therapist must be aware that each partner experiences anxiety differently (the narcissist needs specialness and appreciation and the borderline suffers fragmentation/ abandonment).
4. The therapeutic alliance (bonding) must be joined with the member who is predominantly narcissistic, because the narcissist's tendency to flight, isolation, and withdrawal can pose a serious threat to treatment. The borderline must be provided empathic responses as the bonding with the narcissist is being accomplished.
5. The therapist needs to apply group formation theory to these couples, who function as does Bion's basic assumption group, to illuminate regressive behaviors (Lachkar, 1984).

A sixth point, one which was not mentioned in my earlier papers, has become apparent with increasing clinical experience: The more primitive and destructive the couple is, the more structure they need.

As has been mentioned in the section about transference, we need to keep in mind there are three transferences that are operant: the two individual transferences and the couple transference. These transferences must always be interpreted within the context and confines of the relationship, and how this affects the functioning of the dyad.

THREE PHASES OF TREATMENT

To elucidate the movement away from circular, painful, and destructive behaviors, I have applied Meltzer's (1967) paradigm of "geographical confusion." The three-phase format for treatment described in this section is superimposed on theoretical principles related to how couples move from one treatment phase to another as determinants of psychological progress.

Meltzer discussed movement from one psychic space to another, stressing the importance of what he termed geographical confusion, particularly to adult borderline patients and the more severe psychopathological borderlines. I attempt to apply ideas from Meltzer's geographical positions to specific developmental stages through which couples move. I believe Meltzer's descriptions of skin boundary and adhesive identification visually and graphically illustrate how one individual can virtually live inside the mental space of another object. In treatment, these three phases, which can occur concomitantly and can overlap, are based on (1) fusion, (2) separation, and (3) interaction. The concepts of Freud, Mahler, Kohut, Klein, Fairbairn, Winnicott, Bion, and Bowlby are integrated and evaluated to help determine psychological development. The concepts from self psychology, which are most useful in conjoint psychotherapy, help the therapist to understand issues of the merger and fusion in the collusively bonded dyad, particularly in Phase 1 (the blaming and attacking stage) to mirror the pain that having a "no self" or a "mindless self" this fusion brings about.

In the initial phase, Meltzer included intense massive projective identification, intolerance of separation, omnipotent control, envy, jealousy, deficiency of trust, and excessive persecutory anxiety.

This phase of parasitic bonding is one in which the individual needs to maintain close physical contact to hold together the parts of the self, and to form an area of life space inside the self that can contain the objects of psychic reality. This is the process Meltzer termed "adhesive identification." The intolerance to separation manifests itself in absolute dependency on an external object. In this initial phase, one object lives inside the external object in order to maintain a sense of cohesion, but although boundaries are blurred it is a two-part functioning. In treatment of couples, this is equivalent to what occurs between the partners when they are immersed in states of fusion. In the early stage, which will be described later in more detail, interpretations are withheld. They are upstaged by therapeutic techniques of involvement, attunement, understanding, mirroring, and containment. Although interpretations take a back seat for the moment, they are recorded for future reference. This requires a certain capacity of the therapist to contain, hold information, deal with very few central issues, and not spill out or evacuate as the patients do.

In Phase 2, the two objects are beginning to separate and are beginning to live side by side. Meltzer distinguished between "real love" and the initial possessive jealousy that appears as a part object. Meltzer assured us that progress is almost always achieved if the analyst can persevere when geographical confusions are in the forefront of the transference and when almost endless patience and tolerance are required.

In Phase 2, I believe the ideas of Klein to be most useful, especially those of splitting, projection, and projective identification, and including the good breast/bad breast versus toilet breast concepts. Bion's notion of the contained and the container and his theories on linking and thinking are also very important here.

Grotstein (1984a) metaphorically and symbolically suggested that the borderline seems to cling adhesively to the surface of the mother's body as well as to other surfaces, as an exaggerated attempt to get a sense of contact, and therefore of skin definition. The borderline experience tends to be moving to and from the mother's skin, whereas the narcissist tends to appreciate the mind, the capacity for introspection, and response to interpretation. The therapeutic task, in this phase, then, is to gradually wean the borderline away from living emotionally inside the narcissist, and the narcissist away from idealized external objects.

Tustin (1981) suggested that autistic and childhood psychotic illness results from premature disruption of primary at-one-ness with the precocious experience of twoness. Developing reliance on another object is a slow process. I concur that emergence from this state not only requires careful scrutiny and understanding of developmental theories, but can be very trying on the therapist's anxiety level.

Phase 3 is more interactional (symbiotic bonding), with the partners showing more understanding that each has the right to subjective experience. The couples are more aware of the collusional bond, and strive more toward healthier symbiotic ties. Prior to this, the sense of separateness has been an undeveloped idea, a nonexistent thought: Separateness is a preconception relating to a sensory perceptional notion that an undeveloped part of the self is missing. If one is pervasively projecting inside another object, one cannot tolerate separation. Separateness is the nonpossessed object (paranoid-schizoid position). The inner world cannot tolerate the frustration of the feeling of nonexistence, and thus strives to seek out others through bonding in clinging, in an unfulfilling manner. In this phase there are fluctuating movements between the paranoid-schizoid position and the depressive position.

I have attempted to synthesize the psychoanalytic theories of Meltzer, Klein, Bion, and Grotstein and to apply them to conjoint treatment within the framework of three specific phases.

Phase 1: Borderline Lives within the Mental Space of the Narcissist—a State of Oneness

Fusion (Blaming/Attacking Phase)

In this phase the borderline partner is living emotionally inside the mental space of the narcissist (see Diagram A). There is considerable fusion and projection, and little distinction

DIAGRAM A
PHASE 1
Borderline Lives within the
Mental Space of the Narcissist

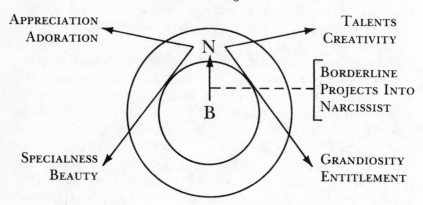

EXTERNAL OBJECTS

APPRECIATION   TALENTS
ADORATION   CREATIVITY

N

BORDERLINE
PROJECTS INTO
NARCISSIST

B

SPECIALNESS   GRANDIOSITY
BEAUTY   ENTITLEMENT

Borderline

Has blurred and fused boundaries

Needs bonding and maternal attachment

Is clinging and parasitic

Uses blaming and attacking defenses

between self and other. There is intense intolerance for separateness, omnipotent control, envy, jealousy, massive projection, and excessive persecutory anxiety. The borderline partner might say, "If she loves me, then I know I am deserving. When she's gone I feel like a nothing! I can't live without her." In this phase couples are heavily engaged in blaming and attacking behaviors and defenses. An intervention might be, "It must be very painful to feel attacked all the time, and to feel that no matter what happens you are the one to blame."

In this phase, the borderline is living inside a vacuum with "no thoughts" (beta elements), living in fear, with the psychotic part of the personality communicating feelings through projection and blame. In this state of isolation, one cannot relate to others, and one drains and taxes other persons as one forcefully tries to invade. During this phase the borderline derives gratification from the fantasy of the narcissist's availability. The paradox is that the narcissist is never available except for self-interest. There is no differentiation between self and other, as in, "If I'm good, Mommy is there. If I'm bad, Mommy leaves me." Good and bad objects are split off where integration between the good and the bad cannot take place, and defenses get in the way of sorting out what is coming from within and what is being projected from without. In this geographical position (as Meltzer would term it), the borderline is preoccupied with not having mommy not part of the time, but all the time!

Toilet Breast

The borderline partner cannot make use of Mommy's breast as a container that has the capacity to hold the baby. For the borderline partner in Phase 1, the therapist often serves as a "toilet breast," as in Klein's (1948c) concept. There must be an object that will contain the depth of the projection and the evacuation of painful affects (beta elements).

The therapist, like the mother, can be used by the couple (child) as a toilet breast or bad breast. These functions occur mostly in the initial stage of conjoint treatment, when the dysfunctional partners of the couple are unable to break out of their circle, and need help in "cleaning up" (toilet training). Part of the "dirt" is initially projected onto the bad breast therapist who is perceived as an inadequate and unavoidable source. In this phase, the therapist must show considerable empathy with the messy dysfunctional parts of the self in order to achieve some sense of mastery and growth.

Excessive demands, such as constant telephone calls, are other ways of using the therapist as a toilet breast. The therapist might interpret, "You keep calling me because there is a part of you that does not feel contained. For now, it is important to know that I am available to you as much as I can possibly be. It's important to acknowledge that you do need help from me and that is the healthy part of you that can express your real feelings, and I am glad that the vulnerable and healthy you can express needing me. It is the attacking, withdrawing, demanding, and blaming you that is messy. The mess is okay for now, but only until we can clean it up or wean you gradually away from this destructive part" (toilet-training the patient). The therapist, used interchangeably as breast and toilet, might explain, "I don't mind being used in this way because it helps me understand things better so we can start sorting things out here."

The concept of the toilet breast is exemplified in the case of the borderline wife who was not able to pay for her individual sessions. It became clear that the narcissistic husband was in charge of the family medical bills and expenses. Instead of taking up the issue with the husband who was essentially the breadwinner of the family, the borderline wife attacked the therapist as being greedy, selfish, and money hungry. The therapist responded, "I think you are seeing me as a 'money doctor,' and if I am a money doctor/mommy, then you feel I am a bad mommy/therapist. It seems hard to imagine that a 'mommy' has needs. It is hard for you to see that I can also be a caring and loving doctor/mommy/me, but, in fact, this bad doctor/mommy/me can also be the caring, loving me! Maybe you feel that you are being greedy if you ask your husband for help" (bonding with the greedy/needy part of the borderline and transforming greed and need into a digestible thought).

Within these preoedipal relationships, the Kleinian technique of referring to the self as the "mommy/doctor/me/therapist" is very effective. Eventually this kind of approach in primitive relationships may lead to further understanding about projections, skin boundaries, and definitions: "So you are not letting me know how bad I am for having needs. So there is a greedy 'me/you' and it is hard to see how the caring part of me can care for you. The greedy-you part is now like the greedy-me part." The therapist/mother must then be available to help the partners in the couple-infant configuration discharge their anxiety into the toilet breast, so that the good breast therapist/ mommy can emerge.

Phase 2: Awareness of Twoness

Emergence of Separation

In the second phase, each partner is beginning to establish a relationship with the therapist as a good reparative object. Some therapeutic bonding and assurance of the therapist's availability is beginning to take place (see Diagram B).

Phase 2 is still in a twilight zone, but there is an awakening of the partners in being able to rely on the therapist as someone who can protect them from the tendency to abrogate their experience. There is developing awareness of life other than through the partner. In this stage of "twoness," there still is very little differentiation between self and other: "My needs are your needs." This is quite different from Phase 1, where there is little awareness of having a life or awareness of needing. In this state of twoness, the narcissist, although still deriving pleasure from the external world, needs constant affirmation, adoration, and approval, and begins to become aware of a consistent denial of needing another object. There is awareness that external gratification, overstepping boundaries, and blaming really do not develop a sense of self.

In this phase, the therapist is able to point out more of the projective processes and to begin to wean the partners away from their blaming and attacking defenses. The therapist might say, "You are now projecting into your (borderline) wife your own feelings of guilt because you can't tolerate facing something within yourself. You're afraid to have your own feelings or to feel vulnerable."

Parasitic Bonding vs. Healthy Dependency

Many countertransferential issues emerge in Phase 2, and the borderline begins to sense, although in a hazy manner (a preconception of an idea) that needs are healthy. In this stage

DIAGRAM B
PHASE 2
Awareness of Twoness: The Filtering Stage
(Beginning of Interaction)

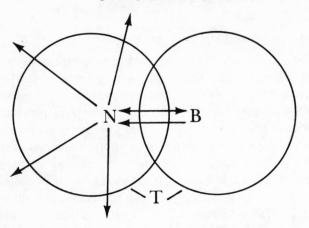

Narcissist	*Borderline*
Develops awareness of need to rely on external objects	Begins to develop relationship with therapist as an external object
Becomes aware borderline provides important function	Becomes aware of separate needs and issues
Develops relationship with therapist	Becomes more interactional
	Becomes aware of need to rely on external object

we begin to differentiate between the forming of a healthy alliance (transitional use of the therapist) and a parasitic alliance with the therapist (therapist being used as a confusional object). I cannot stress how important this distinction is. As an example of confusional use, the borderline partner might say, "Now we can get a divorce! You see I tried everything, even therapy, and it didn't work."

It is not uncommon that in Phase 2 one spouse will drop out. In the case of Vera and Jeffrey, Jeffrey became violent with Vera, and Vera terminated the relationship. Vera's integration and realization of her splitting mechanisms made her aware that the warm Jeffrey she loved was the same Jeffrey who was violent and emotionally unavailable. This enabled her to let go of the parasitic bond. She realized she could not force him to change, but had to accept him as he was (the depressive "realistic" position). Even though Jeffrey no longer attended the sessions, we still dealt with these concepts in the ensuing conjoint sessions. Vera had to face that the Jeffrey she loved was the same Jeffrey who beat her up. "The reason you tolerate this 'beating-up' part is because there is an internal beater inside of you that continually berates you and puts you down. So if there is not an outside beater there is an inside one. Then you need the other part of Jeffrey to love you and relieve and reassure you because you beat yourself up." Vera indicated that there were still things about Jeffrey she loved and admired including his insight and awareness. The work that followed led us to understand how the persecutory part of herself (the beaten-up part) tended to get stuck in clingy, unhealthy relationships.

In order for integration to take place, the beaten-up, persecutory part of the borderline needs constant feeding and nourishment. When one gets rid of an intolerable part within the self, the self never gets fed with the nourishment it needs. The unnourished self becomes clingy and forms parasitic relationships with others. The borderline partner might say, "If only he would see how I'm hurting, he would then love me" (bonding with pain). The therapist must bond with the healthy aspects in order to allow a strong dependency relationship to develop, which then leads to growth and better object choices. Often patients will express concern about becoming too dependent on the therapist and that they want to "do it" by themselves, but using the therapist as a healthy transitional object can occur when one or both of the partners recognize that they need help and can transfer the healthy "needy" aspects of themselves. Unhealthy parasitic relationships lead to hiding, fears, darkness, persecutory anxiety, clingyness, and emptiness. Being clingy is not the same as being needy.

Through expressions of psychosomatic illness, victimization, phobias, suicide ideation, sexual addiction, and other split-off affective areas of experience, one may project massively into the other.

Eventually the couple comes to realize that one partner cannot be the ultimate provider for the other, the rescuer, the reliever of persecutory anxiety, or the one to make up for all losses and deprivation. The partners learn that in order to attain any gratification in the relationship, one has to risk, to ask for what one needs, and not to relieve the other person of responsibility. In Phase 2, considerable support is needed during the weaning process. The therapist might say: "What you did this time was different. You did not take in the bad feelings. Even though what he said sounded perfectly rational and logical intellectually, you know something didn't sound right, and you paid attention to your feelings. You did not run to the bank to take out a loan for him merely to relieve him of his anxiety. Instead you waited while allowing your husband an opportunity to develop his own inner resources, which he did!"

Phase 3: Boundary of Two Emerging Individuals, Separate yet Bonded and Connected, and Interactional

In Phase 3 there is an emergence of separateness (see Diagram C): the realization comes that one can live outside the other's self, with one's own thoughts (better use of transitional objects), and can begin to tolerate one's own fate or destiny (alpha function).

In this phase, both partners are beginning to see that they have their own inner conflicts. There is more tolerance of one partner for the other partner's needs and thoughts as being different. More time is spent talking about fears and individual concerns; sometimes the partners begin to share dreams rather than resorting to talking about what they feel others have "done to them." In taking more responsibility for the past, the partners show a stronger tolerance level for containment of anxiety, and demonstrate an ability to wait and to face their

DIAGRAM C
PHASE 3

Boundaries of Two Separate,
yet Connected and Bonded, Individuals

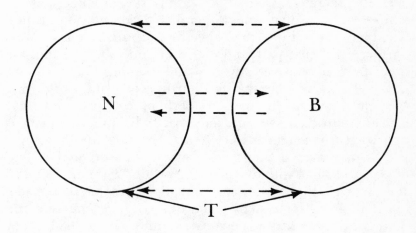

ALPHA FUNCTION

Borderline becomes more narcissistic.

Narcissist develops manic defenses against borderline.

Borderline's rage (better than passive-aggressive tendency to express feelings of betrayal covertly, rather than overtly).

More awareness of need for treatment.

Better and less confusional use of healthy transitional objects.

Encouragement and praise are received for taking more responsibility for behaviors.

Patient has developed appreciation for thinking over "doing" and "acting."

The "understanding" player takes a more vital part.

own faults and deficits. It is during this phase that some couples will drop out or that only one partner will remain in treatment.

In this phase the therapist is experienced more as a feeding/containing/waiting mommy. There is increased interaction with the therapist as a reparative object capable of providing a new experience, and as a vehicle to thinking and linking new ideas.

During therapy sessions, the therapist spends longer periods addressing individual issues rather than dyadic or couple issues. The therapist will find that while there is discussion with one partner, as if that partner were in an individual session, the other partner is actively involved and listening. Often sessions in this phase are reflective and introspective, and it is during this time that one partner, or perhaps both partners, may request individual sessions, and that individual treatment is desired and recommended. Often at this juncture the couple may want to drop out quickly because "all is well," and we find ourselves dealing with the quick fix, or the "flight into health." It must be clarified for the couple that progress has been made, but that taking some steps forward is not the same as a cure or as integration (Mason, personal communication, 1988). They may have acquired some tools, but may not yet have the skills to use them. It must be explained to both partners that when one partner terminates, the other may carry on, and that conjoint treatment may continue even with one person not present, as long as the focus remains on the relationship and transference interpretations are made within that framework. If one of the partners does not continue, "conjoint" treatment may still occur for the individual who stays in therapy within the context of the conjoint treatment, that is, until the formation of a transference relationship with the therapist can occur.

While the partners' behaviors improve, and insights develop, they still need help in understanding how they happened to get in the situation requiring therapy in the first place! They may have symptom relief, but symptom relief is not the same as structural change. The therapist has the task, then, of helping the couple face the past as well as the future. It is in this stage that the partners need to be reminded that to forget the past is like cutting off a part of themselves, and that they need the past in order to survive. Some liken this experience to a marital Holocaust: "We must not forget!" Two separate individuals with separate needs are emerging, two individuals who are aware of uniqueness and differences, but yet who maintain a bond and are connected through their mutual desire to grow and develop. In Phase 3 there is some awareness, only a glimpse perhaps, that one needs the other because each needs the other to play out their drama and to assure that there is a benefit in working things through. There is awareness that one partner stirs up unresolved conflictual issues in the other, and that to destroy the other is tantamount to destroying a part within oneself. The partners learn that to destroy, attack, or get rid of something is not the same as trying to understand something about themselves. What happens in Phase 3 is not to be confused with conflict resolution or with "working through."

During Phase 3 there is massive denial and often a tendency to develop manic defenses. Therapeutic failure may result from those who turn to the quick fix, or deny the help they received. Omnipotence and devaluation—as in, "We went for treatment but it didn't help!" or "We did it all on our own!"— must be interpreted at all times. For example, to one husband who told me he would like to stop because he couldn't afford the treatment, I responded, "And yet all along, while you have said you can't afford the treatment you have been paying regularly for the past 2 years. I think what you are saying is that you may feel you can't afford to face some of the painful feelings you are having. Now that you have acquired some tools from me, you feel that you can do it all by yourself." The partner who drops out often has a sense of failure because of not getting a quick fix. Frequently in this phase, there is great deal of frustration and resistance. The partner might say, "It's not working! I've tried everything. Things are not getting any better!" The therapist can help with this dilemma by responding, "I think that's exactly what happens in the relationship. As soon as there is some difficulty or frustration, there is the impulse to give in or give up. Now it is happening here. But I am not going to give up because I know if I can hold on; help us all wait, then something constructive may happen."

There is more interaction around issues of loss and separation, and healthier use of transitional objects to fill in empty space, the black hole, or the void. There is less taking in of the projections of the other and more awareness that the projection stimulates an unresolved internal part of the self.

Past histories, genetic material, and archaic associative responses often emerge during Phase 3, paralleling mistreatment and transcending the couple experience. There is an amazing replication of archaic anxiety about how they were mistreated as children, and some recognition of similar mistreatment is extended to external objects.

In Phase 3, each partner begins to take more responsibility for the past, and to recognize that what has been done now has a history. The partner recognizes that the memories of these injuries cannot be dissipated or remedied quickly.

It must be clarified that during this phase, defenses against mourning and facing feelings of sadness and pain become evident; however, if feelings of sadness and pain are ignored, part of the self does not heal or develop. Entering the depressive position is the facing up to losses and not to defenses against them. Often conjoint treatment ends at this time. One or both of the individuals may decide to continue for more intensive treatment either with the same therapist or with another. Phase 3 can be a transitional phase, and it plays itself out depending upon the needs of the couple and the capacity of the therapist to deal with both partners individually.

These three phases of conjoint treatment are neither a means to all ends nor a quick cure, but rather provide a transition or preparation for more intensive treatment. A strong therapist can help couples through periods of resistance to treatment and help the partners not disrupt treatment too early, before the individuals are able to face, stand up to, and be accountable for their own behaviors. The therapist must be prepared not only to interpret fears, but to anticipate manic defenses that precede the patient's entering the depressive position. The therapist's own anxiety regarding the wish to cure can get in the way of interpreting these manic defenses, or the therapist can feel too threatened or guilty to help hold on to the treatment. "I can see that for so long you felt helpless and powerless, now what you are doing is the opposite. You either withdraw, or you say or do nothing. Now what you want to do is to do it all—even take over the treatment." Beware of the quick fix, "All is well," "I can't afford it," or "I can do it myself." Be aware that for the narcissist the issue may be omnipotent control, whereas for the borderline it may be a manic defense against the powerless part of the self.

The patient may be trying to get rid of the therapist and the treatment before the patient has integrated that part of the self. "Look Mommy how big I am—I can take over your job!" The only problem with taking over is that the patient does not have the tools (preoedipal conflicts). "See Mommy, Daddy how big I am, I can wear your clothes and become you!" (The problem is that although a little boy can wear daddy's pants, they won't fit.)

Case Illustration of Treatment Phases

The case of Joe and Mary illustrates the three phases of treatment.

Phase 1: A State of Oneness

THERAPIST: So, what brings you here?
JOE: I want to stay married!
THERAPIST: What about you?
MARY: Well, I decided to move out, become independent, and
    do some things on my own.
JOE: Well, then, why don't you get a divorce?
MARY: No, I'm really not ready. I don't know what I want yet.
    I just want to live alone for a while, go out, have fun, be
    independent.

Notice the "grip" Mary has, keeping Joe on hold while she seeks out others to validate, appreciate, and mirror her. Her independence is not a real independence, because she is running away and not facing what she really needs to face.

THERAPIST: Well, tell me how you feel, since Mary hasn't made up her mind.

JOE: I've made up my mind. I'm going to stay married!

THERAPIST: As far as I know, it takes two partners to decide to stay in a marriage.

JOE: Well, since she can't make up her mind, then I have and my decision is to stay married!

MARY: But I don't want to.

JOE (threatening): Then get a divorce.

MARY: No. I'm not ready.

JOE: Then that means you want to stay married.

In this phase there exists a state of oneness between Mary and Joe. Joe is living within the mental space of Mary. He derives his sole sense of himself from whether or not Mary is available to him or not. Mary is the more narcissistic, not only because she is keeping Joe on hold (excessive entitlement fantasies), but because she feels she can use Joe while she remains free to seek out others. Each partner is using the other as a confusional object. Although Mary realizes that the little girl part does not really know how to be independent, her grandiose self believes independence comes from external gratification ("Look at me! I'm a big girl and can be independent.") Joe appears to be the more borderline in that he cannot think beyond his primitive needs, and feels terrified at the prospect of her leaving him. He is clinging, possessive, and retaliatory.

Their circular arguing makes for confusion; it is as if the room were spinning. In their relationship there is no room for empathy or insight. There exists only the behavior of closed minds: blaming/attacking defenses, excessive distorted ideas of grandiose entitlement fantasies, and magical thinking, as in "I want, therefore, I shall have."

After one particular therapy session, Joe and Mary left feeling very romantic, and decided to make a date. At the last minute, Mary called Joe to call the date off, claiming she had a headache. That night, Joe went to her house and caught her with another man. He grabbed her and shook her; afterward, she called and told me she was extremely upset over this incident. In this case, the therapist is used as a toilet breast to contain the negative hostile attacks of Joe onto Mary. The therapist becomes the preoccupied mother worried about Joe's violent and aggressive tendencies.

Phase 2: Emergence of Separateness

In the next session, I offered full support to Mary (the narcissist), while also setting a limit to Joe (the borderline), because Joe had physically shaken her! To Mary I said, "If this ever happens again, you will have my full support in getting a restraining order; no one has a right to hit you, touch you, or shake you." I offered support to Joe by acknowledging, "Mary has no right to make a commitment to you, then let you down at the last minute." I let him know he was perfectly entitled to feel angry, even if she offered him the explanation of a headache. She could have made an effort—taken a nap, or some aspirin. "But more importantly, if Mary didn't want to be with you she could have told you. I think what hurt you was being betrayed." I turned to Mary and let her know that she did let Joe down. This provided a new awareness, and each partner felt understood. Joe and Mary finally were able to start taking in new ideas because they felt relieved, safe, protected, and not blamed.

In this phase there is some awareness for each partner that each stirs up some inner conflict within the other. The projective processes are clarified as contributors to their confusional states. There is a sense, or a preconception, that internal conflicts are distinct and separate, whereas in Phase 1, this preconception is virtually nonexistent.

In this phase the partners were beginning to examine their behaviors introspectively. Within a few sessions, Joe began to cry, and told us that his mother was an alcoholic, and that she had never been emotionally available to him.

Mary's profound withdrawal initially took the form of massive denial about the couple's current financial situation. Mary began by expressing anger and outrage about their financial state. Joe had declared bankruptcy, and he had let her down by not paying back a house loan to her father. Her withdrawal and isolation represented her inability to deal realistically with these issues, and fight for that to which she was truly entitled. The narcissist is never narcissistic enough!

Narcissists never know what they are really entitled to; they go after only their grandiose fantasized entitlement, and not what they are really entitled to.

Mary's withdrawal had a profound impact on Joe. I told him he was now letting us know what it felt like to be emotionally bankrupt. (A transformation of beta elements into alpha function was taking place, transforming poisonous material and detoxifying the feelings into something that could be digested and emotionally useful and helpful.) Joe's capacity to tolerate his own inner badness of being a "bad Joe," could now be seen from a healthier perspective. "You are letting Mary know what it feels like to be emotionally bankrupted, as you have been your whole life. This feeling is so intolerable to you that instead of owning up to it, you project it into Mary. No one ever owned up to letting you down; now it's hard to face that you have let others down."

Joe came to realize why he would not file the divorce papers.

JOE: If I file them, it looks as if I want to get a divorce, and I don't. I want to stay married.

THERAPIST: Now you want to stay married, and I'm trying to help you see what it takes. It's difficult to stay married, because it means we have to do the work for Mary and face the difficulties and work them through. But of course you have a "me" here to help you, and I am not an alcoholic unavailable mother! So you say that if you file, that's the same as wanting a divorce, but as far as I know, the act and the doing are not the same thing as wanting. Just because you file doesn't necessarily mean you want a divorce. Just because you feel like hitting your wife does not justify your doing it. You can feel like shaking her, but you're not allowed really to do it. So just because you file does not mean you want a divorce.

In this phase I had an opportunity to interpret the splitting and I noted that all behavior did not emanate from Mary. Joe was helped to face his internal state of impoverishment, and Mary was beginning to see that her running away from Joe was really avoiding facing up to unresolved money issues with him.

In interpreting the splitting, I said to Mary, "First, there are two Marys, one who loves Joe and another who is let down and doesn't know how to deal with her disappointment. Then there is another Mary who turns to lots of other men as daddies to admire her and to make her feel special." To Joe I said, "There are two Joes. One who feels hurt and betrayed and attacks in order to get even, and one who wants to hold on like glue. Both Joes desperately want to be loved. Both are destructive because neither way makes you be loved; in fact all you'll do with Mary is hook into her rebellious child." I completed the interpretation by showing that there was a cause and effect.

Phase 3: Interactional

Phase 3 is interactional; that is, there is more interchange between patients and therapist than in Phases 1 or 2.

Mary was worried that I would be the one to terminate the sessions, and that I would threaten her, abandon her, get tired of her. She was feeling guilty that she did not show up for one of the appointments. I interpreted that she was afraid that I would withdraw, become "independent," or leave her, but that indeed it would be more likely that she would be the one to leave. She might, I said, have a hard time being able to withstand the rigors of the conjoint sessions, to stand up to me and tell me what she was feeling or thinking, or to stand up to her husband. I pointed out to her that when things got tough she was the one who tended to leave, become silent, or get so enraged she turned away and avoided. I reassured her that I would not leave or withdraw from her as her mother did, but would be emotionally available to her. She was projecting into me that I would be the one who would avoid the issues or go away from her. She also let us both know how painful it felt to be left. Although neither one of us had actually withdrawn from her, she needed to understand how she was projecting a part of herself into me and into her husband. These fears kept her being a little girl and could get in the way of her taking care of her needs, to really learn how to stand up for herself. I interpreted, "The big girl you doesn't know how to defend yourself, but if you walk away or don't 'show up' here, then you will never have a chance because you will never be able to turn to those who can help you, for example, your lawyer, accountant, or financial planner, or those who can really help you 'show up'!"

Mary was hurt and felt that I was not appreciating her. I let her know that I appreciated her, but that she was not appreciating me or herself. Mary thought that by pointing out her deficits, I was putting her down. "In fact," I said, "I see more of a resourceful you than you see in yourself! However, if I don't point out these behaviors to you, then it will seem as though I am the one who is 'not showing up,' and who is withdrawing from what is really happening, and if that were the case, we would continue to go around in a circle, never putting an end to these destructive behaviors." Mary responded, "I don't know how to go after what I am entitled to with Joe because I'm scared and he makes me feel so guilty." "Ah," the therapist might add, "this is the part of you I can appreciate, the part of you who doesn't know everything, the part that can admit to being scared. Now if you can hold on to these feelings, I think that this can lead to something very special."

In the last phase the dynamics become increasingly clear. The role of the therapist takes on a new meaning to each of the partners. Joe became the borderline child, setting up his mommy/wife to be the all-encompassing mother. The child/baby/husband now had a mommy/therapist totally preoccupied with him because of the worry that he might become violent again. I was attempting to provide the necessary holding environment, because when the potential holding environment is threatened, as in divorce, fragmentation can occur.

When the therapist can help the borderline patient contain some of the internal feelings, there is more of an opportunity to face reality and see more clearly that all the badness does not emanate from within. Borderlines can hold on to the more loveable parts of themselves when they can understand that it's what they project that is destructive, and not the contents from within.

Mary's interaction with me in Phase 3 was focused on allowing herself to have more healthy dependency needs. The role of therapist bonds with or "feeds" the healthy resourceful part of the narcissist, while not "feeding" the detrimental parts of the defensive structures. There is an awareness that the grandiose self is destructive, and that this does not lead to a state of cohesion and integration. The therapist might say, "It's good for you to face something you don't know, because if you can face that you don't know, then we have a chance to learn, to develop something together, find a way, and ultimately, you will get to know."

THE IMPOSSIBLE COUPLE

The sixth consideration in the treatment procedure is that the more primitive and destructive the couple is, the more structure is needed. We have all experienced the "impossible couple." These individuals tend not to be motivated because of their impulses to act out, and because their primitive defenses include massive denial, projection, and blaming and attacking behaviors. The couples I term impossible involve partners who are not capable of being in the same session together at the same time. For the impossible couple it may be necessary to see each partner at a separate time, and to state clearly that the process is not to be confused with individual psychotherapy but rather is a precursor to conjoint treatment. The partners need to know that when the couple "grows up," and when the partners can stand to be in a room together, then they will be ready to have conjoint treatment. Until that time, however, it will not be feasible. During this preliminary treatment phase the partners must be reminded that the focus still remains on the couple problem.

It may be that certain individuals are too fused or merged with one another to be treated together. Supportive structured psychotherapy is advisable to prepare the person for contact with the other partner. When couples respond in this way there is no semblance of communication. In working with these types of couples, the therapist must keep in mind that the goal is to help the partners face one another in a conjoint setting, and that the function for the therapist is to serve in this specific capacity. One of the basic elements that emerges in this particular configuration is the notion that these persons cannot tolerate another person having an idea contrary to theirs. For two or more ideas about one issue to exist simultaneously is tantamount to betrayal, abandonment, and abrogation of one's personal experience. The task is to provide understanding that an idea does not take away anything, but in fact can even add something, that if one can stay with one's own experience, ideas can blend and truth can develop. To assure tolerance, one might wish to suggest transitional objects. It may not even be too farfetched to provide a small teddy bear for the patient to hold on to while waiting for another person to state an opposing idea or thought. Sometimes eye contact is needed, a supportive smile, an empathic look, a nod, or whatever it takes to help the person hold on while another idea is being presented.

TECHNIQUES

Directive Approaches vs. a Psychodynamic Approach

Directive approaches put the therapist in the position of placing strong pressures on, and issuing commands to, the patient. It is popular among family therapists, including many treating couples, to assign tasks for the couple to do between sessions, but I personally do not assign homework or exercises. There are advantages and disadvantages to both methods.

Some therapists, for instance, will ask the couple to take turns listening to one another for 15 minutes, merely listening to the other without saying anything. Although these tactics are used to reduce anxiety and to give the patient the feeling that something is being done, they do not actually relieve anxiety because they do not lead to understanding. In fact, assigning tasks can give a false sense of doing something, and this can alleviate the therapist's tolerating a state of messiness and of confusion. "Doing something" takes the task away from understanding, and the therapist may be experienced as abandoning the couple. Cleaning up a mess is not the same as understanding how one got into the mess in the first place. Giving assignments for the narcissist/borderline couple may give the false message that the partners are to provide for one another, rather than that the therapist provides for each. For all these reasons, I choose not to offer direct tasks.

Analogous to the concept of tasks in conjoint therapy is the idea of the person who continually gets into lawsuits and seeks legal counsel to clean up some financial mess. The attorney could help take care of the specific problem, but could serve the client in greater measure by helping the client to understand how the mess was made in the first place. Telling someone what to do in a specific instance is not the same as providing structure and limit setting.

Containment

Earlier containment was described as an invaluable therapeutic tool for conjoint treatment. It takes a "container" to help patients face the intolerable unknown. These patients might ask, "Why am I so lonely? I feel it gnawing away at the depths of me. I can't stand to have anyone see me in this state." The therapist might respond, "Yet even as you say you are experiencing this intolerable loneliness, you still can function, you can walk and think, and there still is a 'you' that can make decisions," and might expand on this with something like, "I think that because you feel so lonely, you become the loneliness for all to see, as if there is no skin boundary or a you to protect or as if that is all of you."

Because of the borderline's readiness to take in the projections of others, borderline patients seem to need containment more than empathy in order to feel safe. A therapist might say, "We are better off trying to understand what it is inside of you that makes you feel bad and that makes you identify with these projections."

The Experience of Truth

In treatment, the therapist needs to be aware that couples need to be understood first and to vent feelings. The therapist must try to be available to both sides, and to allow each to have a personal experience of the "truth" and allow each to confirm that the therapist can understand how each can feel a particular way. One of the most valuable discoveries is that there is room for more than one truth.

Who's right? Who's wrong? They're both right and they're both wrong. Each has a personal experience of the "truth." It is the way these truths are expressed that is dysfunctional. If the therapist engages in the battle or focuses on what or who is right and wrong, then the therapist is participating in the craziness. It is up to the therapist to understand both sides, and the therapist can do this through a process Bion referred to as "detoxification."

We ask ourselves, what it is that occurs intrapsychically at the moment of discovering a psychological truth? What is the truth? Bion has offered the therapist "abandonment of memory and desire" (1977); that is, the ability to give up all memory and desire by putting aside preconceptions and theories, and thus to be totally available, without contamination from previous sessions, other people, or other external influences. We are interested in discovering psychological truth, and that truth can be uncovered only through experience. Bion's work offers us an invaluable tool, and one most useful in couple therapy.

The therapist must protect the partners when one tries to rob the other (or to rape the other person's mind), by letting the offending individuals know that no matter how absurd the other person's view may seem, that person still is entitled to have that view. It is my job to allow more than one view, and to allow differing views to "room" together.

When the partners argue, the therapist must be careful not to get pulled into it, not to engage in a battle. One may instead comment, "If I respond to this then we all will be arguing, and there will be no treatment taking place." In these situations, I advise the therapist not to respond further: It is best to wait and say nothing. Make them curious! Make them think! Make them wait! Look at each of them for a response until they are dying to know. When the timing seems appropriate, then say something like, "I think I have it! It seems clearer to me now what the problem is. It appears that you are in a competition with each other and with me, and as if one idea has to win over the others. It seems intolerable that both of your ideas can live together in the same house or in the same room, and can live with my idea." If the couple denies this is going on I remind them of what I have heard in the session and what I have experienced. To help expand these ideas further I have developed the six-point procedure described earlier.

GENERAL CONSIDERATIONS

Communication

Many theorists, and even many authors of pop psychology books on how to communicate effectively or on "how to teach communication skills," have missed the major focus. What does it mean to teach couples to communicate?

Communication is not merely stating what is on one's mind. To do so, in fact, can be destructive and dangerous to the self. To communicate effectively means first to think and sort out thoughts, ideas, and various confusions before expressing what is on one's mind. These feelings need to be sorted out and organized before they are expressed to a partner or any other person.

In adult communication, it is unacceptable to use the relationship as a toilet (the toilet breast or the toilet relationship). To merely speak out or state whatever is on one's mind is tantamount to spilling out or evacuating. We do not need simply to get rid of ideas, we need to think about them first. In other words, we need to learn how to think before we can clearly express and communicate our feelings.

Secondly, we need to learn how to express ideas not only in a way that can be understood, but in an empathic manner, so that the listener can hold on to the thought, take it inside, digest it, and eventually make use of it.

A patient may say, "As a child I was never able to vent and express my anger to my father. Now that I have grown and am I am not so afraid, I feel it's important that my husband put up with my explosive moods." This is a misuse of the relationship. One needs therapy to work through unresolved issues, not a partner one uses, in the name of communication, as a toilet.

Resistance

Initial resistance to making a commitment to the treatment is commonplace, and includes complaints over costs. The couple needs to be reminded of the reasons that brought them to therapy in the first place. "You mean to say there are arguments, fighting, and economic problems, and now you say you can't afford to come. I don't see how you can afford not to come!"

The couple in treatment for 3 months who then quit because "it didn't do any good" or because they were able to "work it out all by themselves and now are doing just fine" is evidence of denial in the patients of the feeding given to them in the treatment, a denial of the good breast. Bion discussed flight/fight in regressive groups, wherein a couple or a pair bonds together to fight off the enemy—that is, the therapist. The therapist needs to be aware of a quick disruption in therapy that could relate to the patient's "practicing phase" (Mahler, Pine, & Bergman, 1975); when patients are ready, they don't need to reality-test the therapeutic work.

Marital couples may resist for other reasons: envy, greed, or massive denial. They may envy the therapist's capacity for containment, empathy, or other attributes the therapist may have and thereby may disavow the help they receive. Many factors may be involved when a couple terminates treatment prematurely, but termination does not necessarily represent a treatment failure, a therapeutic impasse, or an empathic failure. In fact, even if only one of the partners remains, this can be considered as a positive sign.

If one partner gets angry or annoyed, it is up to the therapist to let both partners know that this is preferable to avoidance, denial, or subjugation of the self, and that the therapist is not disturbed by the anger, but rather welcomes it because it can lead to more understanding. The therapist has an opportunity to become the new object and to protect the borderline from the narcissistic partner who reenacts emotional abuses similar to the ones the narcissist has experienced in the past.

CONCLUSION

Although educating narcissistic and borderline partners about the therapeutic process is complex and confusing, it is essential. Not to do so is unrealistic. These couples need to know that the problem was not formulated overnight, and that it cannot be resolved or cured instantly. Each partner needs the other to play out the drama. If one expresses how one feels, that can be evacuating. If one holds back what one is thinking or feeling, that can be withholding. If we do not express how we feel, it can go against human nature. If we try to think, to relate, and to understand, that is psychoanalytic! In this chapter, I have attempted to outline a more systematic treatment approach with narcissistic/borderline disorders in order to understand treatment successes as well as failures. That a couple may abruptly terminate treatment does not always mean that the treatment has been a failure; in fact, in some instances, it indicates success. If we can understand what constitutes the successes and what differentiates them from the failures, we are better equipped as clinicians to develop an effective treatment approach. Although more research is warranted on these burgeoning relationships. I believe there is a need for a systematic approach to conjoint therapy.

CHAPTER IX

Cases

The cases described in this chapter are included to exemplify the theoretical presentations in this book, and to augment the material on treatment of the borderline/narcissist couple.

CASE 1*

**Diagnostic Distinctions
(Qualitative Differences)**

Albert and Ruth

In this case, the partners demonstrated both narcissistic and borderline symptomatologies. Albert feels overly entitled, but also exhibits many blaming and attacking defenses. Ruth has mainly borderline features, in that she has difficulty holding on to her own experience.

This couple had been married for 4 years and had a 2-year-old child. Albert (the narcissistic husband) had been married three times before. Ruth (the borderline wife) was afraid Albert would leave her. The problem centered on the "lies" he told, which she could not tolerate. Each had a different experience of the "truth" (Lachkar, 1984).

RUTH: Albert has trouble with the truth.
THERAPIST: Oh, in what way?
RUTH: Albert never tells the truth. All he does is lie.

* See Chapter III.

THERAPIST (turning to Albert): Is there any truth to your not telling the truth?

ALBERT: I do tell the truth. I only exaggerate the truth.

RUTH: That's a lie! You don't tell the truth. You lie all the time! (turning toward the therapist) We have an apartment in Redondo Beach, and he tells everyone that we have a million-dollar home in Malibu. We have a rowboat and he tells everyone we have a yacht. Now, do you call that telling the truth? I'm so embarrassed with my friends.

ALBERT (starting to scream): That's why I do it! I exaggerate the truth because that's all you do is bitch, bitch, bitch! You don't understand me and when you're like this I just want to run away from you.

RUTH: I can't trust him. It causes bad feelings inside me. I feel as though I'm not worth anything. He treats me like a nobody. That's how I feel, like a nothing, as if I don't count. I just keep hoping he'll change.

THERAPIST (to Albert): It sounds to me as if you are not getting the appreciation and recognition you would like so you resort to telling her anything to please her.

ALBERT (softening): When I tell her the truth all I get is complaints. So now I just tell her what she wants to hear. She never appreciates the things I do for her. That's when I usually take off. I go off with my friends who value me. But, then I start to feel bad, so I keep coming back.

CASE 2*

Diagnostic Distinctions (Fine-Tuning and Subtle Differences)

Jonathan and Luella

At the onset, it was not clear which partner was predominantly borderline and which, narcissistic. Upon further investigation,

* See Chapter III.

it seemed likely to be a mixed bill. Initially, Jonathan appeared to have many pronounced borderline features, an alcoholic who was incapable of tolerating any frustration or of staying with issues, and at the drop of a hat would blame and attack his wife.

In addition to aggressive acting out and destructive qualities, Jonathan had many narcissistic features. He was irate when he heard his boss had moved Jonathan's desk from the front showroom to the back showroom in the manufacturing plant (perhaps an insult to his grandiose self). Jonathan may not have felt so much abandoned as narcissistically wounded at the notion that his boss did not appreciate him. He blurted out, "I was so upset today that I almost killed a pedestrian!" I needed to determine, in light of borderline versus narcissistic rage, if this was a reaction to his abandonment anxiety or was a personal injury to his sense of specialness.

In contrast, Luella, Jonathan's wife, who also became irate (borderline rage), could not stick to anything, rambled on and on without much insight or awareness, split off her needs, and used her husband as a target. She would criticize her husband and put him down in a punitive and destructive manner. For instance, Luella complained bitterly that Jonathan did not help with the dirty dishes, nor did he take out the trash. The shelf paper was still not finished, he didn't notice her new negligee or that she had lost weight, and he failed to notice she changed the furniture around. On the surface, one could surmise not only that Luella felt abandoned, but that generally she was not being appreciated, and she confirmed this, saying that she was concerned he would withdraw from her, or would go into one of his drinking binges. Still she seemed to be more preoccupied with being recognized and being appreciated than with being abandoned.

I empathized with Jonathan with respect to his feelings of not being appreciated by his boss, and suggested that it might be important to take up this issue with his boss. Jonathan responded defensively that he had "already dealt with" his boss, explaining that his friends "from the next room talked to him." I told Jonathan that his friend talking to his boss is not the same as he himself talking to the boss. He blurted out, "The problem is not the boss, but the problem is all Luella!" To this I responded, "You say that the problem is Luella, while you treat me in the same manner you do Luella: You push me away, and discount me and what I say, as if you don't appreciate me either. This is sort of the way your boss did with you. Maybe you're letting us know what it feels like when you are not being appreciated."

Jonathan shook his head as if to say, "I don't want to bother with it, it's not important anyway" (clearly indicating his devaluation of this interpretation). What I had just said to him was very difficult for him to digest and take inside, and I let him know I understood that. I explained that we were not communicating, that he didn't have to agree with what I said or to "do" what I suggested, but that I was just asking for him to understand. I told him that because he had "hired" me to help him discover new parts of himself, and because, in a way, he was my boss, I would talk to him, directly.

Jonathan smiled and looked quite surprised. He proceeded to tell us how he wished his wife would talk to him more directly. (The borderline responds better to directness and confrontation, and the narcissist to interpretation.) At this point, I was still unsure which partner was the more borderline and which the more narcissistic. I simply continued to interpret the avoidance, the denial, the splitting, and the blaming, attacking defenses.

I attempted to focus, in working with Luella, on her splitting off of her needs. On the surface, it sounded as if she were very certain of her needs, but actually she was disavowing them by spewing out her contents, using words as confusional objects, blocking communication, and not allowing meaningful interchange and expression of affects and feelings.

To Luella I said, "Yes, you either want to talk about everything, tell everything that bothers you about Jonathan, like all the dirty dishes, or else you want to withdraw, give up, and say nothing. The problem with trying to deal with everything is that you end up dealing with nothing. So it is all or nothing" (grandiose fantasies and the splitting mechanisms). "I guess I will have to confess that I am in the same position here as you are, that I can't deal with all the issues right now, but I can deal with some of them, so both of us will have to tolerate putting some of these issues on the shelf for a while, until we can sort out some of these areas" (the couple transference).

In the fourth session, it still wasn't clear as to which partner was more inclined toward borderline and which toward narcissistic organization. I divided the session into three parts. In the first two, each one interacted with me while the other sat back listening and had a chance to comment and give feedback.

As usual, Jonathan decided to start, not because he felt entitled, but because of his lack of tolerance and impulse control. In spite of this, I was impressed how they were able to sit without interrupting. I also had to use my body language and eye contact to help "hold" them in place.

Both Jonathan and Luella had difficulty holding on and waiting. Each partner needed the other because they stirred up something inside one another; their relationship with one another stimulated a halted development that needed to grow.

This case is illustrative of the complexity and ever-changing states of the narcissistic/borderline couple. In one session or at one moment, Jonathan seemed to be more narcissistic, and at other sessions or other moments Luella seemed to be more narcissistic. In the fifth session, Jonathan appeared more grandiose than before, claiming that he had an overwhelming amount of work to do, and that because of his perfectionistic qualities he felt he had to do it all.

In time, it became clear that it was Luella, rather than Jonathan, who was the more inclined toward narcissism. Luella took on the role of a very bossy and aggressive wife, whose superego functions and guilt mechanisms operated at a very punitive and restrictive level. Her grandiosity was expressed by her various attempts to do too much, and to tell Jonathan all the things that were wrong with him. She would then withdraw, never reflecting on or staying with any of the issues. Jonathan, however, was at a more primitive level and had more

borderline features. I came to understand Jonathan's withdrawal and blaming tendencies not as an escape to his inner
world, but rather as a form of evacuation to get rid of anxiety.

CASE 3*

Understanding as a Defense:
Teaching the Couple to Perform Self-Object Functions

Dana and Bob

Dana and Bob had been in treatment with another therapist
for a year. During that time, Dana had been encouraged to
"understand" her husband's passive-aggressive behaviors.
When Dana and Bob first started treatment with me, I let her
know that it was not her role to "understand" her husband's
feelings, and that in this situation her understanding was only
getting in the way of her own development. I encouraged her
to leave the understanding to me.

In this case, the former therapist had served not only as a
self object, but also as a container. For the mate of a passive-
aggressive person to serve as a self object can lead only to
maladaptive functioning.

Bob had a blurred concept of boundaries, and allowed an
intrusive mother and sister to enter his home at any hour of
the day. Dana was very "understanding" of this invasion of the
couple's privacy; however, her understanding became misconstrued as weakness. During therapy, Dana was overly empathic
and sympathized excessively with her husband's pain. This
understanding brought on behavior on her part that colluded
with Bob, and ultimately led to devaluation and to his further
attacks on Dana.

At this point, it was necessary for me to step in and to take
over the function of the strong parent imago, to be available
to protect the couple from outside intruders (fantasied pred-

* See Chapter V.

ators). Dana could then adjust to a normal role of being a wife or even a "child" with normal needs, rather than acting in the defensive role of the little parent or little adult or little therapist. I was able to focus on helping Dana see the real aspects of her role—how she was intruded upon and how her rights were violated. Bob had a right to see his family, but did not have a right to invade Dana's space. When I was able to point out these deficits, Dana was able to respond more positively.

Bob and Dana were in a shared business together. The husband had many fantasies of their being business partners and working together as a team (a parasitic bond, as opposed to a healthy dependency relationship). They denied that the business was failing, and that they were moving into serious debt.

Dana's childhood had included continuing expectations that she function as the little adult. She had had to take over many parental functions for her immature, dependent mother, and in order to achieve any sense of worthiness, she had had to provide for her younger sisters. Dana had developed many compensatory mechanisms by becoming the pseudoparent, the good girl, the good helper, and now the good patient, and this included being the good little therapist. In the marriage she believed that it was her responsibility to make up for the losses of the business, and she felt it was entirely her fault that the business was indeed failing (persecutory anxiety).

In a combination of conjoint and individual treatment, Dana was helped to face that she was not the only one responsible for the business failure, and that she covered up the problems by continually relieving her husband of his responsibility and by paying all the expenses.

Treatment consisted of trying to awaken a sleepy "couch husband." Partway through the treatment, Dana said, "I'll never forget the look on his face when I told him that this time he's to be responsible for half the taxes and for half the loan—that we were, after all, partners. He almost fell off the couch!" The major thrust of the treatment for Dana was to help her stand up for her rights, and to deal with her needs in a way that was more containing and less attacking. The dependent infantile and the pseudoadult aspects of Dana's psychopathological states were illustrative of earlier needs that had been severely subjugated and now were projected onto Bob. Bob initially felt betrayed by both Dana and me. The therapeutic work consisted of trying to help Bob face issues around betrayal. Although we were able to channel Bob's talents and ambitions into more realistic goals and aims, he eventually dropped out. I continued treating Dana.

Dana became aware that she was the one who was betrayed (busily taking in Bob's projections). She said, "I worried about betraying my husband or that I would lose him. You helped me face his anger, and he even respects me more now. I am beginning to see our relationship in more realistic terms."

The therapist must be able to sustain the difficult role of containing painful feelings and affects of the patient's previous injuries—not only through words, but by being able to demonstrate containment with vigor and conviction.

CASE 4*

The False Self

Fred and Mary Beth

In this case, Mary Beth, the borderline wife, was helped to understand that her false self was a means of avoiding feelings of vulnerability, sadness, and mourning. Mary Beth held the distorted view that her "true self" would lead to feelings of unworthiness, when, in fact, it was the projected, split-off part of herself that invariably made her feel unworthy.

As Mary Beth, her husband, Fred, and I began our session, Mary Beth said she was in "the worst state," but that I shouldn't worry because "soon these terrible feelings will pass and then I'll be my other self again" (false self). I reassured her, "This

* See Chapters II and VI.

state of vulnerability and sadness is important, but rather than allowing yourself to have these feelings you cover them up by being a 'good girl,' trying to please others, or 'making nice-nice,' when actually these sad feelings are healthy. When you cover up these feelings, you continually undermine yourself in this relationship and your ability to relate more effectively with Fred." Mary Beth responded that she was upset because her husband said she was worthless for not contributing to the household expenses. I pointed out that she was not feeling worthless because her husband told her she was worthless. Quite the contrary, she felt worthless because she could not hold on to her own feelings (her internal household), and felt she had to live up to the expectations of others. "You need someone like a 'me' here to help you hold on to your real feelings and to help you mourn and face the feelings of sadness" (the mourning process helps one get more in contact with needs and feelings). I explained that the same pattern was being repeated here in this session. "You don't feel worthy here to allow yourself to feel upset, to feel hurt; instead, you tend to cover up your true feelings by bringing in a false self or your 'other self' to make it appear that all is well" (the borderline's inclination toward the abrogation of the self). "That's what makes you feel unworthy. I was very impressed by what happened. Earlier, when you allowed yourself to feel the sadness, the pain, the sensitivity, and the vulnerability, Fred responded very warmly to you. When you did allow yourself to have these experiences, you felt it was tantamount to a psychological death."

I reassured Mary Beth that when she was in this state, which she called the worst state, she was really holding on to her true feelings, and that this was preferable to being in her false self state because there is then an opportunity to grow, to develop, to understand, and to take something inside. When she was in her false self state, she did not have a chance to take in anything, and this was what made her feel worthless. Mary Beth assumed that if she allowed herself to be a needy little girl she would be abandoned or rejected, by me or by her husband. Mary Beth therefore adopted a false self and become the supervisor, manager, therapist, mother, or little adult, but then would end up feeling worthless because the little girl part of her could not maintain those roles. I let Mary Beth know that when she was in the false self state she was like a little girl trying on mommy's clothes only to discover that when wearing mommy's clothes they don't fit and one becomes a caricature instead of a real person. Analogy is a useful tool to point out the absurd and delusional part of the personality.

I spoke to Mary Beth about being in her false self state: "When this happens, you end up persecuting yourself because you give up your own needs and feelings, and then you can't see what your real role as a wife or as a patient is" (persecutory anxiety gets in the way of thinking and seeing reality).

Mary Beth responded tearfully, "My mother always told me I should put on a good front, to look and act as though I knew everything so that I wouldn't humiliate her in front of her friends. I always wanted to have my mother's approval, I would always do anything to get her approval at any price, and now it makes me feel sad to have my husband see me in this way" (we know we are doing well when we get this kind of genetic association). Mary Beth's husband, Fred, spoke up: "Actually, I like you better in this way. You seem softer, more beautiful to me, more sensitive and real.

The case of Mary Beth and Fred illustrates how the interpretation of an internal persecutory mother can help patients face their feelings of vulnerability, and how the "true self" can be experienced in new ways.

CASE 5*

Excitement, Passion, and Magical Thinking

Gerald and Karen

A narcissistic husband, Gerald, was having tremendous sexual fantasies about an old girlfriend. He yearned for excitement and passion, and was thinking about "getting rid" of his wife.

* See Chapters II, III, and VI.

Gerald was disgusted with his wife's chanting, and her preoccupation with gurus and Hare Krishnas. Karen, Gerald's wife,
was a bright, intelligent woman, and Gerald could not understand her excessive interest in these gurus.

Gerald also was very upset that Karen didn't plan anything
for his birthday. Although Gerald did not plan anything for
himself either, he came home hoping Karen would have
arranged to have a cocktail, to go out, to open gifts, and to do
something special. When I asked if he had planned anything,
Gerald said he just assumed that Karen would make the plans,
and he expressed severe hurt that she had not done so.

I said, "I guess you expected your wife to be different, to
suddenly change. Your wife certainly makes a good object for
your projections, because there is also a magical part, a certain
guru, a part of you that hopes that plans will be magically
made and all will go well."

These partners make for good projections, and when an-
gered, the narcissistic partner often wants out of the marriage.
It's extremely important to be able to say, "Yes, there you go
again, wanting to get rid of her, or me, or a part of you that
you cannot tolerate facing the reality. It's easier to get rid of
someone or to find some outside excitement than to find the
excitement within yourself."

Gerald responded to this approach by saying, "I'm just not
turned on by her anymore. I don't feel excited!" I answered,
"But you also turned off to the true passionate part of you, the
part that can face issues, take care of your own needs, stir
things up, hold on to yourself, follow through, find the true
excitement and inner passion within you. That excitement is
impossible to find, especially when the two of you are searching
for gurus (couple myth). This apparently makes you too
anxious, so now you'd like to find it somewhere else. The true
passion is within you." He said, "Yes, I really would like that,
but I don't know how to do it." I responded, "Now this is really
getting exciting! The healthy you can admit that there is no
magical answer, and admit you don't know how. Terrific! This
is the beginning of finding passion."

If these issues had not been dealt with early in the treatment,

I believe the relationship would have resulted not only in a premature disruption of the treatment, but in dissolution of the marriage. To overly empathize with the borderline husband's disappointment, may have led to more fragmentation. Empathy in this case might have been misconstrued as collusion.

CASE 6*

The Nice Guy: Passive-Aggressive Behaviors and How Borderlines Misperceive

Arthur and Margaret

Arthur, a borderline husband, expressed his hostility, anger, and outrage to Margaret, his narcissistic wife, through passive-aggressive actions. He continually would "forget" to follow through with his promises and commitments. When he was asked to go to the market for his wife, he would arrive when the market was too crowded or was closed. When they had scheduled social activities, or went out to dinner, he would forget his wallet and credit cards or claim they were stolen. People from work intruded into his space by calling his personal number. He allowed workers to come into their home at any hour of the day or night. Even worse, business people, creditors, debtors, and marshalls serving warrants would pound on their door in order to collect from Arthur for unpaid bills. This enraged Margaret, who, as the narcissistic wife, was left feeling invaded and infringed upon. She felt the "mess" was too overwhelming and complained bitterly about her rights being violated. Instead of paying attention to what she realistically could do to correct the situation, Margaret would withdraw, walk away, and not talk to Arthur, or would not have sex. He in turn would attack her. "All you ever do is bitch! bitch! bitch!"

Whenever Margaret would express her outrage, Arthur would act as though *he* were the one who was angry. I reminded

* See Chapters III and IV.

Margaret of her tendency to withdraw, saying that I was perplexed that Arthur was turning things around, behaving as if he was the one who was angry with Margaret, "while as far as I know you [Margaret] are the one who is angry with him [Arthur]." (Arthur was using language as a confusional, rather than a transitional, object.) I asked Arthur what Margaret had done to make him angry with her, when it was she who was telling Arthur that she was upset about her rights being violated.

Arthur, true to the role of the passive-aggressive husband, responded, "There are many things I'm upset about," and started to list all of them. Margaret the narcissistic wife again reacted with extreme outrage and was dramatically shocked to hear complaints she had never heard before: "He only brings these things up when I am angry with him!" I reflected, "Oh, you have 'heard' these complaints before, but you 'heard' them indirectly. Now you are hearing them in a more healthy way. I think I know what may be happening." To the husband, "You don't feel deserving or entitled to bring up your complaints unless your wife gives you the entree by being angry with you." Arthur worried that he would "become his wife" or his mother (a form of identification or twinship) if he brought up any of his own issues.

I explained, "If you continue to join with your wife's complaints by voicing your complaints only when she is angry, you will never be able to turn to the internal creditors inside to help you. You do have some healthy needs, but if you keep projecting them into others, you will continue to feel robbed. I'm so glad you are here to get help because this will give us an opportunity to develop a new line of credit." I let Arthur know how very much I appreciated and valued what he was offering us. "I can hear how very much you want to be a 'nice guy,' but that's not being a nice guy! It's being a sucker! In fact, it leaves you feeling not like a 'nice guy' at all, because everyone ends up getting even angrier with you. I hope that while you are coming here, the healthy 'big boy'/'nice guy' you can learn how to express your feelings more directly." Within the context of the couple transference, they both needed to know that the therapist was not going to be a "nice doctor," but rather a helpful doctor who would know the difference between being angry and being bitchy!

CASE 7*

Entitlement Fantasies

Jane and Ron

This case illustrates how the therapist tries to help the couple sort out what each is entitled to.

After 2 years of combined conjoint treatment and individual treatment, a 43-year-old wife, Jane, became very anxious about asking me to hold one of her checks. She had prior knowledge of an interpretation made to her husband, and feared that I would respond similarly to her. Her husband, Ron, had asked me, time after time, to hold checks until he could "make ends meet." I felt it was important to serve for a while in the capacity of a "toilet breast," and I held checks for him until I felt Ron was ready for this interpretation: I told Ron that someday these checks might grow up to become real checks, but right now they were baby checks that hadn't developed or matured. It appeared, I said, that he would like for me to "carry him" and to relieve him of his responsibility (as his wife did). I told Ron that if I continued to relieve him in this way, he would not be able to understand anything about his true entitlement needs. This might momentarily make him feel special to be joined to me in this way, but it wouldn't last. In fact, if I provided for him the things to which he was not entitled, he then might not have a chance to discover to what he indeed was entitled, and so would be unable to "check" out his real needs.

Jane was quite worried that I would offer her the same response if she asked me to hold one of her checks. I assured her that she had different entitlement needs that were separate

* See Chapter VI.

from those of her husband, and that with her there had never been any issue about money. She was reassured that she had been reliable, and had paid on time, and that her husband's issues were separate from hers and were not to be regarded as the same. (Quite the contrary, her issue was not feeling deserving enough to ask for her needs. So far "baby checks" or bad checks were not one of Jane's needs; however, if she never asked, then she would lose out on being a baby in this instance.)

CASE 8*

Guilt vs. Shame

Michael and Francis

This case illustrates how a guilt ridden, overly controlling, narcissistic husband stirs up profound feelings of shame in his borderline wife, and how the borderline wife, in turn, stirs up feelings of guilt in the narcissistic husband. The complicity of the couple entraps them in a primitive bond.

Francis, the borderline wife complained that her narcissistic husband Michael was always late and unavailable. Francis took on the role of a complaining, demanding partner. Issues of separation were viewed as intolerable, keeping her in the role of a helpless victim and handicapped by her lack of impulse control, containment, and inability to hold on to her own feelings and thoughts. The realization that her husband emotionally abused and mistreated her was vehemently denied until she found him in bed with another woman. Until this time, she felt ashamed for distrusting him. "I can't tell how I feel because he doesn't listen. He gets angry and hostile with me when I get angry. How can I get angry when he gets angry?" (projecting his guilt into Francis).

Treatment for this narcissistic husband focused upon the

* See Chapter VI.

incorporation of a controlling mother who gets in the way of his pleasure and fun.

MICHAEL: She is just like my mother. My mother would never listen to me. All she would do was yell, scream, and get in the way of my fun. That's why I need other people. I need excitement. (Turns to the external excitement because he has not found the internal excitement). She drives me away by her demands.

THERAPIST: "Well, now we are getting somewhere. You're looking for excitement, and you're not finding it in your relationship. So your wife is like your mother—controlling, rejecting, getting in the way of your fun, but then you also see me as someone getting in the way of your fun. Setting limits and making demands here. So when your wife gets angry you rebel, and then you can't see if your wife has a legitimate gripe or not. All you see her as is a screaming, yelling, complaining, and controlling mother (guilt tends to distort reality).

In the transference, the therapist became the controlling dominant mother, who ruined all the fun and got in way of his pleasure by making demands upon him. For the borderline wife, I became the "spoiler," the mother who ruined everything.

Feeling overwhelmed by guilt, Michael dropped out of the conjoint treatment, but Francis continued on with weekly individual psychotherapy. The focus eventually shifted from shame to understanding how the internal part of herself readily took in the projections of others. Although the therapeutic interventions essentially had to justify that there was an external abusive, cheating husband (important, especially for borderlines who tend to easily disavow their experience), they also validated that there was also an internal one. "Yes, there does seem to be this external abusive betraying husband who leaves you out, abandons you, makes you feel shameful, there also does seem to be a part that leaves yourself out, robs you of your feelings. This is what makes you feel so ashamed and helpless."

Treatment for this borderline wife had to focus on her delusional fantasies, to go along, to be a "good girl," to always make "nice nice" to recapture the wonderful feeling of a warm safe, soothing womb. In the transference, I became the intruder into her symbiotic world, the "troublemaker," the "spoiler."

Francis began to notice that Michael was beginning to get more "turned on" to her. The therapist remarked, "Yet, your idea was that I was a spoiler, that if I didn't go along things would be catastrophic, and now you tell me that things at home are considerably better. As we can see, this internal mother that continually tells you to be a 'nice girl' or look the other way can interfere with your judgment."

The therapeutic task was to assure her that the therapist was not going to merely stand by and make "nice nice" as she does, while simultaneously reassuring her that the goal was not to spoil things, but to help her have a healthier and richer life.

Al and Lucy

A couple with a 2-year-old daughter recently moved from the East to the West Coast. Al, the borderline husband, could not come to the session during which Lucy, the narcissistic wife, confessed that her husband was not the biological father of the child, that he was sterile and could not conceive. Lucy confessed that she'd fallen in love with another man, become pregnant, and had the child. When I asked her why she wanted me to know this, she responded that she could not stand the guilt, that she was not getting along with her husband and thought he ought to know the truth. I told her, "Certainly it is appropriate to feel guilty. However, although your intention may be to reveal the truth, you are not taking into consideration what is best for your family and the welfare of your child. Rather, you are considering only that you can't stand your own guilt, and now want to get rid of it." I advised that she seek her own individual treatment to deal with this issue. In this treatment, we will focus more on how Lucy had been very angry at her husband's attacking, destructive behavior, and now wanted to retaliate.

Mindful of being a container for Lucy, I continued, "Yes, it's certainly important to tell the truth, but in this instance, it is not clear what the truth is. First of all, there is no proof that your husband is not the biological father of the child, and secondly, you are not really interested in the truth, but rather in both relieving yourself of the intolerable guilt that you feel, and getting back at your husband. I don't see how that is dealing with the truth, especially when the main issue is what is going on between you and your husband that apparently is not being dealt with."

CASE 9*

Confusional, Diversional, and Transitional Objects

Susan and Alex

Susan's husband, Alex, threatened to leave her if Susan continued to use her teddy bears. He saw these objects as getting in the way of their relationship, feeling that her dependency on them was destructive and made her too needy. (Susan's previous therapist also had thought that her dependency on transitional objects would regress her to an infantile state.)

A self-psychological point of view would be focused on the subjective meaning of a transitional object, whereas object-relations theory reinforces the importance and significance of the meaning of transitional objects via one's projections. For instance, Susan became angry when she was told that there would be a charge for missed appointments: She accused me of being a "money-hungry therapist," and said that I didn't really care about her, but only about my money. I responded, "You expect me to respect your transitional objects, those that are related to your needs, and I guess you'll have to consider respecting mine too, my security blanket." To bond is to relate to the healthy way in which one uses transitional objects and

* See Chapters IV, V, and VI.

to join in the experience through understanding what is being projected, transference interpretations, and countertransference (in this instance, her greed and my guilt). It is one thing to validate the couple's experience to talk about something, but quite another to use the material to become immersed in and a part of the experience.

Later in a session, Susan revealed that she was feeling better and was enjoying cuddling up to her teddy bears, particularly when I was away or when her husband was away. They helped her sleep, and helped the transition of the breaks between us.

Friends as Confusional Objects

Don and Danielle

The life of one couple, Don and Danielle, consisted of going to exciting places throughout the world: nightclubs, skiing, safaris, fancy restaurants, Academy Awards dinners, and so forth. Danielle, the borderline wife, yearned to have time alone with Don. She continually felt left out and abandoned, as he would take her with him traveling, and then suddenly leave to go elsewhere with his many "interesting" friends, leaving her behind. Each time Don promised her a nice, quiet, cozy dinner, or dinner for "just the two of them," they would suddenly be bombarded by his friends. Danielle was constantly puzzled as to how these friends would suddenly appear from the woodwork.

Don's friends became confusional objects, exploding and intruding into their relationship, and interrupting their capacity for intimacy. (Transitional use of friends would be, by contrast, their use to fill in the lonely space.) If friends did not "appear from the woodwork," Danielle complained, Don would make telephone calls the remainder of the evening while she impatiently waited or stood idly by. The telephone became, as did the friends, diversional and confusional objects, rather than vehicles to enhance good feelings, communication, and understanding.

I explained to Danielle that in this case it was not delusional that she felt she was being abandoned; indeed she was being abandoned!

Treatment as Transitional

Karl and Lydia

If a couple enters treatment without clear awareness as to who is in need of the treatment; if there is no awareness of the problem; or when the reason for entering treatment is not for the sake of the self, but is directed toward the other, treatment may be considered diversional or confusional. When there is an awareness of the necessity for the treatment of the conflict, and some sense that the therapist can facilitate a transition to mental health, treatment may be regarded as transitional.

Karl, a husband and father of two children, an attorney, entered into treatment with the complaint of his wife's chronic forgetfulness. He bitterly complained about being let down by his wife, Lydia. Lydia responded that she was not the one with the problem, but that Karl was a nag, was boring, and was a constant complainer, and never would leave her alone. Initially, Karl decided that the problem was all his wife's fault—that he was problem-free. Not only was Lydia forgetful, he complained, she was always late, spent too much money, was a compulsive shopper, and chronically would lose things. I slowly moved in by becoming the self object for both of these individuals. I allowed Karl to make use of the treatment by helping him face realistically that he was not responsible for Lydia, that she was not a child, and that there must be some reasons why he felt so responsible. Eventually, Karl was able to face that he was not responsible for his wife's forgetfulness, lateness, and so on. Karl could not deal with Lydia realistically because of his own guilt, and in taking care of his own needs, Karl felt he would be "abandoning" and "betraying" his wife. Eventually Karl began to recognize that he had his own issues to deal with, and started to face the difficulties surrounding his guilt. Karl would go to the party in his own car when Lydia was not ready. If she was unable to find the address, Karl faced that it was not his responsibility to be Lydia's caretaker. He came to realize that it was ultimately more loving not to relieve Lydia with a quick fix, which would only cover up the real issues. In this illustration, forgetfulness is clearly confusional in that Lydia blocked all methods of communication. Entering into treatment might be viewed as transitional, with Karl using his wife as a transitional object. The patient may have a preconception that treatment could be helpful, or, as Tustin might say, he brought in his "bibby."

Making use of the treatment as a transitional object occurs when there is bonding to the therapist as someone helpful (a good breast), as opposed to the perception of the therapist as a toilet breast. An emerging problem cannot be dealt with realistically unless the therapist is willing to be part of the interaction to bond with the healthy parts of the patients. The therapist who has bonded with the healthy parts of patients can truly facilitate real relief from anxiety. In this "transitional" case, relief came about through a differentiation between a "me" and "not-me" with Karl's recognition that he was not responsible for his wife's behavior. This not only led to an healthy emotional separation, but facilitated the bonding with the therapist so that healthy treatment could become a transition to development and growth. The movement from using the treatment as diversional to using it as transitional occurs when there is bonding not only with the therapist, but with the need for treatment.

CASE 10*

Doing Mommy vs. Being Mommy

Abigail and Claude

After several conjoint sessions, it was decided that the wife, Abigail, should be seen individually. Abigail was afraid to use

* See Chapters II and VI.

the couch. She felt that she would have to conform to being the nice little girl her mother wanted her to be, and feared that I would insist that she plunge right in, as her mother used to make her do, and that I would not help her recognize the steps it takes to use the couch. Instead of becoming the doing mother, who would make her simply "go ahead and try it," I tried to help her by becoming the being mother, who seeks to understand what is getting in the way of doing. I tried to help her understand that she felt anxious because this left her in a state of confusion, not knowing when it was safe to risk and when it was not. It turned out that her fear was that if she used the couch I would become a lazy doctor/husband/me and would ignore her, would eat while she was lying down, would talk on the phone, and generally would take my gaze and attention from her. Even worse, Abigail feared that I would look at her as she saw her father—drunk, lazy, and a sleepy "couch father/husband."

I responded to her projections by letting her know that she was not seeing me for who I am because she was projecting a part of herself into me. She needed to understand that she was putting into me a "sleepy and lazy" part of herself that she wanted to get rid of (the part of the self that goes along). "You need to 'do' something rather than just allow yourself to be a little child here and to allow yourself just to 'be.' It is important for me to 'be' here to help you understand what is blocking you from staying in contact with your feelings. Before 'doing' something, we need to understand why you feel I would ignore you, or would see you as you see your father or husband" (states of fusion), "as a lazy, sleepy 'couch patient.' " I explained to Abigail that if she gets rid of the part of her self that has contact with her feelings, she will not be able to turn to her feelings as a vital resource.

CASE 11*

Addictive Love: The Albatross

Mark and Sandy

MARK: I seem to feel this low again. Sandy is back in my life again and she is calling me.

I was silent.

MARK: I seem to hang on to her words like they are everything, like when she says, "I love you." I want to believe these words, yet I know she is away with Bob again.

I listened attentively.

MARK: I know she is with him because I go by her house and check if his car is still there or if she has moved out. I see it, just as I suspected (borderline's inability to rely on experience and need to keep checking, because he can't count on his mind).

THERAPIST: Sounds as though you are doubting yourself and you need to check up to make sure that what you know is so, that you need to check up on yourself. How is it that you can't trust what you know? Every time you have gone by her house in the past, you know you have seen Bob's car there.

MARK: I guess, I can't understand how she always rejects me and loves me at the same time. It affects me so deeply. She is like my mother. She rejects me and accepts me. When I am with her, she is loving and warm, and responsive. But when I call her a few days later, she is cold, aloof, and withdrawn, as if a wall goes up. I say to her, "Hey, wait a minute this is Mark speaking!" But it really doesn't matter

* See Chapter II.

so much (borderline tendency to disavow the experience and the hurt). She reminds me of my mother, she rejects and accepts me at the same time.

THERAPIST: You must be feeling very hurt and confused. Maybe you're worried that there may be something wrong with you.

MARK: Well, I am hurt and confused, my mother said she loved me but didn't show it. I knew she had her own problems with my father and she felt frustrated.

THERAPIST: How old were you?

MARK: Around 3.

THERAPIST: That's when your first sibling was born. That's when you felt displaced by her. Until this time, you had a chance to have a special relationship with your mother, until she came along.

Mark seemed too embarrassed to cry, but shook his head and became very tearful.

THERAPIST: It must have hurt then the same way it hurts now with Sandy, feeling that something is wrong with you that you are being replaced.

MARK: Well, I guess I was different then. I was just too sensitive to cope with my sibling.

THERAPIST: You seem to think there is something wrong with being sensitive and different, or that to have needs and feelings is wrong and makes you out to be the outcast one. And then there is a Sandy who now confirms this view.

MARK: I remember in school, I used to get a check mark for every time I talked too much and my mother would punish me.

THERAPIST: Too bad she couldn't see your talking as ambition, excitement, and enthusiasm—as an opportunity to develop your personality rather than something to be put down for—or that you may have had something important to say.

MARK: Yes, that's true. I feel as though it's still there.

I was silent.

MARK: I feel like a masochist. I feel so impotent. I keep going back to the pain. There are many who do accept me, but I keep going back to those who reject me.

THERAPIST: I guess it's hard to take in and need others, to be fed by them internally, when you believe there is something wrong with you. The only problem is that as long as there is a Sandy out there to stir up these painful feelings then you don't have to face your needs or to face the part in you that needs to understand something about yourself. (Sandy projects into Mark, and Mark identifies with the projection.)

MARK: She is like the devil and the god. She has the power to save and relieve me. She is like an albatross around my neck. I just can't let go of the fantasy. I just love her. I love the way she looks, the way she feels, the way she smells. There simply is no other woman.

THERAPIST (attempt at transference interpretation): Yes, but as you idealize her, you leave yourself out. If she is either the devil or the god, then there is no you. She then has everything and you have nothing. You also leave me out as if I don't count, as if I am impotent and insignificant, and that understanding your mind doesn't count. Only if a Sandy loves you, accepts you, or rejects you counts. That's pretty simple, but it doesn't help us understand why you get into this addictive state. Perhaps you do so that you don't have to face the issues that brought you here in the first place.

CASE 12*

The Affair

Lauren and Jim

Lauren, a narcissistic married female surgeon, fell in love with Jim, a married engineer. They were in their mid-forties, each

* See Chapters VI and VII.

had children, and each had been married for about 10 years. They had been seeing each other on and off for approximately 1 year. Lauren and her present husband had been in combined conjoint and individual treatment. In the initial phase of the affair, Jim called Lauren at least three times each day and said he would "go out of his mind" if he didn't see her. During the course of their relationship, the frequency of Jim's calls and the time he spent with her gradually diminished. He would explain that he was busy working, or had become preoccupied with work and family.

On Thanksgiving day, the lovers arranged to see each other briefly before both families were to gather at their respective homes for dinner. Jim called a few minutes before they were to meet, and said he couldn't meet with her because he was having his entire family over and there was a very special aunt coming whom he hadn't seen for a long time. On another occasion, Jim canceled their date claiming that he was over-loaded with work, and when he worked that was all he could think about. On other occasions, he spent time with his daughter, of whom he was deeply fond. Lauren became extremely hurt, injured, and enraged at this unavailability, which she perceived as a rejection. Her rage led to feelings of envy of her lover, his family, his daughter, his work, and even his aunt. Lauren couldn't imagine that Jim could get excited by events or persons other than her. She wished that events in her own life could fulfill her or satisfy her, but her envy and primitive rage were overwhelming.

Although this patient had many narcissistic features, includ-ing that she needed to turn to the external environment in order to get the excitement she craved, she also exhibited many borderline characteristics. "I feel as though I am a nothing." I interpreted that it was not her lover who made her feel like a nothing, it was that she needed an outside daddy/lover telling her that she was special. Because she felt like "nothing" she idealized him, and she was unable to see the shortcomings and limitations of her lover. The person who really was devaluing Lauren was herself. If Jim, or whoever, as lover, was made out to have everything (idealization), then by contrast she must have nothing (devaluation). That Lauren, although she, too, had important things in her life, had to turn to others to seek validation, made her feel even more worthless.

Lauren continually complained about her mother: Her mother, Lauren reported, didn't have a life of her own, and received all of her gratification from her daughter's accomplishments. I was able to bond with the part of Lauren who detested her mother for "not living her own life," and for imposing herself on her daughter's life. It became apparent that Lauren was reenacting with her lover this scenario of an archaic experience she had with her mother. Lauren feared that, like her mother, she would not be able to have a life of her own. As her mother lived through her, Lauren became aware of how she lived through the life of her lover, and in doing so attempted to control him. How can one feel important when living inside someone else's "internal house"? Since the affair, Lauren had neglected herself, her husband, her children, and her friends and family, yet she needed someone, another daddy/lover, to stir vital issues, to move her to pay more attention to her own "internal house."

In many affairs, wives, husbands, and families do come first, and often the lover feels very much left out. As the material unfolded during Lauren's twice-weekly individual sessions, her history and her background as an only child who always had been the center of attention became apparent. She mistook her lover's unavailability as a severe narcissistic injury to her grandiose self, and as a threat to her exaggerated entitlement fantasies. She fantasized that his caring and preoccupation would fulfill her in the desire to be the number one child she always wanted to be. Her idealization of her lover and the subsequent devaluation of herself resulted in misperceiving the "reality" of their situation (devaluation and idealization get in the way of thinking).

Although I did not see Jim, I felt that some understanding of Jim's dynamics would be useful in helping Lauren see the introjects and projections. I speculated that Jim seemed to have a more realistic grasp of what their relationship meant. His ability to avoid colluding with her demands, provided an opportunity to take a look at Lauren's intrusive nature, and her sense of boundary and space.

I speculated that Jim seemed also to exhibit many borderline and narcissistic features. His behaviors of intense passion were followed by subsequent withdrawal and isolation; this vacillation demonstrated that Jim leaned more toward narcissistic features. His excessive caution, withdrawal from Lauren, and isolation represented Jim's fears of being hurt, touching on a part of himself that panicked whenever his passions and infant needs were stimulated. Jim's desire to try to hold on to himself and the boundaries was interpreted by Lauren as rejection and unavailability. It became apparent that the Jim, as Lauren's lover, exhibited the many traits and behaviors he loudly complained about in his wife. He projected all the needy parts of himself into his lover, and relieved himself by working compulsively (just as his wife did with him, and as he did his own father). His own internalized representation of an unavailable passive father got in the way of confronting his wife, and of showing his feelings and passion more directly. Because Jim was fused with his wife (by exhibiting the same behaviors and defenses as she), he could not separate from her, either emotionally or physically. He turned to working very aggressively in business and to the affair as ways of getting rid of his anxiety and his needs. He projected his real needs onto his wife and onto his lover, making them out to be the needy ones.

I tried to help Lauren understand how she relieved Jim, as she did her husband, by becoming so needy and so desperate that she could not see what parts of these men were truly available to her. Jim frequently used Lauren's spouse as an excuse to withhold intimacy. The bond between Jim and Lauren was the reenactment of his relationship with an intrusive, smothering mother. The internal relationship he held with his mother continually interfered with Jim's ability to maintain healthy relationships. The mother-son interactions as played out in the Lauren/Jim lover relationship would sway back and forth like a dance, until the therapist was able to help the narcissistic Lauren understand that by escaping into a whirlwind of passion, she was losing a big chunk of herself. All the while she was idealizing her lover, she was losing out on finding the real excitement within herself. Reality is not always as exciting as fantasy and passion, but reality has the basic function of being something one can count on that can lead to self esteem and to experiences that are meaningful and important.

The Secret

One therapeutic task is to help the patient learn to wait—that is, that quick responses can destroy. The "secret" also must be viewed within the framework of containment. Does the therapist have the capacity to hold on to a secret, to make use of the secret in a way that is productive, without revealing it or otherwise betraying the patient? In the case of Jim and Lauren, I needed to hold the secret from Lauren's husband during weekly conjoint visits. This modeled for Lauren that the therapist had the capacity to contain her impulses and hold on to the anxiety of Lauren's husband "not knowing." I needed to demonstrate that even though there may be the desire to give in to the impulse to reveal the secret, to do so would be joining Lauren by not holding on; after all, good mommies do not reveal secrets and do not need to evacuate. This is an issue that must be addressed for conjoint therapy, where there are conflicts between the containing of the secret and telling the "truth." It is not up to the therapist to tell the truth. It is up to the therapist to interpret the dynamics surrounding the affair (betrayal, envy, quick fix, approval), but not the secret. The therapist must interpret, not spill over. If the emphasis is placed on strengthening the internal structures, patients, in time, may reveal their own truths. For the therapist to reveal the secret not only would sabotage the narcissistic wife's real entitlement to come to terms with truth and reality, but would undermine the patient's potential to face his or her true self through the art of introspection. The issue of betrayal in this case is not a matter of not disclosing the secret—"Why didn't you tell me about my wife's affair?"—but is more about what is distorted and what is being projected. The therapist, addressing the issues of betrayal rather than the affair itself, might respond, "I did; I've been addressing the betrayal all along, how appointments were not kept, how promises and other commitments were broken, how money was not paid back! Now you are turning to me as if now I am the betrayer."

Through many transference interpretations, I was able to help Lauren face the narcissistic part of her personality. There were times where she became enraged with me and devalued the interpretations. I explained that "although my interpretations may not be 'number one,' at least they still can be helpful. I don't need to be the 'special doctor.' " I told Lauren that I could not provide everything for her (just as she could not provide everything for others, including her lover and her husband); however, I could help. Though I was not omniscient, we had a chance to do good work together and to make progress, and it was important to join together to have a meaningful therapeutic "affair."

In this case, the therapeutic task was to address the notion that Lauren was devaluing the treatment because of her envy and tendency to join with an idealized archaic object. Lauren needed to recognize that she was withdrawing from the treatment, her husband, her work, her own life, her family, and her friends and was turning to a life that was filled with highly charged fantasy. She was engaged in an affair that did not "construct" a rich life for her, but rather one that led her to lifelessness, to mental death, and to kill all the passion within her own internal world.

References

Ackerman, N. W. (1958). *The psychodynamics of family life*. New York: International Universities Press.

Adler, A. (1927). *Understanding human nature*. (W. B. Wolfe, Trans.). New York: Greenberg.

Adler, G. (1985). *Borderline psychopathology and its treatment*. New York: Jason Aronson.

Atwood, G., & Stolorow, R. (1984). Chapter 2, Structure of subjectivity: Explorations in psychoanalytic phenomenology. In *Psychoanalytic Phenomenology*. Hillsdale, NJ: Analytic Press.

Bateson, G., Jackson, D. D., Haley, J., & Weakland, J. H. (1956). Toward a theory of schizophrenia. *Behavioral Science, 1*, 251–261.

Bienenfeld, F. (1980). *My mom and dad are getting a divorce*. St. Paul, MN: EMC Corporation.

Bienenfeld, F. (1983). *Child custody mediation*. Palo Alto, CA: U. S. Science and Behavior Books.

Bienenfeld, F. (1986). Breaking through "impossible" barriers in child custody mediation. *Conciliation Courts Review, 24*, 39–42.

Bienenfeld, F. (1987). *Helping your child succeed after divorce*. Claremont, CA: Hunter House.

Bion, W. R. (1958). On arrogance. *International Journal of Psycho-Analysis, 39*, 266.

Bion, W. R. (1959). Attacks on linking. *International Journal of Psycho-Analysis, 40*, 308.

Bion, W. R. (1961). *Experiences in groups and other papers*. London: Tavistock.

Bion, W. R. (1962). *Learning from experience*. London: Heinemann.

Bion, W. R. (1963). *Elements of Psycho-Analysis*. London: Heinemann.

Bion, W. R. (1965). *Transformations*. London: Heinemann.

Bion, W. R. (1967). *Second thoughts. Selected papers on psycho-analysis*. New York: Jason Aronson.

Bion, W. R. (1970). *Attention and interpretation*. London: Maresfield Reprints, Tavistock.

Bion, W. R. (1977). *Seven servants: Four works by Wilfred R. Bion*. New York: Jason Aronson.

Bowen, M. (1960). Family concept of schizophrenia. In D. D. Jackson (Ed.), *Etiology of schizophrenia*. New York: Basic Books.

Bowlby, J. (1969). *Attachment and loss* (3 Vols.). New York: Basic Books.

Boyer, L. B. (1987). Regression and countertransference in the treatment of a borderline patient. In J. Grotstein, M. Solomon, & J. Lang, (Eds.), *The borderline patient: Emerging concepts in diagnosis, psychodynamics and treatment* (Vol. II. pp. 41–57). Hillsdale, NJ: Analytic Press.

Brandchaft, B., & Stolorow, R. (1984). The borderline concept: Pathological character and iatrogenic myth. In J. Lichtenberg et al. (Eds.), *Empathy II*. Hillsdale, NJ: Analytic Press.

Campbell, J. (1988). *The power of myth*. New York: Doubleday.

Caper, R. (1988). *Immaterial Facts. Freud's discovery of psychic reality and Klein's development of his work*. New York: Jason Aronson.

Clayman-Cook, C. (1987). *Melanie Klein, How her personal life affected her theories*. Unpublished paper.

DeMause, L. (1974). *The history of childhood*. New York: Psychohistory Press.

Demos, V. E. (1985). *Affect and the development of the self: A new frontier. Cambridge Hospital*. Cambridge, MA: Cambridge Press.

Deutsch, H. (1942). Some forms of emotional disturbance and their relationship to schizophrenia. *Contemporary Psychoanalysis, 11*, 301–321.

Dicks, H. (1967). *Marital tensions. Clinical studies toward a psychological theory of interaction*. New York: Basic Books.

Emde, R. N. (1987, August). "Development Terminable and Interminable, II Recent Psychoanalytic Theory and Therapeutic Considerations." *The effective core of the self: Motivational structures from infancy*. Paper presented at the International Psychoanalytic Congress, Montreal, Canada.

Erikson, E. (1950). *Childhood and society*. New York: Norton.

Eyton, A. (1986). *Kafka's "Metamorphosis": A model for schizophrenia*. Unpublished paper.

Fairbairn, W. (1954). *An object relations theory of the personality*. New York: Basic Books.

Ferenczi, S. (1925). Psycho-analysis of sexual habits. In E. Glover (Trans.), *Further contributions to the theory and technique of psychoanalysis*. London: Hogarth Press.

Flicker, M. (1988). *Object relations and the treatment of the seriously regressed borderline patient.* Paper presented at the Los Angeles Psychoanalytic Institute.

Foley, V. D. (1974). *An introduction to family therapy.* New York: Grune and Stratton.

Framo, J. (1972). Symptoms from a family transaction viewpoint. In N. Ackerman, J. Lieb, & J. Pearce (Eds.), *Family therapy in transition* (pp. 125–171). New York: Springer.

Freud, A. (1936). *The ego and the mechanisms of defense* (rev. ed., 1966). New York: International Universities Press.

Freud, S. (1940). *An outline of psycho-analysis.* In J. Strachey (Ed. and Trans.), *The standard edition of the complete works of Sigmund Freud* (Vol. 23, 141–207). London: Hogarth Press. (Original work published 1938)

Freud, S. (1953–1974). In J. Strachey (Ed. and Trans.), *The standard edition of the complete psychological works of Sigmund Freud* (24 vols.). London: Hogarth Press and The Institute of Psycho-Analysis.

Freud, S. (1955). Notes upon a case of obsessional neurosis. In J. Strachey (Ed. and Trans.), *The standard edition of the complete works of Sigmund Freud* (Vol. 10, pp. 153–318). London: Hogarth Press. (Original work published 1909)

Freud, S. (1955). Totem and taboo. In J. Strachey (Ed. and Trans.), *The standard edition of the complete works of Sigmund Freud* (Vol. 13, pp. 1–161). London: Hogarth Press. (Original work published 1912–13)

Freud, S. (1955). Group psychology and the analysis. In J. Strachey (Ed. and Trans.), *The standard edition of the complete works of Sigmund Freud* (Vol. 18, pp. 67–143). London: Hogarth Press. (Original work published 1921)

Freud, S. (1957). On narcissism: An introduction. In J. Strachey (Ed. and Trans.), *The standard edition of the complete works of Sigmund Freud* (Vol. 14, pp. 69–102) London: Hogarth Press. (Original work published 1914)

Giovacchini, P. (1975). *Psycho-analysis of character disorders.* New York: Jason Aronson.

Giovacchini, P. (1984). *Character disorders and adaptive mechanisms.* New York: Jason Aronson.

Grinberg, L., Sor, D., & de Bianchedi, E. T. (1977). *Introduction to the works of Bion: Groups, knowledge, psychosis, thought, transformations, psychoanalytic practice* (A. Hahn, Trans.). New York: Jason Aronson.

Grosskurth, P. (1986). *Melanie Klein: Her world and her work.* New York: Knopf.

Grotstein, J. (1980). A proposed revision of the psychoanalytic concept of primitive mental states. *Contemporary Psychoanalysis, 16,* 479–546.

Grotstein, J. (1981). *Splitting and projective identification.* New York: Jason Aronson.

Grotstein, J. (1983). A proposed revision of the psychoanalytic concept of primitive mental states. II. The borderline syndrome. Sec. 1. *Contemporary Psychoanalysis, 16,* 570–604.

Grotstein, J. (1984a). A proposed revision of the psychoanalytic concept of primitive mental states. II. The borderline syndrome. Sec. 2. *Contemporary Psychoanalysis, 20,* 77–118.

Grotstein, J. (1984b). A proposed revision of the psychoanalytic concept of primitive mental states. II. The borderline syndrome. Sec. 3. *Contemporary Psychoanalysis, 20,* 266–343.

Grotstein, J. (1987a). *Meaning, meaninglessness, and the "Black Hole": Self and interactional regulation as a new paradigm for psychoanalysis and neuroscience. An introduction.* Unpublished paper.

Grotstein, J. 1991. (Personal communcation).

Grotstein, J., Lang, J. A., & Solomon, M. F. (1987b). Convergence and controversy: II. Treatment of the borderline. In J. Grotstein, M. Solomon, & J. Lang (Eds.), *The borderline patient: Emerging concepts in diagnosis, psychodynamics and treatment* (Vol. II. pp. 261–310). Hillsdale, NJ: Analytic Press.

Guntrip, H. (1971). *Psychoanalytic theory, therapy, and the self.* New York: Basic Books.

Haley, H. (1967). Toward a theory of pathological systems. In G. Zuk & I. Boszormenyi-Nagy (Eds.), *Family therapy and disturbed families.* Palo Alto, CA: Science and Behavior Books.

Hartmann, H. (1958). *Ego psychology and the problem of adaptation* (D. Rapaport, Trans.). New York: International Universities Press.

Harwood, I. (1983). The application of self psychology concepts to group psychotherapy. *International Journal of Group Psychotherapy, 33,* 460–487.

Hawking, S. W. (1988). *A brief history of time from the big bang to the black holes.* New York: Bantam Books.

Hedges, L. (1983). *Listening perspectives in psychotherapy.* New York: Jason Aronson.

Hegal, G. W. (1821). *Hegel's philosophy of right* (T. M. Knox, Trans.). Oxford: Clairendoon.

Heimann, P. (1950). On countertransference. *International Journal of Psycho-Analysis, 31,* 81–84.

Isaacs, S. (1943). The nature and function of phantasy. In M. Klein, P. Heinman, S. Isaacs, & J. Reviere (Eds.), *Development in psycho analyses.* London: Hogarth Press.

Jackson, D. D. (1959). Family interaction, family homeostasis, and some implications for conjoint family psychotherapy. In J. H. Masserman (Ed.), *Individual and familial dynamics*. New York: Grune & Stratton.

Jackson, D. D., & Weakland, J. H. (1961). Conjoint family therapy: Some considerations on theory, technique and results. *Psychology, 24* (Suppl 2), 30–45.

Jacobson, E. (1964). *The self and the object world*. New York: International Universities Press.

Kafka, F. (1972). *Metamorphosis*. New York: Bantam. (Original work published in 1915)

Kernberg, O. (1975). *Borderline conditions and pathological narcissism*. New York: Jason Aronson.

Kernberg, O. (1976). *Object relations theory and clinical psychoanalysis*. New York: Jason Aronson.

Kernberg, O. (1980). Regression in groups. In O. Kernberg (Ed.), *Internal world and external reality*. New York: Jason Aronson.

Kernberg, O. (1982). In J. O. Cavenar & K. H. Brodie (Eds.), *Supportive psychotherapy with borderline patients. Clinical problems in psychiatry* (pp. 100–202). Philadelphia: Lippincott.

Kernberg, O. (1984). *Object relations theory and clinical psychoanalysis*. Northvale, NJ: Jason Aronson.

Kernberg, O. (1989). Sadomasochism, sexual excitement, and perversion. *Journal of the American Psychoanalytic Association, 333*–362.

Kernberg, O. (1990). Between conventionality and aggression: The boundaries of passion. Presented at *The cutting edge 1990. The heart of the matter: Helping improve vital relationships*. University of California, San Diego, Department of Psychiatry, School of Medicine, San Diego, California, April 28–29.

Kernberg, O., Selzer, M., and others. (1989). *Psychodynamic psychotherapy of borderline*. New York: Basic Books.

Klein, M. (1946). Notes on some schizoid mechanisms, developments in psycho-analysis. *International Journal Psycho-Analysis, 27,* 111.

Klein, M. (1948a). *Contribution to psycho-analysis, 1921–1945*. London: Hogarth Press.

Klein, M. (1948b). The development of a child. In *Contributions to psychoanalysis 1921–1945*. London: Hogarth Press. (Original work published in 1921)

Klein, M. (1948c). Mourning and its relation to manic states. In *Contribution to psycho-analysis 1921–1945* (pp. 311–338). London: Hogarth Press. (Original work published in 1940)

Klein, M. (1957). *Envy and gratitude*. New York: Basic Books.

Klein, M. (1975a). A contribution to the psychogenesis of manic-depressive states. In R. E. Money-Kryle (Ed.), *Love, guilt and reparation and other works 1921–1945* (pp. 262–289). New York: Free Press. (Original work published in 1935)

Klein, M. (1975b). The psychological principles of early analysis. In R. E. Money-Kryle (Ed.), *Love, guilt and reparation and other works* (pp. 126–138). New York: Free Press. (Original work published in 1926)

Klein, M. (1975c). Weaning. In R. E. Money-Kryle (Ed.), *Love, guilt and reparation and other works 1921–1945* (pp. 290–305). New York: Free Press. (Original work published in 1936)

Klein, M. (1975d). On identification. In R. E. Money-Kryle (Ed.), *Love, guilt and reparation and other works 1921–1945* (pp. 141–175). New York: Free Press.

Klein, M. (1975e). Love, guilt and reparation. In R. E. Money-Kryle (Ed.), *Love, guilt and reparation and other works 1921–1945*. New York: Free Press. (Originally published in 1937)

Kohut, H. (1966). *Forms and transformation of narcissism.* New York: International Universities Press.

Kohut, H. (1971). *The analysis of the self.* New York: International Universities Press.

Kohut, H. (1977). *The restoration of the self.* New York: International Universities Press.

Kohut, H. (1984). (A. Goldberg & P. Stepansky, Eds.). *Does analysis cure?* (Kohut's final book, published posthumously). Chicago: University of Chicago Press.

Lachkar, J. (1983). *The Arab-Israeli conflict. A psychoanalytic study.* Doctoral dissertation. Los Angeles, CA: International College.

Lachkar, J. (1984). Narcissistic/borderline couples: A psychoanalytic perspective to family therapy. *International Journal of Family Psychiatry. 5*(2), 169–189.

Lachkar, J. (1985a, Spring). Panel discussion: The victimization of human rights. *Bulletin of the Southern California Psychoanalytic Institute and Society, 72,* 17–21.

Lachkar, J. (1985b, Fall/Winter). Narcissistic/borderline couples: Theoretical implications for treatment. *Dynamic Psychotherapy, 3*(2), 109–127.

Lachkar, J. (1986). Narcissistic/borderline couples: Implications for mediation. *Conciliation Courts Review, 24*(1), 31–43.

Lachkar, J. (1989). *Narcissistic/Borderline Couples: A Psychoanalytic Perspective to Marital Conflict* (unpublished paper presented to the Los Angeles Psychoanalytic Society and Institute, Los Angeles).

Lachkar, J. (1991). Primitive Defenses in the Persian Gulf (unpublished paper presented at the International Psychohistorical Association, John Jay Collage, New York).

Langs, R. (1989). *Rating your psychotherapist: Everything you need to know to find the therapist who's right for you—from getting referrals to ending treatment*. New York: Ballantine Books.

Lansky, M. (1981). *Family therapy and major psychopathology*. New York: Grune and Stratton.

Lansky, M. (1987). Shame in the family relationships of borderline patients. In J. Grotstein, M. Solomon, & J. Lang (Eds.), *The borderline patient: Emerging concepts in diagnosis, psychodynamics and treatment* (Vol. II). Hillsdale, NJ: Analytic Press.

Lindon, J., & Gabbard, G. (1991). Does technique require theory? *Bulletin of the Menninger Clinic, 55* (1).

Loewenberg, P. (1985, Spring). The Victimization of Human Rights. *Bulletin of the Southern California Psychoanalytic Institute and Society, 72,* 20.

Magrid, B. (1984, Fall/Winter). Some contributions of self psychology to the treatment of borderline and schizophrenic patients. *Dynamic Psychotherapy, 2,* 101–111.

Mahler, M. S., Pine, F., & Bergman, A. (1975). *The psychological birth of the human infant*. New York: Basic Books.

Mason, A. (1981). The suffocating super-ego: Psychotic break and claustrophobia. In J. Grotstein (Ed.), *Do I dare disturb the universe? A memorial to Wilfred Bion* (p. 141). Beverly Hills, CA: Caesura Press.

Masterson, J. F. (1981). *The narcissistic and borderline disorders*. New York: Brunner/Mazel.

Meltzer, D. (1964–1965). *Sexual states of mind. Scotland*. Adapted lectures read at the Institute of Education. London: University of London.

Meltzer, D. (1967). *The psycho-analytic process*. London: William Heinemann Medical Books.

Minuchin, S. (1974). *Families and family therapy*. Cambridge, MA: Harvard University Press.

Money-Kryle, R. E. (1961). *Man's picture of his world*. London: Duckworth.

Rice, A. K. (1965a). Rice Institute. *Journal of Personality and Social Systems, 1*(3).

Rice, A. K. (1965b). *Learning for leadership*. London: Tavistock.

Rinsley, D. B. (1978). Borderline psychopathology: A review of etiology, dynamics and treatment. *International Review of Psychoanalysis, 5,* 45–54.

Sander, L. W. (1962). Issues in early mother-child interaction. *Journal of the American Academy of Child Psychiatry,* 141–166.

Satir, V. (1964). *Conjoint marital therapy.* Palo Alto, CA: Science and Behavior Books.

Schain, J. (1985, Winter). Can Klein and Kohut work together in a group? *Clinical Social Work Journal, 13,* 4, 293–303.

Scarf, M. (1987). *Intimate partners.* New York: Random House.

Scharff, D. & Scharff, J. S. (1987). *Object relations family therapy.* New Jersey: Jason Aronson.

Schwartzman, G. (1984). Narcissistic transferences: Implications for the treatment of couples. *Dynamic Psychotherapy, 2*(1), 5–14.

Segal, H. (1964). *Introduction to the works of Melanie Klein.* New York: Basic Books.

Sharpe, S. A. (1981). The symbiotic marriage: A diagnostic profile. *Bulletin of the Menninger Clinic, 45*(2), 89–114.

Sharpe, S. A. (In Press). The oppositional couple: A developmental object relations approach to diagnosis and treatment. In R. A. Nemiroff & C. A. Colarusso (Eds.), *New dimensions in adult development.* New York: Basic Books.

Silverman, D. (1988, June 9). *Art psychotherapy: A treatment approach to borderline adults.* Paper presented at the Los Angeles Psychoanalytic Institute, Los Angeles, California.

Slipp, S. (1984). *Object relations: A dynamic bridge between individual and family treatment.* New York: Jason Aronson.

Solomon, M. (1985, July). Treatment of narcissistic and borderline disorders in marital therapy. Suggestions toward an enhanced therapeutic approach. *Clinical Social Work Journal, 13*(2), 141–156.

Solomon, M. (1986). The application of self-psychology to marital therapy. *Clinical Social Work Journal,* 141–156.

Spitz, R. A. (1958). On the genesis of superego components. *Psychoanalytic study of the child. 13,* 375–404.

Spitz, R. A. (1965). *The first year of life.* New York: International Universities Press.

Stolorow, R., & Lachmann, E. (1980). *Psychoanalysis of developmental arrests, theory and treatment.* New York: International Universities Press.

Strean, H. S. (1980). *The extramarital affair.* New York: Free Press.

Strean, H. S. (1985). *Resolving marital conflicts: A psychodynamic perspective.* New York: John Wiley and Sons.

Sullivan, H. S. (1953). *The interpersonal theory of psychiatry.* New York: Norton.

Tustin, F. (1981). *Autistic states in children.* Newtown Road: Routledge, Kegan Paul, Ltd. and Broadway House.

Watzlawick, P. (1974). *Change.* New York: Norton.

Watzlawick, P., Beavin, J. H., & Jackson, D. D. (1967). *Pragmatics of human* communication: A study of interactional patterns, pathologies, and paradoxes. New York: Norton.

Willi, J. (1982). *Couples in collusion: The unconscious dimension in partner relationships.* Claremont, CA: Hunter House.

Winnicott, D. W. (1953). Transitional objects and transitional phenomena in a study of the first not-me possession. *International Journal of Psycho-Analysis, 34*(2), 89–97.

Winnicott, D. W. (1965a). *The maturational process and the facilitating environment: Studies in the theory of emotional development.* New York: International Universities Press. London: Hogarth Press.

Winnicott, D. W. (1965b). Psychoanalysis and the sense of guilt. In *The maturational process and the facilitating environment: Studies in the theory of emotional development* (pp. 15–28). New York: International Universities Press.

Winnicott, D. W. (1965c). The capacity to be alone. In *The maturational process and the facilitating environment: Studies in the theory of emotional development* (pp. 29–36). New York: International Universities Press.

Winnicott, D. W. (1965d). The theory of the parent-infant relationship. In *The maturational process and the facilitating environment: Studies in the theory of emotional development* (pp. 37–55). New York: International Universities Press.

Winnicott, D. W. (1965e). Ego distortion in terms of the true and false self. In *The maturational process and the facilitating environment: Studies in the theory of emotional development* (pp. 140–152). New York: International Universities Press.

Winnicott, D. W. (1965f). Communicating and not communicating leading to a study of certain opposites. In *The maturational processes and the facilitating environment: Studies in the theory of emotional development* (pp. 179–192). New York: International Universities Press.

Wolstein, B. (1987). Experience, interpretation, self-knowledge: The lost uniqueness of Kohut's self psychology. (In Book Review. H. Kohut, How Does Psychoanalysis Cure? Chicago: Univ. of Chicago Press, 1984). W. A. White Institute, New York.

Name Index

Adler, A., 35
Adler, G., 6, 19, 20, 28, 65
Atwood, G., 39

Bergman, A., 14, 19, 37, 86, 186
Bienenfeld, F., 143, 144, 145
Bion, W., x, xii, 7, 14, 19, 24, 25, 28, 31, 41, 49, 52, 57, 58, 60, 81, 92, 102, 104, 107, 109, 124, 132, 133, 134, 135, 137, 138, 146, 160, 161, 162, 163, 184, 186
Bowlby, L., 12, 14, 23, 161
Brandchaft, B., ix, 6, 7, 38, 51, 72, 115, 116

Campbell, J., 135, 136
Caper, R., 8
Clayman-Cook, C., 23, 24, 110

de Bianchedi, E., 25
DeMause, L., 79, 133
Deutsch, H., 18
Dicks, H., xi, 133, 134

Emde, R., 76, 77
Erikson, E., 35
Eyton, A., 30

Fairbairn, W., 3, 12, 35, 161
Flicker, M., 131
Freud, S., x, xii, 2, 3, 14, 19, 31, 32, 33, 36, 37, 38, 76, 84, 88, 97, 109, 110, 115, 117, 124, 133, 161

Gabbard, G., 116
Grinberg, L., 25, 27

Grosskurth, P., 23
Grotstein, J., xii, 3, 12, 13, 14, 19, 22, 28, 33, 81, 87, 88, 102, 104, 113, 117, 125, 162, 163

Hartmann, H., 35, 36, 38
Hawking, S., 28
Hedges, L., 35, 113
Hegel, G., 11
Heimann, P., 98

Isaacs, S., 11

Jacobson, E., 19, 35

Kafka, F., 30
Kant, I., 25
Kernberg, O., x, 3, 8, 9, 10, 19, 20, 32, 33, 38, 94, 109, 133, 134
Klein, M., xii, xiv, 7, 11, 12, 14, 19, 23, 33, 36, 37, 38, 72, 84, 85, 87, 88, 89, 90, 91, 92, 94, 95, 98, 102, 109, 110, 111, 112, 113, 115, 116, 117, 118, 122, 123, 124, 161, 162, 163, 165, 166
Kohut, H., ix, xii, xiv, 3, 5, 6, 8, 9, 11, 12, 20, 32, 33, 36, 38, 39, 77, 87, 88, 95, 96, 97, 101, 103, 114, 119, 126, 161

Lachkar, J., x, xi, xii, 6, 17, 18, 39, 40, 49, 58, 64, 72, 78, 79, 84, 118, 133, 135, 137, 146, 160, 189
Lachmann, E., ix, 6, 38, 39, 51
Langs, R., 7
Lansky, M., xi, xii, 6, 62
Lindon, J., 116
Loewenberg, P., 84, 120

Subject Index